BOOKS BY

H. L. Mencken

THE AMERICAN LANGUAGE

THE AMERICAN LANGUAGE: *Supplement One*

THE AMERICAN LANGUAGE: *Supplement Two*

HAPPY DAYS ⎫ *which, taken together,*

NEWSPAPER DAYS ⎬ *constitute* THE DAYS

HEATHEN DAYS ⎭ OF H. L. MENCKEN

A NEW DICTIONARY OF QUOTATIONS

TREATISE ON THE GODS

CHRISTMAS STORY

A MENCKEN CHRESTOMATHY

(with selections from the *Prejudices* series, *A Book of Burlesques, In Defense of Women, Notes on Democracy, Making a President, A Book of Calumny, Treatise on Right and Wrong,* with pieces from the *American Mercury, Smart Set,* and *Baltimore Evening Sun* and some previously unpublished notes)

MINORITY REPORT: *H. L. Mencken's Notebooks*

THE BATHTUB HOAX *and Other Blasts and Bravos from the* Chicago Tribune

These are Borzoi Books

PUBLISHED BY   Alfred A. Knopf   IN NEW YORK

THE BATHTUB HOAX

and Other Blasts and Bravos

THE
BATHTUB HOAX

AND OTHER

BLASTS & BRAVOS

FROM THE *CHICAGO TRIBUNE*

BY

H. L. Mencken

EDITED,

WITH AN INTRODUCTION AND NOTES,

BY ROBERT McHUGH

ALFRED · A · KNOPF

NEW YORK · 1958

L. C. Catalog card number: 58–12629

© Alfred A. Knopf, Inc., 1958

THIS IS A BORZOI BOOK,
PUBLISHED BY ALFRED A. KNOPF, INC.

FIRST EDITION

The only way that democracy can be made bearable is by developing and cherishing a class of men sufficiently honest and disinterested to challenge the prevailing quacks. No such class has ever appeared in strength in the United States. Thus, the business of harassing the quacks devolves upon the newspapers. When they fail in their duty, which is usually, we are at the quacks' mercy.

—H. L. Mencken, *in* MINORITY REPORT

ABOUT H. L. MENCKEN

SINCE THE DEATH of H. L. Mencken on January 29, 1956, there have been a few probing but somewhat uneasy attempts to find a place for him in history.

Some tidy arrangement ought to be within reach, it would seem, so that generations to come might glance at his label and file him safely away as writer, critic, philologist, or merely phenomenon of the twenties.

But specimens like Mencken are much too complex to be classified easily. Or perhaps the range is still too short to evaluate properly his influence on American literature and his efforts to encourage the development of a national tongue unembarrassed by a debt to England.

Gerald W. Johnson believes there is evidence that the philologist is beginning to overshadow all other manifestations of Mencken. It is true that his books on the American language show signs of enduring. But if we agree with Mr. Johnson, do we not relegate to shadows the leader of the American literary rebellion from which rose such writers as Sinclair Lewis and Theodore Dreiser?

Seeing this need of a broader basis for remembering Mencken, William Manchester has compared him to Samuel Johnson.

The idea is tempting. Mencken's inquiry into the origins of our speech in *The American Language* and its supplements was as monumental and scholarly a task as Johnson's dictionary.

Each man was inordinately famous in his day as writer, dictator of literary tastes, and critic of the mores of his times. Cults of followers, alike in their fatuous devotion, grew up around both. Johnson had a faithful echo in Boswell, and Mencken had his echoes too. In fact, so widely quoted and aped was he that a friend protested in despair the creation of too many noisy and inferior "Menckenoids."

Johnson was a hypochondriac. And, similarly, a disorder as minor as a pimple could plunge Mencken into a mood of near despair. The two men even died at the same age—seventy-five.

Yet, the differences are quite as striking. Johnson's prose seems frequently involved and ponderous, while Mencken's robust style is a model of lucidity. Mencken vivified his expressions with agreeable mirth, but Johnsonian wit often was weighted with asperity.

Fastidious about his diet, Johnson was given to munching dainty cakes. Mencken could devour a duck. The Sage of Baltimore was an atheist who welcomed death as a relief from the torments of a final illness. Johnson lived in mortal terror of hell.

Indeed, Ambrose Bierce comes to mind as far more a kindred spirit for comparison, though there seems little doubt that Mencken was the superior stylist.

Both were audacious critics of many of the ideas held dear by their countrymen. And, at least on the West Coast, Bierce became a literary arbiter in the manner of a Mencken, albeit a much less influential one.

But Bierce was an angry and bitter man, and, as such, the antithesis of Mencken, who was so delighted with the world that the daily miracle of a fresh egg for breakfast could stir his buoyant zest for life.

Analogizing even further, the name of Samuel Butler crops up for consideration. Mencken and Butler were both newspapermen and rebels against the clergy, and both had an interest in music and science.

The author of *Erewhon* and *The Way of All Flesh* was a satirist of a different stripe, however, and a comparison on this ground collapses into an image of Mencken brandishing a broadsword and Butler deftly flexing a slender foil.

On still another level, Shaw's name has been raised in the search for a pattern to which Mencken's protean form might be fitted. Alistair Cooke notes that Mencken obviously learned much from his early observations of the Irish playwright, and terms both men "superior popular educators who kick up a terrific dust on the intellectual middle plateau between the philistine and the first-rate scholar."

Both were outstanding stylists, he observes, then retreats from prolonging the comparison because of Shaw's "superior intellect and satirical power."

Where, then, does one turn for a proper yardstick to take the measure of this man?

It will not be found for some time, I believe, as the dust has yet to settle from the explosions he caused as the rage of the twenties. I speak here of Mencken as author, literary critic, and student of the American language.

It is quite a different matter to consider him in yet one more role—the one he plays in the pages to follow—that of newspaperman.

Mr. Cooke, no mean journalist himself, has described Mencken as "possibly the greatest, certainly the most volcanic newspaperman our country has known."

Few practitioners of the trade will disagree with this, though many may be plagued by the uneasy notion that Mencken broke too many journalistic rules to be accepted unreservedly as a *bona fide* member of the fraternity.

What reputable newspaperman today, for instance, could survive as such after deliberately writing for publication an outright lie? Mencken did it with scarcely a backward glance to see if he had got away with it.

This supreme violation of the code is the bathtub hoax featured in this book. It is a transient essay written when World War I and Mencken's Teutonic sympathies had made the discussion of more serious issues difficult for him, to say the least.

It was a time when misguided patriots harassed harmless old men with German names in Mencken's native Baltimore; when propagandists spread stories about an enemy given to crucifying Canadian soldiers and happily committing infanticide. In some quarters these stories were solemnly published.

Mencken, in this atmosphere, selected a plebeian household fixture and confected a whopping lie about it that all too many of his readers believed. The misinformation he so puckishly broadcast still may survive in some remote quarters despite his subsequent efforts to acknowledge the fraud.

This fake history of the bathtub in the United States was first published in the now defunct New York *Evening Mail*.

If Chaucer's Nun's Tale, more than five centuries old,

can be looked to still as the classic spoof on atrocity stories, then in a much smaller way the bathtub hoax merits preservation today.

For the two stories are analogous at least to this extent—Chaucer provided a snicker at the expense of the creators of atrocious propaganda, and Mencken uttered a horse laugh in the faces of those gullible enough to swallow that which is obviously untrue.

The English poet and narrative artist covered a superior smirk with an elegant sleeve during the appallingly ignorant Middle Ages. And Mencken's pie-throwing practical joke was played on a people just emerging from a wartime hysteria no less medieval for its nescience.

Mencken, because he was willing to disregard the holy doctrines of his trade, provided an amusing and instructive lesson in human credulity.

Still another canon he saw fit to violate surrounds the editorial pages. The feeling has existed for years that newspapers must be courageously outspoken, and that to prove they are so, they must proclaim editorial opinion every day.

Obviously, this attitude does not take into account the embarrassing possibility that there may be days when even the most informed editor will lack a sensible idea worth expressing. Mencken scandalized his colleagues by admitting the likelihood of this and by offering the merciful suggestion that on such barren days editorials should be eliminated.

Worse, he went even further. He denied that editorial writers can perform competently from lonely ivory towers. He insisted that instead they should leave their offices frequently to contact the people and issues they write about.

If this was a sensible thought, to many it was also revolutionary.

Equally subversive was his stand that objective reporting is impossible. There is nothing wrong with opinion in a news story as long as the writer signs his name and is willing to back it up, Mencken has said.

I believe history records that a sports editor once had a finger bitten off for advancing this theory to an aging police reporter during an informal seminar in a Keokuk, Iowa, beer stube.

If the tale is true, I am not surprised, for it is widely known that the type of controversy H. L. Mencken could generate frequently led to heated argument. A prolonged discussion of this skill is made unnecessary by the samples to follow, in which the reader may find a few of his own pet images smashed.

It is, to be sure, journalism from another age. But it glows with timelessness owing to the writer's faculty for ferreting out the essence of each contemporary furor.

For example, a report on an all but forgotten controversy over birth control still stands up as a comment on our deadly tendency to stifle free discussion when dissent is in the minority.

In another of the essays gathered here, Mencken opposed the Lord's Day Alliance, but placed his real critical stress on the injunctive process its leaders employed to enforce blue laws. He saw recurrent danger in any move designed to abrogate the right to trial by jury.

Included also are discussions of literary figures whose works are still read, meditations on ideas still under debate, and comments on the American scene which can stand repeating today.

Most of Mencken's newspaper writing was done for the Baltimore *Sunpapers*, where he hung his hat for nearly his entire journalistic life of a half-century. But these essays, all but the one that is featured, were written for the *Chicago Tribune* in the late twenties.

Mencken was in that gay era a man who had been damned by presidents and described by *The New York Times* as "the most influential single citizen" in the country.

Less extravagant evaluations, prepared in the perspective that only the passage of time can bring, await him in the years to come.

Evidence for composing such judgments lies in some two dozen books Mencken wrote or helped to write, and to a lesser degree in at least four books about him.

Meanwhile, here is the eloquent foe of all quacks in the role he liked best—that of newspaperman.

It is appropriate that Mencken should have written the script for the part himself. He did this when he said the ideal reporter "should have the widest conceivable range of knowledge, and he should be the sort of man who is not easily deluded by the specious and the fraudulent."

ROBERT McHUGH

Columbia, South Carolina

CONTENTS

ABOUT H. L. MENCKEN, *by Robert McHugh*   vii

I. *American Credulity*   3

A Neglected Anniversary (The Bathtub Hoax)   4
Melancholy Reflections   10
Hymn to the Truth   15
The Believing Mind   20

II. *Land of the Free*   25

The Bill of Rights   26
The Comstockian Imbecility   31
The Anatomy of Wowserism   36
Padlocks   41
The Battle of Ideas   46
The Birth Control Hullabaloo   51
Equality Before the Law   55

III. *The Arts*   61

Essay on Constructive Criticism   62
Hints for Novelists   67
Yet More Hints for Novelists   71
Poe's Start in Life   76
The Case of Dreiser   81
H. L. Mencken on Mark Twain   86
Robert Louis Stevenson   91
Beethoven, Obit. March 26, 1827   96
The Music of the American Negro   100
On Realism   105
View of Literary Gents   110
The Avalanche of Books   115

IV. *Religion, Ethics, and Science*   121

Fundamentalism: Divine and Secular   122
The Rev. Clergy   126

Cousin Jocko   131
Jacquerie   136
Man as a Mammal   141
Havelock Ellis   145
On Eugenics   150
Human Monogamy   155
Another Long-Awaited Book   160
Holy Writ   165

V. *Politics, Government, Jurisprudence* 171

The United States Senate   172
The National Conventions   177
Notes on Government   182
Blackmail Made Easy   186
A Long-Felt Want   191
Vive le Roi!   196

VI. *Education, Philology* 203

The Pedagogue's Utopia   204
On Going to College   209
The Language We Speak   214
Babel   219
The Emperor of Dictionaries   223

VII. *Miscellany* 229

The American Scene   229
On Connubial Bliss   234
Dreams of Peace   239
On Human Progress   244
The South Rebels Again   249
The Sad Case of Tennessee   254
The Movies   259
The Telephone Nuisance   264
Victualry as a Fine Art   269
On Controversy   274

GLOSSARY   279

THE BATHTUB HOAX

and Other Blasts and Bravos

I. AMERICAN CREDULITY

Ours is a curious culture indeed. Moon-rocketry flourishes compatibly with such necromantic practices of the Middle Ages as palmistry and astrology.

Only recently, protective legislation was sought in one southern state to outlaw fortune-telling, so serious is the financial loss among the gullible.

Elsewhere in the nation, shop clerks happily consult their horoscopes and maiden ladies tremulously submit their palms to gypsies while a scientist next door plots the course of a man-made satellite hurtling through space.

Mencken would never have questioned the congruity of this arrangement had he survived into the space age. For he believed that, scientific and intellectual progress among a minority notwithstanding, most of his countrymen were afflicted with a compulsion to accept as gospel that which is obviously untrue.

"A Neglected Anniversary," the now famous but fake bathtub history that follows, was first published December 28, 1917, in the New York Evening Mail *as an amusing if somewhat vacuous whimsicality.*

To Mencken's delight, it began cropping up periodically as a sound reference source over the next ten years, and

3

he was obliged to admit that it was fiction. These admissions are included in this section along with "The Believing Mind," which has nothing to do with the bathtub hoax but everything to do with the principle it illustrates.

A NEGLECTED ANNIVERSARY

ON DECEMBER 20 there flitted past us, absolutely without public notice, one of the most important profane anniversaries in American history—to wit: the seventy-fifth anniversary of the introduction of the bathtub into these states. Not a plumber fired a salute or hung out a flag. Not a governor proclaimed a day of prayer. Not a newspaper called attention to the day.

True enough, it was not entirely forgotten. Eight or nine months ago one of the younger surgeons connected with the Public Health Service in Washington happened upon the facts while looking into the early history of public hygiene, and at his suggestion a committee was formed to celebrate the anniversary with a banquet. But before the plan was perfected Washington went dry, and so the banquet had to be abandoned. As it was, the day passed wholly unmarked, even in the capital of the nation.

Bathtubs are so common today that it is almost impossible to imagine a world without them. They are familiar to nearly every one in all incorporated towns; in most of the large cities it is unlawful to build a dwelling house without putting them in; even on the farm they have begun to come into use. And yet the first American bathtub was installed and dedicated so recently as December 20, 1842, and, for all I know to the contrary, it may be still in existence and in use.

Curiously enough, the scene of its setting up was Cincinnati, then a squalid frontier town, and even today surely no leader in culture. But Cincinnati, in those days as in these, contained many enterprising merchants, and one of them was a man named Adam Thompson, a dealer in cotton and grain. Thompson shipped his merchandise by steamboat down the Ohio and Mississippi to New Orleans, and from there sent it to England in sailing vessels. This trade frequently took him to England, and in that country, during the 30s, he acquired the habit of bathing.

The bathtub was then still a novelty in England. It had been introduced in 1828 by Lord John Russell and its use was yet confined to a small class of enthusiasts. Moreover, the English bathtub, then as now, was a puny and inconvenient contrivance—little more, in fact, than a glorified dishpan—and filling and emptying it required the attendance of a servant. Taking a bath, indeed, was a rather heavy ceremony, and Lord John in 1835 was said to be the only man in England who had yet come to doing it every day.

Thompson, who was of inventive fancy—he later devised the machine that is still used for bagging hams and bacon—conceived the notion that the English bathtub would be much improved if it were made large enough to admit the whole body of an adult man, and if its supply of water, instead of being hauled to the scene by a maid, were admitted by pipes from a central reservoir and run off by the same means. Accordingly, early in 1842 he set about building the first modern bathroom in his Cincinnati home —a large house with Doric pillars, standing near what is now the corner of Monastery and Oregon streets.

There was then, of course, no city water supply, at least in that part of the city, but Thompson had a large well in his garden and he installed a pump to lift its water to his house. This pump, which was operated by six Negroes, much like an old-time fire engine, was connected by a pipe with a cypress tank in the garret of the house and here the water was stored until needed. From the tank two other pipes ran to the bathroom. One, carrying cold water, was a direct line. The other, designed to provide warm water, ran down the great chimney of the kitchen and was coiled inside it like a giant spring.

The tub itself was of new design and became the grandfather of all the bathtubs of today. Thompson had it made by James Guiness, the leading Cincinnati cabinet maker of those days, and its material was Nicaragua mahogany. It was nearly seven feet long and fully four feet wide. To make it water tight the interior was lined with sheet lead, carefully soldered at the joints. The whole contraption weighed about 1,750 pounds, and the floor of the room in which it was placed had to be reinforced to support it. The exterior was elaborately polished.

In this luxurious tub Thompson took two baths on December 20, 1842—a cold one at 8 a.m. and a warm one some time during the afternoon. The warm water, heated by the kitchen fire, reached a temperature of 105 degrees. On Christmas day, having a party of gentlemen to dinner, he exhibited the new marvel to them and gave an exhibition of its use, and four of them, including a French visitor, Col. Duchanel, risked plunges into it. The next day all Cincinnati—then a town of about 100,000 people—had heard of it, and the local newspapers described it at length and opened their columns to violent discussions of it.

The thing, in fact, became a public matter, and before long there was bitter and double-headed opposition to the new invention, which had been promptly imitated by several other wealthy Cincinnatians. On the one hand it was denounced as an epicurean and obnoxious toy from England, designed to corrupt the democratic simplicity of the republic, and on the other hand it was attacked by the medical faculty as dangerous to health and a certain inviter of "phthisic, rheumatic fevers, inflammation of the lungs, and the whole category of zymotic diseases." (I quote from the *Western Medical Repository* of April 23, 1843.)

The noise of the controversy soon reached other cities, and in more than one place medical opposition reached such strength that it was reflected in legislation. Late in 1843, for example, the Philadelphia common council considered an ordinance prohibiting bathing between November 1 and March 15, and it failed of passage by but two votes. During the same year the legislature of Virginia laid a tax of $30 a year on all bathtubs that might be set up, and in Hartford, Providence, Charleston, and Wilmington, Del., special and very heavy water rates were levied upon those who had them. Boston early in 1845 made bathing unlawful except upon medical advice, but the ordinance was never enforced and in 1862 it was repealed.

This legislation, I suspect, had some class feeling in it, for the Thompson bathtub was plainly too expensive to be owned by any save the wealthy. Indeed, the common price for installing one in New York in 1845 was $500. Thus the low caste politicians of the time made capital by fulminating against it, and there is even some suspicion of political bias in many of the early medical denunciations. But the invention of the common pine bathtub, lined with zinc, in 1847, cut off this line of attack, and thereafter the bathtub made steady progress.

The zinc tub was devised by John F. Simpson, a Brooklyn plumber, and his efforts to protect it by a patent occupied the courts until 1855. But the decisions were steadily against him, and after 1848 all the plumbers of New York were equipped for putting in bathtubs. According to a writer in the *Christian Register* for July 17, 1857, the first one in New York was opened for traffic on September 12, 1847, and by the beginning of 1850 there were already nearly 1,000 in use in the big town.

After this medical opposition began to collapse, and among other eminent physicians Dr. Oliver Wendell Holmes declared for the bathtub, and vigorously opposed the lingering movement against it in Boston. The American Medical Association held its annual meeting in Boston in 1859, and a poll of the members in attendance showed that nearly 55 per cent of them now regarded bathing as harmless, and that more than 20 per cent advocated it as beneficial. At its meeting in 1850 a resolution was formally passed giving the imprimatur of the faculty to the bathtub. The homeopaths followed with a like resolution in 1853.

But it was the example of President Millard Fillmore that, even more than the grudging medical approval, gave the bathtub recognition and respectability in the United States. While he was still Vice President, in March, 1850, he visited Cincinnati on a stumping tour, and inspected the original Thompson tub. Thompson himself was now dead, but the bathroom was preserved by the gentleman who had bought his house from his estate. Fillmore was entertained in this house and, according to Chamberlain, his biographer, took a bath in the tub. Experiencing no ill effects, he became an ardent advocate of the new invention, and on succeeding to the presidency at Taylor's death, July 9, 1850, he instructed his secretary of war, Gen. Charles M. Conrad, to invite tenders for the construction of a bathtub in the White House.

This action, for a moment, revived the old controversy, and its opponents made much of the fact that there was no bathtub at Mount Vernon or at Monticello, and that all the Presidents and other magnificoes of the past had got along without any such monarchical luxuries. The elder Bennett, in the *New York Herald*, charged that Fillmore really aspired to buy and install in the White House a porphyry and alabaster bath that had been used by Louis Philippe at Versailles. But Conrad, disregarding all this clamor, duly called for bids, and the contract was presently awarded to Harper & Gillespie, a firm of Philadelphia engineers, who proposed to furnish a tub of cast iron, capable of floating the largest man.

This was installed early in 1851 and remained in service in the White House until the first Cleveland administration, when the present enameled tub was substituted. The example of the President soon broke down all that remained of the old opposition, and by 1860, according to the newspaper advertisements of the time, every hotel in New York had a bathtub, and some had two and even three. In 1862 bathing was introduced into the army by Gen. McClellan, and in 1870 the first prison bathtub was set up at Moyamensing prison in Philadelphia.

So much for the history of the bathtub in America. One is astonished, on looking into it, to find that so little of it has been recorded. The literature, in fact, is almost nil. But perhaps this brief sketch will encourage other inquirers and so lay the foundation for an adequate celebration of the centennial in 1942.

MELANCHOLY REFLECTIONS

ON DECEMBER 28, 1917, I printed in the *New York Evening Mail*, a paper now extinct, an article purporting to give the history of the bathtub. This article, I may say at once, was a tissue of absurdities, all of them deliberate and most of them obvious. I alleged that the bathtub was unknown in the New World until the 40s of the last century, and that it was then invented in Cincinnati. I described how the inventor, in the absence of running water in the town, employed Aframericans to haul it up from the Ohio river in buckets. I told how a tub was put into the White House in the 50s, and how Millard Fillmore took the first presidential bath. I ended by saying that the medical men of the United States unanimously opposed the new invention as dangerous to health, and that laws against it were passed in Massachusetts and Pennsylvania.

This article, as I say, was planned as a piece of spoofing to relieve the strain of war days, and I confess that I regarded it, when it came out, with considerable satisfaction. It was reprinted by various great organs of the enlightenment, and after a while the usual letters began to reach me from readers. Then, suddenly, my satisfaction turned to consternation. For these readers, it appeared, all took my idle jocosities with complete seriousness. Some of them, of antiquarian tastes, asked for further light on this or that phase of the subject. Others actually offered me corroboration!

But the worst was to come. Pretty soon I began to encounter my preposterous "facts" in the writings of other men. They began to be used by chiropractors and other such quacks as evidence of the stupidity of medical men. They began to be cited by medical men as proof of the progress of public hygiene. They got into learned journals. They were alluded to on the floor of congress. They crossed the ocean, and were discussed solemnly in England, and on the continent. Finally, I began to find them in standard works of reference. Today, I believe, they are accepted as gospel everywhere on earth. To question them becomes as hazardous as to question the Norman Invasion.

And as rare. This is the first time, indeed, that they have ever been questioned, and I confess at once that even I myself, their author, felt a certain hesitancy about doing it. Once more, I suppose, I'll be accused of taking the wrong side for the mere pleasure of standing in opposition. The Cincinnati boomers, who have made much of the boast that the bathtub industry, now running to $200,000,000 a year, was started in their town, will charge me with spreading lies against them. The chiropractors will damn me for blowing up their ammunition. The medical gents, having swallowed my quackery, will now denounce me as a quack for exposing them. And in the end, no doubt, the thing will simmer down to a general feeling that I have once more committed some vague and sinister crime against the United States, and there will be a renewal of the demand that I be deported to Russia.

I recite this history, not because it is singular, but because it is typical. It is out of just such frauds, I believe, that most of the so-called knowledge of humanity flows. What begins as a guess—or, perhaps, not infrequently, as a downright and deliberate lie—ends as a fact and is embalmed in the history books. One recalls the gaudy days of 1914–1918. How much that was then devoured by the newspaper readers of the world was actually true? Probably not one per cent. Ever since the war ended learned and laborious men have been at work examining and exposing its fictions. But every one of those fictions retains full faith and credit today. To question even the most palpably absurd of them, in most parts of the United States, is to invite denunciation as a bolshevik.

So with all other wars. For example, the revolution. For years past American historians have been investigating the orthodox legends. Almost all of them turn out to be blowsy nonsense. Yet they remain in the school history books and every effort to get them out causes a dreadful row, and those who make it are accused of all sorts of treasons and spoils. The truth, indeed, is something that mankind, for some mysterious reason, instinctively dislikes. Every man who tries to tell it is unpopular, and even when, by the sheer strength of his case, he prevails, he is put down as a scoundrel.

As a practicing journalist for many years, I have often had close contact with history in the making. I can recall no time or place when what actually occurred was afterward generally known and believed. Sometimes a part of the truth got out, but never all. And what actually got out was seldom clearly understood. Consider, for example, the legends that followed every national convention. A thousand newspaper correspondents are on the scene, all of them theoretically competent to see accurately and report honestly, but it is seldom that two of them agree perfectly, and a month after the convention adjourns the accepted version of what occurred usually differs from the accounts of all of them.

I point to the Republican convention of 1920, which nominated the eminent and lamented Harding. A week after the delegates adjourned the whole country believed that Harding had been put through by Col. George Harvey: Harvey himself admitted it. Then other claimants to the honor arose, and after a year or two it was generally held that the trick had been turned by the distinguished Harry M. Daugherty, by that time a salient light of the Harding cabinet. The story began to acquire corroborative detail. Delegates and correspondents began to remember things that they had not noticed on the spot. What the orthodox tale is today, with Daugherty in eclipse, I don't know, but you may be sure that it is full of mysterious intrigue and bold adventure.

What are the facts? The facts are that Harvey had little more to do with the nomination of Harding than I did, and that Daugherty was immensely surprised when good Warren won. The nomination was really due to the intense heat, and to that alone. The delegates, torn by the savage three cornered fight between Lowden, Johnson, and Wood, came to Saturday morning in despair. The temperature in the convention hall was at least 120 degrees. They were eager to get home. When it became apparent that the leaders could not break the deadlock they ran amok and nominated Harding, as the one aspirant who had no enemies. If any individual managed the business it was not Harvey or Daugherty, but Myron T. Herrick. But so far as I know Herrick's hand in it has never been mentioned.

I turn to a more pleasant field—that of sport in the grand manner. On July 2, 1921, in the great bowl at Jersey City, the Hon. Jack Dempsey met M. Carpentier, the gallant frog. The sympathy of the crowd was overwhelmingly with M. Carpentier and every time he struck a blow he got a round of applause, even if it didn't land. I had an excellent seat, very near the ring, and saw every move of the two men. From the first moment Dr. Dempsey had it all his own way. He could have knocked out M. Carpentier in the first half of the first round. After that first half he simply waited his chance to do it politely.

Yet certain great newspapers reported the next morning that M. Carpentier had delivered an appalling wallop in the second round and that Dr. Dempsey had narrowly escaped going out. Others told the truth, but what chance had the truth against that romantic lie? It is believed in to this day by at least 99.99 per cent of all the boxing fans in Christendom. Carpentier himself, when he recovered from his beating, admitted categorically that it was nonsense, but even Carpentier could make no headway against the almost universal human tendency to cherish what is not true. A thousand years hence schoolboys will be taught that the frog had Dempsey going. It may become in time a religious dogma, like the doctrine that Jonah swallowed the whale. Scoffers who doubt it will be damned to hell.

The moral, if any, I leave to psycho-pathologists, if competent ones can be found. All I care to do today is to reiterate, in the most solemn and awful terms, that my history of the bathtub, printed on December 28, 1917, was pure

buncombe. If there were any facts in it they got there acci-
dentally and against my design. But today the tale is in the
encyclopedias. History, said a great American soothsayer, is
bunk.
(May 23, 1926)

HYMN TO THE TRUTH

ON MAY 23 last, writing in this place, I told the strange, sad
story of an article that I printed in the *New York Evening
Mail*, a paper now happily extinct, on December 28, 1917.
The article, thrown off as a relief from the patriotic libido
of war time, was, in substance, a burlesque history of the
bathtub. I may confess that, when it was done, I fancied it
no little. It was artfully devised, and it contained some buf-
fooneries of considerable juiciness. I had confidence that
the customers of the *Evening Mail* would like it.

Alas, they liked it only too well. That is to say, they
swallowed it as gospel, gravely and horribly. Worse, they
began sending clippings of it to friends east, west, north,
and south, and so it spread to other papers, and then to
the magazines and weeklies of opinion, and then to the
scientific press, and finally to the reference books. Its transparent wheezes got themselves converted into sober history.
It accumulated corroborative detail. To this day it is in circulation, and, as I say, has broken into the reference books,
and is there embalmed for the instruction and edification
of posterity.

On May 23, writing here, I exposed it at length. I
pointed out some of the obvious absurdities in it. I con-

fessed categorically that it was all buncombe. I called upon the historians of the land to take it out of their books. This confession and appeal was printed simultaneously in nearly thirty great American newspapers. One of them was the eminent Boston *Herald*, organ of the New England illuminati. The *Herald* printed my article on page 7 of its editorial section, under a four column head, and with a two column cartoon labeled satirically, "The American public will swallow anything." And then on June 13, three weeks later, in the same editorial section but promoted to page 1, this same *Herald* reprinted my 10 year old fake—soberly and as a piece of news!

Do not misunderstand me: I am not seeking to cast a stone at the *Herald* or at its talented and patriotic editors. It is, I believe, one of the glories of American journalism. It labors unceasingly for virtue and the flag. If it were suppressed by the Watch and Ward society tomorrow New England would revert instantly to savagery, wolves and catamounts would roam in Boylston street, and the Harvard Law school would be engulfed by bolshevism. Little does the public reck what great sums such journals expend to establish and disseminate the truth. It may cost $10,000 and a reporter's leg to get a full and accurate list of the guests at a Roxbury wake, with their injuries.

My point is that, despite all this extravagant frenzy for the truth, there is something in the human mind that turns instinctively to fiction, and that even journalists succumb to it. A German philosopher, Dr. Hans Vaihinger, has put the thing into a formal theory, and you will find it expounded at length in his book, *The Philosophy of As If*. It is a sheer impossibility, says Dr. Vaihinger, for human beings to think exclusively in terms of the truth. For one thing, the stock of indubitable truths is too scanty. For another thing, there is the instinctive aversion to them that I have mentioned. All of our thinking, according to Vaihinger, is in terms of assumptions, many of them plainly not true. Into our most solemn and serious reflections fictions enter—and three times out of four they quickly crowd out all the facts.

That this is true needs no argument. Every man, thinking of his wife, has to assume that she is beautiful and amiable, else despair will seize him and he will be unable to think at all. Every American, contemplating Dr. Coolidge, is physically bound to admire him: the alternative is anarchy. Every Christian, viewing the clergy, is forced into a bold theorizing to save himself from Darwinism. And all of us, taking stock of ourselves, must resort to hypothesis to escape the river.

What ails the truth is that it is mainly uncomfortable, and often dull. The human mind seeks something more amusing, and more caressing. What the actual history of the bathtub may be I don't know: digging it out would be a dreadful job, and the result, after all that labor, would probably be a string of banalities. The fiction I concocted back in 1917 was at least better than that. It lacked sense, but it was certainly not without a certain charm. There were heroes in it, and villains. It revealed a conflict, with virtue winning. So it was embraced by mankind, precisely as the story of George Washington and the cherry tree was embraced, and it will live, I daresay, until it is displaced by something worse—and hence better.

In other words, it was poetry. And what is poetry? Poetry is simply a mellifluous statement of the obviously untrue. The two elements are both important, and perhaps equally. It is not sufficient that the thing said be untrue: it must also be said with a certain grace—it must soothe the ear while it debauches the mind. And it is not sufficient that it be voluptuous: it must also offer a rock and a refuge from the harsh facts of every day. All poetry embodies a lie. It may be an objective lie, as in "God's in His heaven; all's well with the world." Or it may be a subjective lie, as in "I am the master of my fate." But it must be a lie—and preferably a thumping one.

Poets, in general, protest against this doctrine. They argue that they actually deal in the truth, and that their brand of truth is of a peculiarly profound and esoteric quality—in other words, that their compositions add to the sum of human wisdom. It is sufficient answer to them to say that chiropractors make precisely the same claim, and with exactly the same plausibility. Both actually deal in fictions. Those fictions are not truth; they are not even truths in decay. They are simply better than truths. They make life more comfortable and happy. They turn and dull the sharp edge of reality.

It is commonly held that the vast majority of men are anesthetic to poetry, as they are alleged to be anesthetic to other forms of beauty, but this is a fiction, devised by poets to dignify their trade, and make it seem high toned and mysterious. The fact is that the love of poetry is one of the most primitive of human traits, and that it appears in children almost as soon as they learn to speak. I do not refer here to the love of verbal jingles, but to the love of poetry properly so-called—that is, to the love of the agreeably not so. A little girl who nurses a rag doll is a poet, and so is a boy who plays at soldiers with a box of clothes pins. Their ma is another poet when she brags about them to the neighbors, and their pa when he praises the cooking of their ma.

The more simple minded the individual, indeed, the greater his need of poetry, and hence the more steady his demand for it. No poet approved by the intelligentsia ever had so many customers as Edgar A. Guest. Guest's dithyrambs are laughed at by the intelligentsia, not because the things they say are not so, but because the fiction in them is of a kind not satisfying to sniffish and snooty men. It is fiction suitable to persons of a less critical habit. It preaches the joys open to the humble. It glorifies their dire necessities. It cries down their lacks. It promises them happiness, and if not happiness, then at least contentment. No wonder it is popular! No wonder it is intoned every time Kiwanians get together and the reassuring slapping of backs begins. It is itself a sort of back slapping.

And so is all other poetry. The strophes of Robert Browning elude the Kiwanian, but they are full of soothing for the young college professor, for they tell him that it is a marvelous and exhilarating thing to be as intellectual as he is. This, of course, is not true—which is the chief reason why it is pleasant. No normal human being wants to hear the truth. It is the passion of a small and aberrant minority of men, most of them pathological. They are hated for telling it while they live, and when they die they are swiftly forgotten. What remains to the world, in the field of wisdom, is a series of long tested and solidly agreeable lies.
(*July 25, 1926*)

THE BELIEVING MIND

SOME TIME ago I received a letter from an elderly Socialist, once very active in the movement, but long since retired. It was stuffed with circulars advertising a new sure cure for all human ills, from bellyache to cancer. This invention, the Socialist assured me, was no fake. He had personally seen it snatch back men and women from the brink of the grave. It would be in use everywhere, he said, and saving hundreds of thousands of lives a year, if it were not for the hellish conspiracies of the American Medical Association.

It all seemed familiar. More, it all seemed quite natural. For who has ever heard of a Socialist who did not also believe in some other quackery? I have known all the principal gladiators of the movement in my time, at least in America; I have yet to meet one who was not as gullible as a Mississippi darkey, nay, even as a Mississippi white man. Didn't Karl Marx himself carry a madstone and believe in astrology? If not, then it was strange, indeed. Doesn't Debs believe that quinine will cure a cold? If not, then he is not a genuine Socialist.

The leading living Socialist of this great republic is Upton Sinclair. Perhaps, indeed, he is the only leader the movement has left, for Debs is over 70 and all the rest leaped down the sewers during the late war. Well, Sinclair believes in so many different kinds of nonsense that it takes a thick book to record them. He was one of the earliest believers in the fasting cure for catarrh, and he was one of the first dupes to be roped in by the late Dr. Albert Abrams, the San Francisco swindler. I do not hold all this against Sinclair. He is a charming fellow, otherwise. I merely say that it is natural to Socialists. Turn to England, where the current hero of the movement is young Oliver Baldwin, son of the prime minister. On June 20 last the Associated Press reported from London that Oliver had taken to spiritualism and was hearing "spirit voices coming from all parts of the room in no fewer than five languages."

As I have said, practically all of the more eminent Socialists of the United States took to the sewers in 1917. When the gunmen of the Hon. A. Mitchell Palmer began rounding up the lesser comrades, and federal judges began sending them to Atlanta for five, ten, and even twenty years, the high toned members of the movement saw a great light, and began to bawl and sob for the flag. Now, with the danger over, they can't get back; the surviving comrades won't have anything to do with them, and even denounce them bitterly as scabs.

But if the Marxian grove is thus closed to them, there is plenty of room for them around other flambeaux, and all of them seem to be crowding up. A considerable number, in 1920, became violent prohibitionists, and began predicting that the country would be bone dry in two years. Others became chiropractors. Yet others announced that they were converted to the league of nations. Many became spiritualists, and a few, I believe, followed Sinclair in succumbing to Dr. Abrams. The rest went in for free love, fundamentalism, mental telepathy, the Harding idealism, Texas oil stocks, numerology, the poetry of T. S. Eliot, the music of Eric Satie, or the ouija board. One or two became professional sorcerers.

The point is that every one found some sort of satisfaction for the imperative need of his nature—every one found something outlandish and preposterous to believe. For all of them, as ex-Socialists, had believing minds. They could get rid of their socialism, especially when helped by the Polizei, but they could no more get rid of their believing minds than they could get rid of the shapes of their hands. A Socialist is simply a man suffering from an overwhelming compulsion to believe what is not true. He yearns for it as a cow yearns for the milkman, lowing in the cool of the evening. He pines for it as a dry congressman pines for a drink.

Of all the things that are palpably not true, socialism is one of the most satisfying to men of the romantic kidney, and so nine-tenths of them, at one time or another in their lives, are Socialists, or, if not Socialists, then at least Progressives, or single taxers, or evangelists of farm relief. But socialism, though it is sweet, is never enough for them, and neither is the single tax. They always reach out for something else. They always succumb to some other and worse Marx, with longer whiskers and dirtier fingernails.

Years ago, when the single taxers were still making a noise in the land, I made a roster of the princes of the movement, setting down beside each name the varieties of balderdash that its owner believed in. There was not a single name without two entries, and some of them had a dozen. One of the leading single tax agitators was also president of the League for Medical Freedom, a verein of quacks organized to oppose vaccination. Another was a militant anti-vivisectionist, and proposed that the Johns Hopkins Medical school be closed by the police. A third was an anthropophagous atheist of the kind that proselytes, especially among peaceable old ladies. A third [sic] was a table tapper, and a fourth got messages from the ghosts of Martin Luther, Lucy Stone, and Sitting Bull. A fifth deserted his wife for a cutie with pansy eyes, and lost, in consequence, his job as a college professor. A sixth, believing that he was Millard Fillmore, was put away by his family.

I know very few single taxers. They are, in fact, very unpleasant people to know, for they never take a holiday from their delusion, and so their conversation tends to be trying. But the few I know all run perfectly true to type. If they don't believe in osteopathy, then they believe in international peace. If they don't believe in international peace, then they believe in the recall of judges. If they don't believe in the recall of judges, then they believe in sending hijackers to comfortable lunatic asylums and treating them on the theory that they are temporarily out of their minds. Always they believe in something beautifully idiotic, and always they believe in at least two such things.

What lies beneath all this is simply an ancient fact, noted long ago by William James, and before him by Friedrich Wilhelm Nietzsche, and before him by the Greeks, and before the Greeks by the first human politicians. It is the fact that the race of men is divided sharply into two classes: those who are what James called tough minded, and demand overwhelming proofs before they will believe, and those who are what he called tender minded, and are willing to believe anything that seems to be pleasant.

It is the tender minded who keep quacks of all sorts well fed and active, and hence vastly augment the charm of this world. They find it wholly impossible to distinguish between what is subjectively agreeable and what is objectively true. Would it be nice if the whole world turned sober overnight, and even flappers put away the jug? If so, then there must be a quick and sure way to accomplish it. Does prohibition promise to do so? If so, then prohibition must be true. This is precisely the route by which Sinclair became a prohibitionist—one of his follies that I forgot to mention above. And this is the route by which multitudes of his tender hearted brethern and sistern followed him—into the jaws of the Anti-Saloon league.

Socialism, when it was still vague and untested, appealed powerfully to all such persons. Fifteen or twenty years ago it was making immense progress in the United States, vice free silver, deceased. All the young college professors, in those days, were Socialists, as they are now birth controllers. It swept and enchanted the tender mind. Fat women wept over it, as they now weep over the Armenians. But one day it collided slambang with the harsh and horrible facts. One day it was put to the test—and promptly blew up. Even the tender minded could not dodge the appalling proofs. So they fled in this direction and that. Some took to spiritualism, some to chiropractic, some to Genesis. Some, like Sinclair, took to prohibition, the single tax, fasting, and the electronic vibrations of Dr. Abrams. But not one, so far as I can make out, took to sense.

(August 8, 1926)

II. LAND OF THE FREE

Mencken as an advocate of free expression differs in one particular from many newspapermen of today who share his libertarian views.

The Sage of Baltimore not only bawled in a bellicose manner for the right to be heard, but he also practiced without restraint those liberties which he insisted were his.

In these times of more refined journalism, committees of editors meet tirelessly to talk about freedom of speech.

But do they all practice it as assiduously as they discuss it? Not in any real manner, it is certain, on those newspapers which maintain "black lists" of names not to be mentioned in a manner reflecting credit.

And surely the cause of free expression is not well served by those carefully editing material that might be deleterious to a favored few.

These practices look exceedingly dreary when compared to the unholy gusto with which Mencken slaughtered the sacred cows of journalism as he inveighed against censorship and other forms of restraint.

He employed a thumb-to-nose attitude toward the conventions of public and publisher alike. Sent once to perform a journalistic hatchet job on a university president un-

acceptable to his editors, he returned with a piece that had the opposite effect. The intended victim, he explained, wasn't really a bad sort at all.

When considering the hairy-chested type of journalism Mencken frequently employed, however, justice dictates this added observation:

Fearless editorializing does not, after all, demand excessive heroism of the writer. The main requirements are simply a fairly thick skin and the patience to endure the complaints of the outraged.

But it is quite another thing for a publisher to essay the role of champon of free expression. It is his property that is endangered when indignant advertisers threaten a boycott; it is upon him that the genuine pressure from the powerful is brought to bear.

A completely unfettered Mencken was first turned loose upon the public in the "Free Lance" column written between 1911 and 1915 for the Baltimore Evening Sun.

The name of the publisher who supported this venture deserves to be remembered.

It was Charles H. Grasty.

THE BILL OF RIGHTS

Now AND THEN one encounters an excellent book which fails of its purpose because it is based upon an erroneous assumption. Such a book is Congress, *the Constitution, and the Supreme Court,* by Charles Warren, an eminent jurisconsult of Boston, whose previous work, *The Supreme Court in United States History*, won the Pulitzer prize in 1922. The excellence of the volume flows out of the author's profound and philosophical knowledge of American legal history. He understands completely the important part that the courts, and especially the appellate courts, have played in our national development, and he is eloquent and convincing in his argument against those reformers who would hobble them. But he quite misapprehends, I believe, the primary causes of that rising discontent with them which is so plainly visible today.

His error, of course, has plausible foundations. If he assumes that the courts are unpopular because they limit the output of so-called progressive legislation, then he assumes only what has been accepted as a fact by his chief opponents: Senator Borah, the late Dr. La Follette, and the late Col. Roosevelt. Roosevelt's whole attack upon the Supreme court was based upon that notion. The learned justices, wrapped in their funereal shrouds, stood firmly against his plan to stretch the constitution to fit his policies, and he accordingly denounced them as senile, anti-social, and under the hoof of the plutocracy. La Follette echoed the charge, and elaborated it. It bobs up anew in the somewhat muddled speculations of Dr. Borah.

But does it cause any genuine excitement among the generality of Americans? Are they actually fevered by the fact that the child labor act of 1919 was upset by the Supreme court in 1922? Is there any widespread indignation because the same puissant tribunal knocked out the District of Columbia minimum wage act a year later? I think not. Certain specialists in utopian legislation may be wrought up and full of bile, but surely not the average man. What

annoys that average man is something quite different—
something diametrically opposite. He doesn't bellow because the Supreme court guards the constitution too jealously; he bellows because it doesn't guard the constitution
jealously enough.

In other words, the current discontent with the courts,
and especially with the federal courts, rests at bottom upon
a fear of congress, not upon a fondness or respect for congress. No one believes in its *bona fides* any more; no one
believes that its typical member has any thought save for
his own hide. When that hide is menaced he will do anything that is wanted of him, and if the constitution stands
in the way then so much the worse for the constitution. The
legislative process becomes a mere leaping of cowards and
mountebanks. Given a lobby pertinacious enough, almost
anything imaginable may be put through.

Of late this putting through has been going on at a
dizzy rate, and so the statute books are cluttered with oppressive legislation, most of it supported by penalties that
clearly violate the guarantees of the bill of rights. Every one
knows how the right to free speech, for example, has been
invaded and made a mock of. And the right to free assem-
blage. And the inviolability of domicile. And the guarantee
against unreasonable seizures. And the ancient right to a
jury trial. Under the pressure of ruthless fanatics, willing to
go to any length to satisfy their lust to bludgeon and ter-
rorize their fellow men, congress has violated every one of
these rights, and some of them it has violated repeatedly.

The constitutional remedy lies in the courts. They were
set up in the fond belief that they would curb the excesses
of the legislature. They were given a written constitution—
written in the plainest of plain English—to guide and sus-

tain them. In it the inalienable rights of the free citizen were set forth clearly, and the judges were bidden to maintain them. How have they done their job? It must be obvious that, in late years, they have done it very badly. They have not only let congress run amok; they have not infrequently run amok themselves. In most federal jurisdictions today the bill of rights is worth no more than the statutes of Hammurabi. The fact, I believe, is not lost upon the people. It explains their increasing dissatisfaction with the courts—their growing willingness to listen to reformers who propose to reduce the whole judicial system to impotence and absurdity.

Congress began this invasion of the bill of rights very early. The first ten amendments were submitted in 1789 and ratified by the end of 1791, but by 1798 they were already flouted by the alien and sedition acts. The Supreme court, at that time, was not yet in full function, and so the people, passing it over, turned to political action for a remedy. But in 1803 came the great case of Marbury vs. Madison, and thereafter the court's right to police congress was recognized, and it exercised that right steadily and effectively—so effectively that there was no other considerable effort to get around the bill of rights until the stormy period of the civil war.

But even during that stormy period the court upheld the guarantees of the citizen with great jealousy, as the celebrated Milligan case sufficiently proved, and during the years following it kept congress rigorously in order. In 1870, for example, a law was passed setting up a sort of double jeopardy in civil cases—that is, allowing the federal courts to retry actions already decided in state courts. The Supreme court promptly declared it unconstitutional—and it was never heard of again until our own time. In 1890 congress tried to get around the fifth amendment, with its prohibition of prosecution for infamous crimes save after indictment of the accused by a grand jury—and again the Supreme court came to the rescue.

So in other cases. In 1886 congress passed an act which provided for searches and seizures in violation of the fourth amendment, and the Supreme court knocked it out. In 1899 congress passed an act destroying the right of a man accused to be confronted with the witnesses against him, and the Supreme court knocked it out. In 1867 congress tried to put an *ex post facto* law on the books, and the Supreme court knocked it out. In 1909 congress tried to set up appeals by the government in criminal cases, and the Supreme court said nay.

This went on down to the end of the first decade of the present century. Then came a sudden change—how caused I don't know. Holes began to be punched in the bill of rights, and new laws of a strange and often fantastic shape began to slip through them. The hysteria of the late war completed the process. The espionage act enlarged the holes to great fissures. Citizens began to be pursued into their houses, arrested without warrants, and jailed without any form of trial. The ancient writ of *habeas corpus* was suspended; the bill of rights was boldly thrown overboard.

Here was the most noble opportunity that the Supreme court in all its history ever faced. It had a chance to do something, perhaps transiently unpopular, that would be of more value to human liberty in this world than a dozen bogus wars to save democracy. How did it meet the challenge? If you want to find out, and crave an authoritative view, go read the dissenting opinions of the war years and immediately thereafter—that is, go read the opinions of those justices who stood out for the bill of rights in the face of all pressure and uproar and were defeated only by the votes of their illustrious colleagues.

In those minority opinions, chiefly by Justices Brandeis and Holmes, there is much melancholy history. And in that history lie the roots of the evil esteem in which the courts are held today. Few Americans, I believe, want to upset them altogether, in the manner proposed by Roosevelt and La Follette. Their theoretical value in the state is too vast, however lamentable their practical failure. But few Americans, regarding that practical failure calmly, can escape the conclusion that some way to improve them is needed and that it must be found.

(*January 17, 1926*)

THE COMSTOCKIAN IMBECILITY

THE COMSTOCKS, whatever their defects otherwise, at least show great gifts as clowns; they never get into motion without making thumping asses of themselves. I point to the recent onslaughts upon *Judge,* the comic weekly. The smellers of the postoffice department, taking alarm at certain harmless jocosities that it ventured to print, barred it from the mails. And on that very day and date, in the pursuit of their statutory duty to spread the enlightenment, the colleagues of these smellers hauled something over a thousand tons of magazines given over to frank and unmitigated filth—magazines so wholly foul, and so widely known to be foul, that if any one of them ever printed a clean number there would be riots in every Christian community in America.

The name of the Dogbery who fell upon *Judge* I don't know; if I knew it I'd embalm it in this present stream of literary amber. Whoever he was, he was obviously both a comstock and a bureaucrat, a snouter and a job holder—in brief, one toting through life a double burden of cerebral bilge. No doubt he had complaints to support him, or, at all events, a complaint. But from whom? The postoffice never tells; the victim is slaughtered anonymously. Any psychopathic old maid, male or female, is free to turn the official smuthounds loose. If the victim escapes, he has no redress. Would he sue for damages, he must sue a miserable postoffice clerk—and with the courts and their decisions heavily against him.

His remedy, once he has paid his lawyers, is simply to laugh. For the business is almost invariably farcical. In the present case it runs true to type. All the newsstands of the republic are burdened to groaning with smutty magazines. They penetrate to the remotest country towns. They are carried in the mails. And yet the postoffice, bestirred at last to moral indignation, makes its first strike at *Judge*, one of the cleanest periodicals in the country. I have read it for years, and have yet to encounter any obscenity in it. Least of all could I find any in the issue that was barred from the mails.

But the comstockian logic, as every one should know by this time, is not that of ordinary men. The smellers, whether official or unofficial, have tests and standards of their own. One of their principles, I believe, may be disentangled from the *Judge* case: they are against humor—save, of course, when it is made by the collision of the ceiling with their own docuses. *Judge* presumed to poke fun at the loose French comic sheets which circulate so widely among us. The text of these sheets is unintelligible to the Americano; he can grasp only the indecency of their pictures. They are thus (to him) serious works of pornography. Ergo, they go through the mails. But *Judge* jibed at them—and at their readers. Ergo, it was barred.

The thing sounds absurd, but if you will turn to the drama you will quickly find that its roots are in the facts. Every Broadway manager knows that if he would get away with smut all he has to do is to make it indignant. The comstocks will never bother him; nay, most of their clerical allics will praise him. But the moment he ventures into jocosity he is on dangerous ground, and if his jocosity has genuine humor in it he is lost. Has any one ever heard of a raid on a Biblical play? Certainly not. But has any one ever heard of a Biblical play without an uproarious hoochiecoochie in it, and a scene showing the hero being tempted to sin by the première danseuse? Such gross and undisguised lasciviousness is safe. But every time another harmless bedroom farce comes along, and audiences begin to roar with mirth, there is renewed talk of setting up a censorship.

The proprietors of the smutty magazines are well aware of this comstockian principle. The worst of such magazines are violently moral in tone. They describe the seduction of poor working girls, lingeringly and in detail, only to denounce it furiously. They discuss all the blushful mysteries in terms of indignation. Thus they are free of the mails, and every high school boy and girl in the land has access to them. But if one of them ever loosed a cackle, the comstocks would be down upon it at once.

Comstockery, indeed, is nothing but imbecility. It never works, and no wonder, for the fanatics behind it are unanimously fools. Its ostensible objects are never attained; its actual achievements are always ridiculous and usually pernicious.

Consider, for example, its effects upon the book trade in the United States. During the last dozen years practically every publisher of any dignity in the country has been harassed by its agents, and more than one such publisher has been put to great expense to defend himself. Author after author of honest purpose and honorable position has been attacked wildly as an enemy of virtue and a perverter of youth. The courts have been filled with such cases—always against men of unquestionable *bona fides*, always against shining marks.

And meanwhile the country has been flooded with smut—smut by the bale, carload, and trainload. Shyster publishers have got rich printing it—and gone unscathed. All the better known pornographic books have come out in countless editions, and there have been numerous additions to the list. Many of them are advertised boldly, and sold openly. Any boy with a few dollars in his pocket can get all he wants. And what have the comstocks done about it? They have done exactly nothing. The trade grows under their very noses. They waste their energies trying to put down good books.

So with the magazines. They have failed so signally to stop the deluge of smut that there are complaints from all parts of the country. In at least a hundred American towns the local police have been forced to act. They are, of course, idiots, but they are surely not so idiotic as the comstocks. No one, as yet, has heard of their trying to suppress the *Atlantic Monthly* and the *Literary Digest*—and letting *Hot Tales* go. But that, almost precisely, is what the professional comstocks have done. And that is what the postoffice smellers did in the *Judge* case.

Perhaps there is more in all this, after all, than mere imbecility. The comstocks, like all other such public nuisances, live on the money they can cadge from fools—and the liberality of fools, as of wise men, runs in direct ratio to the gaudiness of the show that is offered to them. An onslaught upon a book by a Dreiser or a Cabell is sure of making the first pages, and, what is more, of staying there for several days. Collections, thereafter, ought to be good. But a raid upon a puerile piece of smut by some unknown hack is worth only five lines on an inside page, and so it cannot be trusted to get the mazuma.

Thus the comstockian gladiators are tempted to neglect their proper business—if they may be said to have any proper business at all—and to spend their time harassing honest men. They operate under federal laws, and, in many of the states, under state laws, that make this harassing of honest men quite safe for them. It is difficult for a victim, once he has got out of their clutches, to bring responsibility home to them; it is almost impossible for him to get substantial damages out of them. The smutty old men who chiefly support them are securely hidden behind a corporate screen, erected by law. They can thus afford to take chances. If they fail, nothing happens to them, no matter how great the damage to the man they have assaulted.

Obviously, such laws stand squarely against the com-

mon rights of the citizen and the peace and dignity of the
state. They are incentives to the worst sort of oppression.
Worse, they accomplish no good, direct or indirect. I have
pointed to their gross failure in the case of the smutty magazines. Their failure has thrown responsibility upon the police, where it belongs, and they are meeting it very competently, half-wits though they be. It ought to be upon them
everywhere. Comstockery is useless and it is vile.
(*December 20, 1925*)

THE ANATOMY OF WOWSERISM

TWICE OF LATE wowserian statutes have been repealed in
the republic, and both times in states celebrated for their
Christian rectitude and ferocity. First the legislature of
Tennessee, the same that amazed and amused Christendom
with the anti-evolution law, repealed the act prohibiting
the sale of gasoline on Sunday. And then the legislature of
Kansas repealed the state anti-cigaret law. Both events
brought forth deluges of heavy moralizing by the gifted editorial writers of the nation. The drift of that moralizing was
that the wave of evangelical legislation has reached its crest
and that saner days are ahead.

I can only say that I find myself unable to assent to this
conclusion. There was, in fact, nothing in either repealer
to indicate that the yokels of the land have lost or are losing
their congenital frenzy to flay and harass the rest of us.
There was only proof of an old and familiar fact: that their
lust for righteousness always abates when their own ox is
gored. If automobiles were owned only by city men then

the hinds of Tennessee would never have repealed the law closing filling stations on Sunday. And if the late crusade for democracy had not taught the young peasants of Kansas to smoke cigarets then there would have been no repeal of the state's anti-cigaret act.

The moral muzhik never advocates laws to put down his own vices. Even the Volstead act, as every one knows, still permits him to make hard cider, and even wine. And his rage against the cigaret began as a rage, not against tobacco in general, but simply against city men, for they in those days were the only persons known to him who used the coffin nails. Has any one ever heard of country pastors advocating a law against corn cob pipes or against chewing tobacco? Certainly not. The yokel smokes a pipe and so he is not against it. He chews tobacco and so he is not against it. Now, it appears, he has begun to smoke cigarets, and so the cigaret, too, becomes more and more Christian.

The history of the Kansas anti-cigaret act deserves to be recorded at length, for it throws an illuminating light upon the processes of the evangelical mind. The campaign for the statute was launched in the days of those immortal prairie statesmen, Whiskers Peffer and Sockless Jerry Simpson, when the state was suffering from a profound agricultural depression and half of its people were on the verge of starvation. The chief stock in trade of every Kansas demagogue in that era was the wickedness of the cities. The plutocrats of Wall and State streets, it appeared, were sucking the very lifeblood of the farmers. The latter worked from dawn to dark, gouging the reluctant soil, feeding the voracious hog, following the laborious plow horse. The former, seizing all the profit, lavished it upon wine, women, and song.

To this trio the cigaret had been recently added. It was then relatively new in America and only the opulent and sinful employed it in their debaucheries. The spectacle of a woman smoking in that fevered age had the same effect upon the average pastor as the spectacle of a woman naked from ankles to knees. It sent him leaping to his Bible as if the devil were after him. As for men smokers, he had their number too. They were semi-effeminate scoundrels and voluptuaries, dissipating the just usufructs of honest farmers in the arms of harlots, bartenders, musicians, dancers, and other such emissaries of hell. In brief, the cigaret was the sign and symbol of urban licentiousness.

It was thus quite easy for the hedge preachers to arouse the yokels against it, and once the yokels had begun to sweat, the job seekers who sought to prey upon them naturally got converted. There followed the Kansas anti-cigaret act. The theory under it was that the cigaret was full of opium, and that if its use were not checked by moral legislation it would presently debauch the youth of the whole state and convert every sun boiled young plow hand into a second Heliogabalus, with gangs of dancing girls hidden in the barn and atheism in his heart. The fact that the cigaret symbolized the superior prosperity and happiness of the city man was thus revolting to Christian peasants, along with the cocktail, the leg show, and the week-end trip to Atlantic City.

After awhile the return of prosperity to the steppes began to dissipate this primal rage. The bolder students in the evangelical "colleges" that dot the Kansas prairies bought cigarets from bootleggers, found them tasty, and so became devotees. But the statute remained on the books, as travelers found to their astonishment when they crossed the Kansas line. The Pullman porter, while the train rushed through that depressing vacuum, was forbidden to supply cigarets officially; he had to bootleg them.

Then came the war to liberate the Croats, Letts, Serbs, Czechs, and Montenegrins, and thousands of young Kansas yokels were yanked from the plow and manure fork and put into uniforms. Once herded into camps, they found to their amazement that cigaret smoking was almost universal therein. Not only did the commanding general smoke them; even the female nurses, including many of mature age, smoked them. Yet worse, they were vended openly by the Y.M.C.A., and at good round prices. The camp movies showed Gen. Pershing smoking one. Later on, in France, it appeared that Marshal Foch carried a package in his saddlebag, along with his Bible.

These Kansas heroes learned certain other things in France, and when the war was gloriously over brought them home. There was, for example, the science of necking—but that is another story. Today I discuss only cigaret smoking. They left the banks of the Kansas, at worst, timid experimenters behind the barn or chapel; they came back incurable addicts. The opium, manganese, formaldehyde, Glauber's salts, and other hellish drugs in the coffin nails had done their deadly work—and at bootleg prices even the cheapest cigarets were expensive. So the heroes began agitating for the repeal of the law, morals or no morals, Bible or no Bible. In this crusade the American Legion took the lead. After a long struggle the law was duly repealed. Once more a change in *mores* had undone the consecrated work of moralists.

The whole episode is immensely amusing and profoundly instructive. It suggests the possibility that the Volstead act in years to come may go the same way and by much the same process. If ever the science of moonshining and the art of bootlegging come to such a development that decent drinks are obtainable in the villages of the cow states, then the yokels will lose their bilious envy of the city man and turn against prohibition. They were for it in the first place because the old system gave the city man an advantage over them. He had cocktails and champagne to drink and they had only hard cider and rotgut. So they rose against him—at the same time reserving the cider for themselves and keeping a prudent hold on the rotgut. Good whisky would convert them, as the cigarets of the Y.M.C.A. converted the embattled peasant lads of Kansas.

Such is the typical history of moral endeavor, at all times and everywhere. What lies under it nine times out of ten is simply envy of some one who is having what seems to be a better time. Homely women and farmers are the immemorial proponents of moral legislation, for every homely woman wishes in her heart that she were a man and every farmer wishes that he lived in one of the great Sodoms and Babylons and shared in its deviltries. When the agitation against the sale of gasoline on Sunday started in Tennessee, automobiles were few and practically all of them were owned by city men. The complaisant judiciary of the state quickly found a way to apply the ancient blue laws to the relief of the yokels' envy. But when autos began to multiply in the swamps and mountains and every farmer began to drive one, the old heat of moral passion died out. Presently the rustics were murmuring. In the end they dragooned the legislature into changing the law.

There is at the moment a growing protest against the obscene "art" magazines which now flood the country. Has it been observed that this protest does not come from the farms? That is because the young yokels, by the beneficent work of the postoffice, share in the "art." But if the post-office ever bars these magazines from the mails so that only city sinners may procure them, then every country pastor in the land will be moved to demand that they be suppressed altogether.

(February 27, 1927)

PADLOCKS

THE NOTORIOUS Lord's Day alliance, seeking in several states to adorn the statute books with new blue laws, bor-rows very naturally and gracefully a device from the Anti-Saloon league. This is the device of the injunction. Its pur-pose is plain and undisguised. In all the largest cities of the United States, and indeed in almost all communities above the level of a wayside hog chute, it is impossible to induce juries to convict under the blue laws. No matter how plain the evidence against the boys accused of playing baseball on Sunday afternoon, or the druggist charged with selling chewing gum, or the news agent taken in the act of deliv-ering a Sunday newspaper, the jury says "not guilty," and once it has said "not guilty" that is the end of it.

But judges, for many reasons, are much easier—that is, much easier for the janissaries of chemical purity. Many of them are old men and crabbed—too old to play ball or to chew gum. Many others, practicing law for years, have got themselves so enmeshed in legal technicalities that they can no longer grasp the concept of human rights. And still more, at least in the state courts, want to be reëlected when their terms expire, and know by experience what damage organized malignancy can do to a candidate. Thus they are far more disposed than juries are to jail men for imaginary crimes. If the prosecution is noisy enough and determined enough, they commonly succumb.

Hence the injunction process, now grown so common in our courts. The aim of the injunction is to take the case away from a jury and hand it over to a judge. Once the writ is issued, all the constitutional rights of the accused disappear. He is now completely at the mercy of the judge—and the judge is not only judge but also complainant, prosecuting officer, catchpoll, and executioner. A simple and beautiful process, and very attractive to the legal mind.

Who invented it I don't know. My researches indicate that it goes back pretty far—to the early 80s of the last century, at least. But at the start it seems to have had hard sledding. The Appellate judges of that remote era had a high respect for the bill of rights. In particular they had a high respect for the guarantee of trial by jury. The injunction scheme, as I have said, was plainly a device to get around that guarantee. Its obvious intent and effect were to put the accused at the disposal of the trial judge. So the Appellate courts, for some time, frowned upon it.

But finally, after a hard struggle, it was wriggled through. This was in Massachusetts, in 1887. In form, the injunction act passed there in that year was almost identical with the injunction clause of the Volstead act. It was aimed, like the latter, at bootleggers and blind tigers. Four of the seven judges of the state Supreme court held that it was valid, a majority of one. The other three voted against it, and the dissenting opinion of Mr. Justice Field, afterward chief justice of the court, was an exhaustive review of the whole scheme, its purposes and effects, and a vigorous denunciation of it.

Thereafter, in Massachusetts, it seems to have fallen into disuse, but in the moral middle west it was soon flourishing. Iowa eventually became the scene of its gaudiest triumphs. Vice crusading, so-called, was a popular sport out there; the evangelical pastors led, and a mob of half-wits, eager for salacious adventure, followed. Unluckily, the juries of the towns often failed to convict the victims. In some towns they refused almost every time. So a bright young district attorney at Fort Dodge, William S. Kenyon by name, revived the injunction scheme, and the result was what came to be known through all the cow country as the Kenyon act. Under the Kenyon act a judge could issue an injunction against any one accused of keeping a disorderly house, and thereafter the accused was at his mercy and could be jailed for contempt of court whenever the judge and the vice crusaders thought it ought to be done.

The pious peasants of Iowa, who greatly enjoyed vice crusading, rewarded Kenyon by making him a judge and then a United States senator. In 1922 the sainted Harding took him from the scene and gave him a federal circuit.

Meanwhile, there stand the fifth and sixth amendments to the constitution—and in practically all of the state constitutions they are repeated. The fifth provided that no one shall be made to answer for an "infamous crime"— and this means any crime for which the punishment may be confinement in a prison or penitentiary—"unless on a presentment or indictment of a grand jury," and the sixth provides that "in all criminal prosecutions the accused shall enjoy the right to a speedy and public trial by an impartial jury of the state and district wherein the crime shall have been committed."

It is hard, indeed, for a layman trained in the ordinary processes of logic to reconcile these plain and specific prohibitions with what is now going on in the federal courts, under the Volstead act, every day. If they mean anything at all, they certainly mean that no man shall be sent to prison until two juries have heard the evidence against him and decided that it is sufficient. But under the Volstead act he may be sent to prison if only a federal judge, already admittedly suspicious of him and hence prejudiced against him, decides that he should go. In the one case he has what has been regarded for a thousand years as a fair trial. In the other case he is simply bumped off.

That these judges have the power to punish summarily for contempt is, of course, known to every one. They must have the means in their hands to preserve decorum in their courtrooms, and they must have the means to enforce their reasonable decrees. But the writ of injunction is a remedy in equity, and even lawyers, I suppose, must be aware that equity does not begin to run until the law leaves off. Is there any lack of law for prosecuting bootleggers? Obviously there is not. They may be indicted by a grand jury, tried and convicted by a petit jury, and sent to prison like any other offenders. It is done every day. Why, then, should judges be authorized to try them without a jury and send them up as precipitately as if they had been taken red handed in open court? And why, if bootleggers may be so bumped off, may not all other federal offenders be so bumped off?

The answer I have already given. The injunction

clause of the Volstead act is simply and solely a device to get around the constitutional guarantee of trial by jury—that is, to get around the uncomfortable fact that, in most jurisdictions, at least in the cities, juries are against prohibition and will not convict save in the presence of overwhelming proof. It is one of the most dishonest dodges ever heard of. If it goes unchallenged, it will reduce the whole bill of rights to an absurdity, and in the end an American citizen will have no rights that a federal judge is bound to respect.

For, as I have said, the fact that it is in force and use has not escaped the fanatics who rove the land, seeking ever new means to rowel and oppress the people, and they are already planning to put it into other acts and so shape it to their anti-social ends. If it is turned upon bootleggers, why shouldn't it be turned upon Sunday movies; if it is turned upon Sunday movies, why shouldn't it be turned upon the sort of books that tender imbeciles regard as obscene? It opens the way to a reign of terror hitherto unheard of in the world. It is the negation of all reasonable law and order.

So far, I believe, the Supreme court of the United States has not passed upon its validity—that is, specifically. By inference it has been upheld, but not in plain terms. If, when the time comes, the decision is in favor of it, then the people of the United States had better tear up the bill of rights and bow their necks docilely to the collars of slavery.

(January 31, 1926)

THE BATTLE OF IDEAS

ONE OF THE curses of the United States is the fact that a great deal of its public opinion, and perhaps most, is formulated by men who are not free to express their honest views, even assuming them to be intelligent. I allude to public job holders, from the President down, and to newspaper editorial writers, college professors, and so on. Such men, as every one knows, spend a lot of time discussing economic theories, often indignantly. But of what value is the opinion, say upon socialism or the federal reserve system, of an economist whose job depends upon the good will of a board of trustees made up of bankers and manufacturers? And of what value is that of an editorial writer whose boss is a speculator on the stock exchange?

Here, obviously, the freedom of the expert is quite as important as his honesty, or even his competence. If he is not free, then he is scarcely worth hearing, however ingeniously he may argue his case. I long ago made a private rule about such fellows, and have followed it, I think, to profit. When I hear any one arguing violently for this or that, I always inquire into his private circumstances. If I find that he is perfectly free, should he be so inclined, to express an exactly contrary view, then I am glad to listen to him. But if I find that the expression of a contrary view would lose him his job, or bring down some other swift and harsh punishment upon him, then I am always too busy to give ear to him.

This rule works very well, and saves me much vain listening. The opinions of Gov. Peay of Tennessee on the evolutionary hypothesis are barred out by it, for Peay would have to go back to work if he changed them. The opinions of congressmen about prohibition go in one of my ears and out the other, for the drys among them would lose their jobs if they turned wet, and the wets would be retired if they turned dry. Such men are like lawyers; they argue beautifully, perhaps, but what they say is not worth hearing.

My rule has the curious effect of making me listen with special attention to the ranting and moaning of a class of men whose ideas are very far from my own, to wit, the class of liberals, radicals, and other such dreamers. I am against them congenitally, as I am against wowsers, and the more I hear from them the more I am against them. Nevertheless, I always give heed to them politely, for they are at least free men—it at least costs them something to cherish their brummagem notions. They would suffer no punishment if they changed; on the contrary, they would gain something valuable.

All this is not mere theory: I point to the cases of many American Socialists, now docile ex-Socialists. Down to 1917 or thereabout these gentlemen bawled for the Marxian millennium with great passion, and were denounced for it violently by all good men. When the United States got into the war, and the jails began to yawn, they got converted over night, and began to belabor Marxism just as passionately. The flop was very profitable to them. Their own books had to be peddled laboriously among the comrades, few of whom had any money; their new books became best sellers, and got into all the libraries. More, they were appointed to gaudy boards and commissions, and invited to dinner by Judge Elbert H. Gary. The newspapers, having reviled them for years, suddenly took to greasing and tickling them.

Nevertheless, their new books did not convince me,

though I was in favor of the doctrine they set forth. I preferred their old books, which were idiotic and preposterous, perhaps—but at least honest. Those old books cost them something; their new books got them something. If they switched back to the Marxian rumble-bumble today it would ruin them; hence I am not interested in hearing their reasons for staying where they are. But in the old days they were perfectly free, without damage, to throw Marx overboard, and so I was interested in their reasons for whooping him up.

Their successors of today—that is, their successors in heresy—take on all the attractiveness that used to attach to them. There is something about, say, a Scott Nearing that you will look for in vain in the ordinary economist. The man, I believe, is mainly wrong, and part of his wrongness is downright foolish. When he talks of getting rid of the capitalistic system he is almost as foolish as if he talked of getting rid of the human liver. But if I am thus forced to reject his ideas, I can at least admire the man—and an admirable man is far rarer than a sound idea, and far more valuable.

Nearing started out in life with everything in his favor. He came of good stock, he had a charming personality, he had been educated to a razor edge, and he had a good job in a rich university. If he had stuck to the orthodox economics, he would have been a full professor by now, with four hours' work a week, a vacation of three months every year, and fine pickings in the way of consultation fees. He would be sitting on gaudy committees with ample expense accounts, and writing sound books for the instruction of sophomores and the consolation of investment securities magnates. He would be fat, respectable, and happy.

Instead he is roving the back lands, lecturing futilely to small and penurious audiences of advanced thinkers, most of them obviously dotty. The newspapers, when they mention him at all, speak of him as if he were a sort of criminal. His books are barred from the colleges, lest they inflame the students and force the professors to answer questions. The chautauquas have him on their blacklist, along with Senator-elect Vare and Earl Carroll. He is depicted universally as an enemy to idealism. Yet it must be plain that it is precisely idealism that moves him. Let him give three cheers for the United States Steel corporation tomorrow, and he will be back at the University of Pennsylvania before nightfall, with a life job and a mail full of invitations to dinner. Let him admit categorically that Dr. Coolidge is a greater man than the late Lenin, and his crimes will be forgiven instanter, and money will flow into his coffers. But he refrains, and it is at great cost.

I confess that such resolution seems to me to be very attractive. The question is not whether it is lavished on a sound cause, but whether it is genuinely honest and unselfish. The question is whether there is only policy in them, or actual courage. Such courage, when it is encountered, almost always carries intelligence with it. The man who stands against the majority has to have sharp wits to survive at all: the business is not for dunderheads. Dunderheads are always very orthodox. Every one of them believes in precisely what all the rest of them believe.

What all this leads to, of course, is the doctrine that causes cease to be plausible and charming when they prevail. It may seem like a paradox, but it is really almost a platitude. In the old days of the czar the revolutionists of Russia were admired by everybody, including even American bank presidents. They were not only heroic fellows; they were also very persuasive. Nobody seriously questioned their politics. When they issued a philippic against the czar the whole world applauded; when they knocked off a grand duke only a few specialists in law and order were shocked.

But once these revolutionists disposed of the czar and got into office themselves their whole philosophy began to wobble, and now it is accepted gravely only by a few fanatics. What ails it is that there is no longer any heroism in it. An army is behind it, with a mob behind the army, and so it is official, which is to say, safe, which is to say, unconvincing. A bolshevik, in the old days, had everything to gain by renouncing his nonsense; hence it took on a certain dignity, even when it was most palpably idiotic. Today he has everything to gain by sticking to it, and so no one wants to hear it any more.

We have had an example nearer home. Ten years ago the cause of temperance was making very fast progress in the United States. Drinking was diminishing everywhere; even congressmen, horse doctors, and newspaper reporters were growing sober. Hard liquor was on the slide; light wines and beer were triumphant, with even softer things coming in. It took some courage to renounce the cup, but on all sides it was being done. Then the silly prohibitionists forced the eighteenth amendment into the constitution, and set out to execute it with clubs. Now the country is boozy again—and the brave and enterprising young fellow packs a flask of gin on his hip.

(*August 1, 1926*)

THE BIRTH CONTROL HULLABALOO

THE GROTESQUE FAILURE of the campaign to put down propaganda for birth control has a lesson in it for the optimists who believe that in the long run, by some mysterious hook or crook, and perhaps with divine help, prohibition will be enforced. They will not heed that lesson, but it is there nevertheless. Church and state combine to baffle and exterminate the birth controllers. They are threatened with penal servitude and their customers are threatened with hell-fire. Yet it must be obvious that they are making progress in the land, for the birth rate continues to slide downhill.

Incidentally, it is amusing and instructive to observe that it diminishes most rapidly among the educated and highly respectable classes, which is to say, among those who are ordinarily most law abiding. The same thing is to be noted when one turns to prohibition. The majority of professional crooks, now as in the old days, are teetotalers, but when one comes to the good citizens who scorn them and demand incessantly that the *Polizei* butcher them and so have done with them, one comes at once upon a high density of scofflaws. I know many men of easy means, some of them greatly respected and even eminent. Not two per cent of them make any pretense of obeying the Volstead act. And not two per cent of their wives are innocent of birth control.

The reason is not far to seek. Both the Volstead act and the statute aimed at birth control invade the field of private conduct. They take the roof off a man's house, and invite the world to look in. Obviously, that looking in is unpleasant in proportion as the man himself is dignified. If

he is a low fellow, he doesn't care much, for he is used to
such snooping by his low neighbors. But if he is one who
has a high opinion of himself, and is accustomed to seeing
it ratified by others, then he is outraged. And if he has any
natural bellicosity in him and resistance seems reasonably
safe, he resists with great diligence and vigor.

Here, perhaps, we come upon an explanation of the
fact that prohibition and all other such devices for making
men good by force are far less opposed in the country than
they are in the cities. The yokel is trained from infancy to
suffer espionage. He has scarcely any privacy at all. His
neighbors know everything that is to be known about him,
including what he eats and what he feeds his quadrupedal
friends and associates. His religious ideas are matters of
public discussion; if he is recusant the village pastor prays
for him by name. When his wife begins the sublime biological process of giving him an heir, the news flies around.
If he inherits $200 from an uncle in Idaho every one knows
it instantly. If he skins his shin, or buys a new plow, or
sees a ghost, or takes a bath, it is a public event.

Thus living like a goldfish in a glass globe, he acquires
a large tolerance for snoutery, for if he resisted it his neighbors would set him down as an enemy of their happiness,
and probably burn his barn. If an official spy or two is
added to the volunteer pack he scarcely notices it. It seems
natural and inevitable to him that every one outside his
house should be interested in what goes on inside, and that
this interest should be accompanied by definite notions as
to what is nice and what is not nice, supported by pressure.
So he submits to governmental tyranny as he submits to
the village inquisition, and when he hears that city men re-

sist it, it only confirms his general feeling that they are scoundrels. They are scoundrels because they have a better time than he does—the sempiternal human reason.

But the city man is differently trained. He is used to being let alone. Save when he lives in the slums, his neighbors show no interest in him. He would regard it as outrageous for them to have opinions about what goes on within the four walls of his house. If they offered him advice he would invite them to go to hell; if they tried force he would bawl for the police. So he is doubly affronted when the police themselves stalk in. And he resists them with every means at his command, and believes it to be his high duty to do so, that liberty may not perish from the earth.

The birth control fanatics profit by this elemental fact. It is their great good fortune that their enemies have tried to put them down, not by refuting their ideas, but by seeking to shove them into jail. What they argue for, at bottom, remains very dubious, and multitudes of quite honest and intelligent persons are against it. They have by no means proved that a high birth rate is dangerous, and they have certainly not shown that they know of any sure and safe way to reduce it—that is, any way not already known to every corner druggist.

But when an attempt is made to put them down by law, the question whether they are wise falls into the background, and the question whether their rights are invaded comes forward. At once the crowd on their side is immensely reinforced. It now includes not only all the persons who believe in birth control but also all the persons who believe in free speech, and this second group, it quickly appears, is far larger than the first one, and far more formidable. So the birth controllers suddenly find themselves supported by heavy battalions, and that support is sufficient to make them almost invulnerable.

Personally, I am inclined to be against them. I believe that the ignorant should be permitted to spawn *ad libitum*, that there may be a steady supply of slaves, and those of us who are more prudent may be relieved of unpleasant work. If the debate were open and fair, I'd oppose the birth controllers with all the subtlest devices of rhetoric, including bogus statistics and billingsgate. But so long as they are denied their plain rights—and, in particular, so long as those rights are denied them by an evil combination of theologians and politicians—I am for them and shall remain so until the last galoot's ashore. They have got many more allies on the same terms. And I believe that they are winning.

The law which forbids them to send their brummagem tracts through the mails is disingenuous and oppressive. It is a part of the notorious postal act, put on the books by Comstock himself and supported by every variety of witch burner. I know of no intelligent man or woman who is in favor of the principle of such grotesque legislation; even the worst enemies of the birth controllers would not venture to argue that it should be applied generally. It is favored only by fanatics, most of them pathological cases.

The way to dispose of such laws is to flout them and make a mock of them. The theory that they can be got rid of by enforcing them is nonsense. Enforcing them simply inspires the sadists who advocate them to fresh excesses. Worse, it accustoms the people to oppression, and so tends to make them bear it uncomplainingly. Wherever, in the United States, there has been any sincere effort to enforce prohibition, the anti-evolutionists are already on the war-path, and the Lord's Day alliance is drumming up recruits. No, the way to deal with such laws is to defy them, and thus make them ridiculous. This is being done in the case of the Volstead act by millions of patriots, clerical and lay. It is being done in the case of the Comstock act by a small band, but one full of praiseworthy daring and resolution.

Thus I deliver myself of a whoop for the birth con-trollers, and pass on to pleasanter concerns. Their specific Great Cause, it seems to me, is full of holes. They draw extremely questionable conclusions from a highly dubious body of so-called facts. But they are profoundly right at bot-tom. They are right when they argue that any one who tries to silence them by force is the common enemy of all of us. And they are right when they hold that the best way to get rid of such opposition is to thumb the nose at it.
(*April 4, 1926*)

EQUALITY BEFORE THE LAW

OF ALL THE IDEAS associated with the general concept of democratic government, the oldest and perhaps the sound-est is that of equality before the law. Its relation to the Christian scheme of ethics is too obvious to need state-ment. It goes back, through the political and theological theorizing of the middle ages, to the early Christian notion of equality before God. The true believer, throwing off his earthly habiliments, stood before Omnipotence as the equal of every other true believer, no more and no less. There were no kings in that Stupendous Presence, and there were no slaves.

The debt of democracy to Christianity has always been underestimated. Most historians, indeed, depict it as a product of the French skepticism of the 18th century—that is, as a product of the very negation of Christianity—or as something thrown off from the English philosophical speculation of the century preceding. But that sort of thing is very superficial. Long centuries before Rousseau was ever heard of, or Locke or Hobbes, the fundamental principles of democracy were plainly stated in the New Testament, and elaborately expounded by the early fathers, including St. Augustine. Whatever Nietzsche urges against Christianity is also an argument against democracy, and vice versa. Both are primarily schemes to offset and nullify the savage injustice of nature.

Today, in all Christian countries, equality before the law is almost as axiomatic as equality before God. A statute providing one punishment for A and another for B, both being guilty of the same act, would be held unconstitutional everywhere, and not only unconstitutional, but also in plain contempt of common decency and the inalienable rights of man. The chief aim of most of our elaborate legal machinery is to give effect to that idea. It seeks to diminish and conceal the inequalities that divide men in the general struggle for existence, and to bring them before the bar of justice as exact equals.

In all this, is seems to me, there is little to which rational objection may be offered. All other democratic ideas have a flavor of the fantastic and the disingenuous in them, but here, at least, there is something that is workable and honest. When a man is haled into court he is in the presence of a power that is theoretically irresistible, just as God is theoretically irresistible. If he is treated badly he must submit. Thus it is of the first importance that he be treated fairly, and the only way to treat him fairly is to treat him precisely as every other man is treated.

Nor is it impossible to do so, or even difficult. We have, in the main, accomplished the thing very successfully. Save in England, where it lingers as an anachronism, there is no longer in any civilized country a special court for the trial of noblemen, nor is there any special body of law for them. They must obey the same laws that every one else obeys. If an English duke committed murder tomorrow, he would go to the gallows like any other man, special court or no special court. It would make no difference whether the man he killed was another duke or a garbage man, and it would make no difference whether the witnesses who saw and testified to the crime were nobles or commoners.

The duke, in truth, would probably have a rougher time of it than the common man, just as an American millionaire, accused of felony, has a rougher time of it than a common man. If Harry Thaw had been a poor clerk or some other such humble fellow, the defense he offered would have acquitted him on his first trial, and to the tune of sentimental nose-blowing and loud hosannas. But there we come to a humane weakness: the natural sympathy of common men for their kind, the natural distrust and dislike of superiors. The theory of equality before the law remains unaffected. And the machinery for enforcing it is usually unaffected, too. Thaw did not escape. He was taken

promptly and prosecuted vigorously. The devices that he
employed to avoid execution were open to all men, and
poor men take advantage of them every day.

As I say, this idea of equality before the law has merit.
It is grounded upon a sound concept of justice, natural to
the civilized man. It dignifies human nature by setting a
level below which, in the eyes of mankind in general, it
cannot fall. It is an antidote to that common folly whereby
a dull and trivial man (I allude to King George V, not to
Mr. Coolidge) is venerated because chance has thrown
him into a gaudy and transient office, or because he takes a
good photograph and is thus successful in the movies, or
because his father left him money, or because he is more
like a gorilla than the rest of us.

It is a sound idea, but, being sound, it naturally has
hard going. The sad fact is that the concept of justice is too
recent, phylogenetically, to have many honest devotees in
this imperfect world. It is cherished, perhaps, theoretically,
but it is only too often reduced to a hissing and a mocking
in practice. I have spoken of the Thaw case. Its obscenities
are repeated every time an unpopular man comes to trial.
For unpopularity can no more be kept out of a courtroom
than air can be kept out. Once it has marked a man, he has
lost some appreciable part of his right to justice, and not
all the theorizing on earth can conceal the plain fact.

Worse, even theorizing sometimes fails. We have, indeed, a bold theorizing on the other side. Hasn't everyone
heard the doctrine that so-called reds should be stood up
against a wall and shot—that is, that they should be punished first and tried afterward—that is, that they should be
denied justice altogether? Ah, that such gabble were confined to irresponsible fools! But it begins to penetrate to

higher levels—higher, at least officially. During the Scopes trial in Tennessee the chief prosecuting officer of the state argued in open court, and with the obvious approval of the judge, that a defendant not a Christian had no rights there. And only a few weeks ago, in the Cathedral of St. John the Divine in New York, a Methodist bishop, preaching there as a guest, argued that atheism was treason, and that one accused of it "should not be defended by any specious claim for immunity under the constitutional guarantees of the right of free speech."

The thing even gets into statutes, and they are enforced with scarcely a challenge. I point to the Volstead act, that source unparalleled of constitutional corruption. Does any lawyer argue that a man accused under it enjoys equality before the law—that his rights are precisely the same as those of his brother tried under some other statute? If so, then there is one more lawyer in the world who has not troubled to read the law.

The injunction clause of the Volstead act, in truth, was deliberately designed to put men accused under it into a special class, and to take from them the safeguards and guarantees that surround other defendants. It is an integral part of their punishment that they should not have a fair trial, as a fair trial is described in the fourth, fifth, and sixth amendments, and that special punishment of theirs begins to run against them the instant they are accused, which is to say, against the innocent and guilty alike. Suppose the same device were turned against men accused of murder? Would public opinion tolerate it? Or would there be an outcry?

I am not sure of the answer. The common man, if he had any sense, would instantly challenge every such invasion of the common rights of all men. Unluckily, he has no sense. The bloody show enchants him, and so he forgets the principle. Here what is foul in democracy devours what is good. We assume falsely that all men are intelligent, and hence that all men are just. Our error is made manifest every time justice is rolled in the mud.

(February 28, 1926)

III. THE ARTS

Mencken was not a bloodless critic of literature who felt that his only function was to pass judgment from a distance on the artistic merit of the works of others.

Such a role was far too passive for so vital a figure. Consequently, his status as a littérateur was used as the means to an end, revolutionary in concept, grandiose in scale.

What he sought was a change in the temper of literary expression in America from what seemed to him dilettantism to a robust reflection of the realities of life.

American letters, when Mencken exploded upon the scene, indeed looked blushingly upon what he called "the primary mysteries of existence, the unsolved and ever fascinating problems at the bottom of human life."

It was too busy trying to be morally elevating, Mencken thought, when it ought to be more concerned with satisfying the "curiosity of man in man." His aim was to inject into American literature heady doses of candor and honesty to give it new vigor and scope.

To do so, he doubtless acclaimed too much authors whose approach to their art suited that purpose, and scorned unfairly some whose ideas were of no use in his scheme.

*Whether this reflected upon him as a critic seems
moot at this distance. It is difficult to argue with success,
and the revolution he stirred was a resounding one.*

*Theodore Dreiser, the subject of one of the essays to
follow, was among the chief co-conspirators of that rebellion. Dreiser is also most likely the unnamed author mentioned in "On Realism," contained in this section.*

ESSAY ON CONSTRUCTIVE CRITICISM

KIWANIS, like golf, is a symbol of the business man's natural desire to break the dreadful monotony of his days. And
when I say business man I include also, of course, the doctor, the dentist, the lawyer, and all the other bored and
laborious walking gents of the human comedy. Many of
them achieve opulence and some of them also achieve a
sort of celebrity, at least in their own neighborhoods, but
their work, in the last analysis, is bound to be dull, for
there is little if any difference between what it is today and
what it will be tomorrow. A man may practice law or medicine from end to end of a long life, and do it very competently, without once experiencing the joy of formulating
and testing a new idea. And a man may make a fortune in
some well organized and customary business without ever
feeling even the banal thrill that fires a gambler when he
turns up four aces.

So all the fellows who do the routine work of the
world have to seek for spiritual compensation outside. The

magnificent satisfaction of the free artist can never be theirs; they always know, deep down in their hearts, that what they are doing is not really important, and they also know, every time they begin a new day, that it is not genuinely interesting. So, if they are down near the bottom of the ladder, they go to the movies, put in a radio, and begin payments on a Ford. And if they are half way up they buy a set of golf sticks and try to convince themselves that chasing the ball is great fun—nay, a sort of hygienic measure, like eating six apples a day or taking some one's salts. And if they are at the top, they make idiotic speeches, endow idiotic universities, and announce idiotically that wealth is a sacred trust.

These poor fish, great and small, suffer from one common complaint: they have not discovered how to make life amusing. Worse, they have not discovered how to make it important. This last lack is the harsher of the two, for all of us, above the rank of earthworms, like to think that what we do is important, that our lives are of some consequence to the world. Thus one beholds yokels flocking from their dunghills to hear candidates for the United States senate tell them that they are God's noblemen. And thus one observes earnest men rising at Rotary meetings to argue that the one aim of the automobile accessories business is Service.

It is my impression, gained by observation and prayer, that all such devices of escape are failures, at least in the cases of the more intelligent half of those who employ them. Even in Kiwanis, unless the letters that reach me are forged, there is a great deal of lingering discontent. The first time, perhaps, it is pleasant to hear the visiting idealist argue that John the Baptist was the first Kiwanian, and to blow spitballs at him afterward. But soon or late, save to actual morons, such sports are bound to grow tiresome. The trouble with them is that they are hollow and senseless. They offer no more consolation to the ego than is to be found in the hay and feed business.

It is in far different fields that a good time is really to be had. It is in fields that are occupied, professionally, by men whose dignity is indubitable. In other words, the test of a recreation is the human worth of the men who pursue it for a living, or, at all events, as a serious vocation. So tested, golf blows up instanter: the golf professional, in the human scale, ranks almost as low as a trolley motorman or a congressman. And Service goes the same route, for when one gets among men who feed and clothe themselves upon it one finds one's self among chautauqua orators, drive managers, charity mongers, itinerant evangelists, Y.M.C.A. secretaries, town boomers, and so on—in brief, among mountebanks. It is not much fun, taking one day with another, to meet mountebanks. And it is even less fun to imitate them.

What is needed, in order that the soul may be lifted, is better company. Where is it to be found? It is to be found, it seems to me, in the domain of the arts and sciences. Has the artist, as a man, certain notorious defects? Perhaps. (So, indeed, has every man, including the hay and feed dealer.) But there is one thing about him that sets him off sharply from the great herd of dull men, and that is the fact that he enjoys his job—that he has a roaring good time doing his day's work. He may be, as artists go, only third rate, but he has more fun in the world than any Babbitt who ever lived.

The moral for Babbitt himself is plain. Let him, when

he tires of his dull routine, seek surcease among the artists. Let him try to be an artist himself. Let him get a fiddle and make some music. Or grease his nose and essay Judge Brack at the Little Theater up the alley. Or lay in a box of paints and smear them elegantly upon canvas. Or take a stiff drink and try *vers libre*. Or, if his tastes run to more sober things, let him collect early American humor, or Methodist hymnals, or old theater programs, or set himself down to write a decent life of George Washington—a horrible want for lo! these many years.

But suppose he has no talent for any of these things? Bosh! I am not proposing that he become an expert; I am simply proposing that he amuse himself charmingly, and so grab some share of honest happiness before the lodge brothers file in to view his remains. In order to get pleasure out of the arts it is not necessary to be a master, nor even an adept. I throw myself upon the table as Exhibit A. Though I have no more talent for music than a cow, and can scarcely, at forty-six, tune a banjo or run a decent C major scale, I have devoted myself to music exercises all my life, and get an immense and undiminished pleasure out of them. It would give me little additional satisfaction, I believe, to be a virtuoso.

For what keeps me going is not a desire to be applauded by strangers, most of them not worth knowing, but a desire to spend my leisure joyfully in the company of men I like, and under the shadow of great artists. Beethoven has been dead for long years, but I can still visit him, listen to him, and get the feeling that I know him. I'd rather know one such man than all the golf professionals and Rotary orators since the days of the apostles.

I know many business and professional men who cherish precisely the same notion, and put it into effect with great success. The work they have to do in the world leaves them, somehow, unsatisfied. They do it well, and perhaps, in a way, they like it, but it doesn't give them the lift that a free artist gets. So they seek that lift where and how a free artist gets his. Some of them fiddle, or struggle with the piano—or the saxophone. Others paint or etch. Yet others write books: I met one recently who had just published a Life of Christ!—and it was a best seller! The rest collect books, or ceramics, or prints, or they devote themselves to history.

Such men, I believe, have a vastly better time of it than the golfers and Kiwanians. Their hobbies are more dignified, and take them into much more charming society. The fiddlers among them have Kreisler to admire, and Brahms standing behind him—not some former ice wagon driver turned golf coach. The painters miss the gay spitball battles of a Lions club meeting, but they are in the company of Rubens, Velasquez, and El Greco, and so do not have to listen to bad speeches. The collectors are innocent of the spirit of Service, but they leave something noble and valuable behind them, and are thus remembered with respect by the husbands of their daughters.

What puzzles me is that so few such men go for recreation to the sciences. The arts get almost all of them. But isn't there good sport, too, in the laboratory? Isn't bacteriology, for example, quite as interesting as playing string quartets? And isn't there plenty of room for the amateur of small equipment, inside and outside his head? I think of Robert Koch, and of what he accomplished in his wife's kitchen. But more of that anon.

(March 28, 1926)

THE EXAMPLE that Sinclair Lewis set to them in *Babbitt* seems to be lost upon his fellow American novelists. He showed them in that remarkable work how a novel could be simple and yet very profound—a character sketch of a single individual, and yet a vivid and penetrating portrait of a whole civilization. They seem to be shy of the formula, perhaps because it presents difficulties that go beyond the general skill.

In the fine arts, indeed, simplicity is full of snares. Any first year student of architecture can manufacture Gothic ornament by the acre, but it takes a genius to design a genuinely Gothic structure. So in music. Any one who can write it at all can write tone poems in which the time signature changes with every measure and the tonality with every chord, but the composition of string quartets in strict sonata form is reserved to the masters. So, again, in poetry. Free verse, at bottom, is nothing but an escape for poets too incompetent to manage the pentameter.

Thus, the average novelist sticks to incident, which is the adornment of the novel, and tries to get along without character, which is the fundamental bone and sinew, liver and lights. We have, therefore, a series of trivial situations, irrationally strung together, and signifying nothing. Most of them are sexual—a sheer absurdity, for sexual situations, in real life, are relatively few and mainly unimportant. I know of no man, above the mental level of a movie actor, whose life may be described in terms of a love affair. But novelists go on describing the lives of their creatures in precisely that way.

They do so because it is easy—because it is easy to imagine an infinitude of sexual situations, and easy to get attention by imagining them. In the most innocuous of them, under our Christian civilization, there is bound to lurk a certain impropriety. When kissing begins, inhibitions fly out of the window. Thus the reader reads on, hoping always for the worst, and it is not difficult to hold his custom and get his money. The popular novel, at bottom, is nothing but an aphrodisiac. Its chief practitioners are comparable to the chorus girls who dance naked through bawdy revues.

But writing such banal rubbish must be very unsatisfying to an amitious man or woman, and so I marvel that more of our novelists do not devote themselves to the more dignified and fascinating novel of character. It is, as I have said, difficult. It demands not merely a facile fancy, but sharp powers of observation, a coherent philosophy of life, and the great gift of human sympathy. The novelist who essays it must keep outside his hero, and yet see inside him. The job is surely not one for idle tale spinners.

It offers, however, immense opportunities, for the materials needed for it are lying all about, and most of them remain wholly untouched. The country, indeed, swarms with unworked Babbitts. Babbitt himself was on full view for years, incessantly in function and known to every one. He was American from snout to heels; he was typically, exclusively American in every detail; no one who surveyed the national scene could escape him. And yet it remained for Lewis to put him into a book, vividly, caressingly, understandingly, and at length. All the rest of the novelists, gaping at him daily, overlooked him.

But his brothers remain, and some of them, it seems to me, are quite as characteristic of the republic as he is, and quite as charming, and quite as tempting. I point, as an obvious example, to the American university president. I mean the university president of the new model, half the quack, half the visionary, and wholly the go-getter—the sort of brisk, businesslike fellow who harangues Rotary and Kiwanis, extracts millions from profiteers by alarming them about bolshevism, and so builds his colossal pedagogical slaughter house, with its tens of thousands of students, its professors of cheese making, investment securities and cheer leading, its galaxy of football stars, and its general air of Barnum's circus.

Why has this astounding mountebank not got into a book? He fairly yells for loving embalming a la *Babbitt*. He is not only stupendously picaresque and amusing in himself—the final heir at once of Abelard, Cagliostro, Increase Mather, the Fox sisters, Pestalozzi, Dr. Munyon, Godey of the *Ladies' Book*, and Daniel Drew; he is also thoroughly and magnificently characteristic of the great land we live in. No other country has ever produced anything quite like him. No other country, I suspect, would tolerate him. But here he lives and flourishes, a superb and perfect American —and yet our novelists all neglect him.

Now and then, to be sure, there is a glimpse of him in a book. But it is never a full length portrait; it is never done with the vast competence and unctuous charm that Lewis got into his portrait of Babbitt. We do not think of the university president in terms of any such imaginary archetype of the whole species as we think of the whole race of Kiwanians in terms of Babbitt. The job has not been done by a novelist equal to it. Do we lack one equal to it? I don't think so. We have many highly skillful novelists, and a few of the first talent. But they all waste themselves—or nearly all—upon the trivialities of amour.

I offer them the university president, with his six cylinders and his balloon tires, and to him I add the American politician and the American clergyman—the new high powered, ink burning, rah-rah-rah man of God of the evangelical type. A hundred novelists have tackled the politician—but who has really done him? I can think of no one. They have all come to grief by depicting his life as a sort of battle of ideas. Thus they have disemboweled him and left him a mere inanimate shell. What remains to be done is an authentic portrait of the man as he actually is— true brother to Babbitt, full of soaring yearning and childish imbecilities, and as devoid of ideas as a cashier in a bank.

The American clergyman of the new order deserves not one solitary book, but a whole shelf of books. He is not to be confused with the brutal, dogmatic Puritan of our Paleozoic age, nor with the hard praying, circuit riding soul snatcher of a later time. Something of both these archaic pastors is in him, but there is a great deal more of the modern business man. He is the apostle of efficiency in the holy temple. His aim is to save the world by the devices of Florida realtors. He cannot function without his general staff of trained go-getters. He dies as rich as a railroad purchasing agent.

There was a glimpse of him in *Babbitt*, but only a glimpse. He cries aloud for limning in a grander, gaudier manner. If I were a novelist, I think he'd tempt me more than any other star of the national circus—more even than the university president. There is something beautifully American in his belief in his own hocus-pocus; he admires and trusts himself as innocently as Dr. Coolidge admires and trusts himself. And there is something beautifully American, too, in his colossal futility. We live in a land of

furious lost motion. We hunt streptococci with Busy Ber-
thas. But what a show! What a show! And what figures
stalk through it!

I close with another: the American policeman. Why
has he never got into a book? I offer him to the novelists
at once, and provide them simultaneously with all the plot
they will need. A moron with an IQ of 53, despairing of
ever getting a better job, goes on the force and begins
pounding a beat. A chance favor to a saloonkeeper makes a
sergeant of him, and thereafter he slowly mounts the ladder. At the end he is an inspector and in charge of operations against a fabulous crime wave, imagined by the city
editor of a tabloid newspaper.

Isn't that enough? What a vivid and exhilarating picture of American life could be got out of it! What humors
are there, and what genuine drama! Nor are the materials
esoteric. Every newspaper reporter's head is stuffed with
them. I myself could do such a work in forty volumes folio.
Nine young journalists out of ten, I believe, aspire to the
novel. Well, here is a chance to write a novel as good as
Babbitt.

(*December 27, 1925*)

YET MORE HINTS FOR NOVELISTS

ON THE PURELY technical side the American novel has obviously made immense progress. As ordinarily encountered,
it is very adeptly constructed and not infrequently it is also
well written. The old time amorphous novel, rambling all
over the place and ending with pious platitudes, has pretty

well gone out. The American novelists of today, and especially the younger ones, have given earnest study to form—perhaps, indeed, too much. For in concentrating their powerful intellects upon it they have lost sight of something that is far more important. I allude, of course, to the observation of character. Thus the average contemporary American novel, though it is workmanlike and well mannered, fails to achieve its first business. It does not evoke memorable images of human beings. One enjoys reading it, perhaps, but one seldom remembers it.

I have said this before, but it will bear saying two or three hundred times more. Our fiction, it seems to me, tends more and more to waste itself upon trivialities of technique and manner. The human transactions that it depicts are, in the main, trivial and tedious, and its people are odd fish who might be transported to Norway or Arcadia without suffering any appreciable change. It is only in an occasional *Babbitt* that one encounters an authentic and unmistakable Americano, corn fed and glorious. It is only now and then that one gets away from the drug store smell of Anatole France and George Meredith and sniffs the honest reek of *Homo cooligensis*.

Why this should be so I don't know. The republic swarms with creatures who are intimately national and immensely amusing, and they cry plaintively for the services of the novelist. Yet our current fictioneers neglect all of them, from the university president to the police captain, and from the go-getting pastor to the realtor. Worst and most incredible of all, they neglect the American of Americans, the very *Ur-Amerikaner*—to wit: the malignant moralist, the Christian turned cannibal, the snouting and preposterous Puritan.

I know of no American novel in which this most typical and gorgeous of all Americanos is even half limned.
There are glimpses of him in *The Song of the Lark,* by
Willa Cather, and in *Babbitt,* and there is a more elaborate
but still incomplete sketch in E. W. Howe's *The Story of
a Country Town,* a book published forty years ago, but still
well worth reading. Howe, unfortunately, had other fish to
fry: he slapped in his bucolic wowser brilliantly and then
passed on to melodrama and the agonies of young love. So,
too, with Lewis and Miss Cather. The Puritan father lies
embalmed in the pages of Hawthorne, but his heir and as-
sign of the present day, the high powered uplifter, the
prophet of harsh and unenforceable laws, the incurable reformer and nuisance—this sweet fellow yet awaits his
anatomist.

What a novel is in him! Indeed, what a shelf of novels! For he has as many forms as there are varieties of human delusion. Sometimes he is a tin-pot evangelist, sweating to transform Oklahoma City or Altoona, Pa., into the
New Jerusalem. Sometimes he is a hireling of the Anti-
Saloon league, sworn to Law Enforcement. Sometimes he
is a strict Sabbatarian, bawling for the police whenever he
detects his neighbor washing bottles or varnishing the Ford
on Sunday morning. Again he is a vice crusader chasing the
scarlet lady with fierce Christian shouts. Yet again he is a
Comstock, wearing out his eyes in the quest for smut. He
may even be female—a lady Ph.D. in a linoleum hat, pa-
trolling the cow towns and the city slums, handing out edifying literature, teaching poor Polish women how to have
babies.

Whatever his form, he is tremendously grotesque and
tremendously amusing—and always he drips with national

juices, always he is as thoroughly American as a bootlegger
or a college yell. If he exists at all in other lands it is only in
rudimentary and aberrant forms. Try to imagine a French
Wayne B. Wheeler, or a Spanish Billy Sunday, or a German William Jennings Bryan. It is as impossible as imagining a Coolidge in the Greece of Pericles.

Since the earliest days, as every one knows, American
jurisprudence has been founded upon the axiom that it is
the first duty of every citizen to police his neighbors, and
especially those he envies or otherwise dislikes. There is no
such thing in this grand and puissant nation as privacy. The
yokels out in Iowa, neglecting their horned cattle, have a
right, it appears—nay, a sacred duty!—to peek into my home
in Baltimore and tell me what I may and may not drink
with my meals. A Methodist preacher in Boston decides
what I may read. An obscure job holder in Washington, inspired by God, determines what I may receive in the mails.
I must not buy lottery tickets because it offends the moral
sentiment of Kansas. I must keep Sunday as the Sabbath,
which is in conflict with Genesis, because it is ordered by
persons who believe that Genesis can't be wrong.

Such are the laws of the greatest free nation ever seen
on earth. We are all governed by them. But a government
of laws, of course, is a mere phantasm of political theories:
the thing is always found, in inspection, to be really a government of men. In the United States, it seems to me, the
tendency is for such men to come increasingly from the
class of professional uplifters. It is not the bankers who
run the ostensible heads of the state, as the liberals believe,
nor the so-called bosses, as the bosses themselves believe,
but the wowsers. One Wayne B. Wheeler is now as powerful among us as two J. Pierpont Morgans or a dozen Bren-

nans. I submit the Hon. Andrew W. Mellon as Exhibit A.
Dr. Mellon is himself a banker of the highest tone—perhaps the richest practitioner of that art and mystery in the
country. Moreover, he is a political boss of the first caliber,
albeit temporarily somewhat disabled in that department.
Finally, he is a public official so near the top of the heap
that the deaths of but three men would hoist him automatically into the White House. But when the Anti-Saloon
league speaks he listens.

Thus we are run by wowsers—and wowser is an Australian word that I hereby formally nominate for inclusion
in the American language, that resilient and incomparable
tongue. What does it mean? It means precisely what you
think of inevitably when you hear it. A wowser is a wowser.
He bears a divine commission to regulate and improve the
rest of us. He knows exactly what is best for us. He is what
E. W. Howe calls a Good Man. So long as you and I are
sinful he can't sleep. So long as we are happy he is after us.

I throw off the guess that there are at least forty novels in the wowser—that is, forty good ones. He has as many
forms as the demons who ride him, and every one of them
should make a competent novelist, authentically called to
the vocation, leap in air with loud hosannas and spit upon
his hands. His psychology remains mysterious. The Freudians, I believe, have misunderstood him, and the psychiatrists have avoided him. What are the springs of his peculiar frenzy to harass and punish his fellow men? By what
process of malign eugenics is he hatched? And what is his
typical life history? Here is work for the novelist, which is
to say for the professional anatomist of character.

I believe that Frank Norris, had he lived, would have
tackled it with enthusiasm, and made a great success of its

execution. Norris had a romantic and even a mystical inclination, but at bottom he was a satirist—and the American Puritan was made for satirists as catnip was made for cats. It is easy to laugh at him, but it is hard to hate him. He is eternally in the position of a man trying to empty the ocean with a tin dipper. He will be mauled, and the chance he offers thrown away, if the novelist who attempts him in the end forgets the tragedy under his comedy. I have known many American wowsers in my time, some of them intimately. They were all intensely unhappy men. They suffered as vastly as Prometheus chained to his rock, with the buzzards pecking his eyes. A novelist blind to that capital fact will never comprehend the type. It needs irony—but above all it needs pity.

(*June 27, 1926*)

POE'S START IN LIFE

FOR YEARS it has been known that there existed in Richmond, Va., in the so-called Valentine museum, a packet of letters from Edgar Allan Poe to his foster-father, John Allan. A great mystery was made about them, for what reason I do not know, and few outsiders seem to have ever got a glimpse of them. But now they are all printed in a stately book, at $15 a copy, and so the whole world, or at all events the highly solvent minority, is free to read them at last. They are presented in transcript and in facsimile, and in front of each one there are useful explanations by an estimable Richmond lady, Mrs. Mary Newton Stanard.

As I say, I don't know why they were held back so

long, for certainly there is nothing in them of a scandalous nature—that is, nothing save the news that Poe was once in danger of imprisonment for debt, a common hazard in his time, and his accusation in one letter that old Allan was "not very often sober," certainly nothing astonishing in the Richmond of 1830. After Allan's death, his surviving widow —not Poe's foster-mother, but a successor—gave the letters to her niece's husband, one Mayo, and in 1882 Mayo passed them on to Mann S. Valentine, a cousin of the first Mrs. Allan. This Valentine founded the Valentine museum, and there the letters gathered cobwebs, unread but much gabbled about, until a month ago.

There are twenty-seven letters from Poe to Allan, two from Allan to Poe, one from Mrs. Clemm to Allan, and one from Poe to Sergt. Samuel Graves of the regular army, a friend of Poe's soldiering days, from whom he borrowed money. Graves, evidently in despair of getting it back, sent the letter to Allan, and so the latter became privy to his foster-son's allegation that he was given to the bowl. There was no truce between Allan and Poe after that. The old man simply washed his hands of the young poet. Edgar was at last wholly on his own.

The letters do little credit to either party to the long row. Poe alternates between whining and defiance. In one letter he protests that he is innocent of all the mysterious charges brought against him by his foster-father; in the next he begs maudlinly to be forgiven. Almost always he ends with a demand for money—often for a sum that, in those simple days, was enough to make even a well to do business man wince. Apparently it never occurred to Poe to go to work; a stout lad of 20, he was content to sponge upon Allan and upon his aged and poverty stricken grandmother,

widow of Washington's quartermaster general, rather than
get him a job. His enlistment in the army was mere melodrama. In a short while he was begging Allan to buy his
discharge, and when the transaction was finally arranged
he seems to have made an excellent profit on it.

As for Allan, he makes, in these tattered letters, a ridiculous and ignominious showing. Obviously, he was a Babbitt of purest ray serene: Poe's tendencies toward versifying
not only failed to meet his encouragement, but aroused his
violent opposition. He was apparently convinced that any
young man who made rhymes was full of sin and doomed to
the gallows. When *Tamerlane* came out, he got into a fear-
ful sweat; when the Baltimore volume followed, he excom-
municated his foster-son with bell and book. There is
something downright pathetic, after all these years, in his
tremors. He honestly believed that Poe, as a poet, would
bring eternal dishonor upon the Allan house.

Worse, he was what has come to be called, in the language of modern America, a tightwad, and never yielded up
a cent without a groan. He sent Poe to the University of
Virginia with exactly $110 in hand. It was not enough, by
two-thirds, for the first year's expenses. Poe had to pay $50
down for board and $60 for tuition fees, leaving him with
nothing for room rent, furniture, and books. He sought to
augment his funds by gambling, and was presently stone
broke and in debt. Allan thereupon refused to pay his debts
—some of them regarded by the Virginians of the time as
debts of honor. In consequence, Poe had to leave the university.

Most ambitious young men of today, so used by an un-
intelligent crab, would kiss him good-by and go to work.
There were jobs in those days, as in these. But from some

unknown source Poe had picked up the notion that a literary man needed what he called "a liberal education," and so, instead of going on his own, he renewed his efforts to squeeze it out of the right thinking Allan. Even his enlistment in the army as a common soldier was a device to that end; he believed Allan would promptly buy his discharge and return him to the university. When the scheme failed, he began his long effort to get into West Point.

It must be obvious, in retrospect, that this faith in "education" was mistaken—that Poe would have escaped some of his worst faults and so made his fame even more secure than it is if he had never gone to college at all. The University of Virginia, in his time, had just been started; its faculty was small and the courses it offered were old fashioned and meager. It was nothing like the great American universities of today; it was rather like the forlorn one building "colleges" of the prairies. All it had to teach Poe was a smattering of this and a smattering of that. It gave him the delusion that he was an educated man without actually teaching him anything worth knowing.

The fruits of that delusion appear in all that Poe wrote, and especially in his criticism. He was a shrewd and able critic—perhaps the ablest America has ever produced—but his critical writings were so heavily burdened with pedantic affectations that they had no influence in his day and have been forgotten since. He could not write ten lines without trying to display his learning—and most of it was bogus learning, schoolmasters' learning. Day after day he dished up his stale scraps. He wanted people to admire him as a linguist, as a scientist, as a philosopher. And the only result was that they failed to see his genuine worth as a critic.

But the notion that Poe had to wait long for recogni-

tion and that he had a hard time getting it is mainly sentimental. True enough, he was never properly appreciated
in his lifetime as a critic, but all that belonged to the latter
part of his life, long after his celebrity as a poet and writer
of stories was nation-wide. His poetry got notice almost instantly, and from competent men. His first book was
printed when he was but 18 years old; by the time he was
22 he had three volumes behind him. And they were read
and praised.

One of the first to hail him was John Neal, editor of
the Boston *Literary Gazette* and perhaps the foremost
American critic of the era. Poe sent Neal some of his early
poems and Neal gave them a friendly notice in the *Literary
Gazette*. Moreover, it was intelligent as well as friendly, for
it pointed out Poe's tendency to put words above ideas.
The things on his table, said Neal, were "rather exquisite
nonsense"—but still nonsense. A profound criticism, and
never bettered since. The best poems of Poe are lovely
things, indeed, but they are as devoid of logical content as
so many college yells.

Poe must have told Neal all his troubles, for the latter,
in a subsequent issue of the *Literary Gazette*, gave him
some excellent and much needed advice. It was to the general effect that a young poet's chief need in life is a "mag-
nanimous determination to endure the present," letting the
future take care of itself. The advice was wasted. Poe kept
on hammering old Allan for money and posturing melo-
dramatically as an ill used fellow. It became, in the end, his
fixed character. He saw himself always as a pearl cast before
swine. In the days, later on, when every American magazine
was printing his stuff and the blue stockings of the time
were flocking to hear him lecture—that is, whenever he was

sober enough to perform—he indulged himself in maudlin debauches of self-pity and saw the whole world in conspiracy against him. A genius, and if not of the first rank, then at least near the top of the second—but a foolish, disingenuous, and often somewhat trashy man.

(*November 1, 1925*)

THE CASE OF DREISER

FEW MEN in profane history have been more fortunate in their enemies than Theodore Dreiser; as for his friends, that is another story. His first book, *Sister Carrie*, was suppressed in alarm by a timorous publisher, and so gained an immense surreptitious vogue; his worst, *The "Genius,"* was assaulted by the Comstocks to such good effect that it sold 30,000 copies eight years after publication. He has been denounced steadily for twenty-four years, often with extreme rancor. He stands isolated today, a figure weatherbeaten and lonely. Yet I can think of no American novelist who seems so secure or so likely to endure.

From the start, Dreiser provoked the fury of all the schoolmarm critics of the republic, male and female, and they fell upon him with astounding violence. The attack took forms that were strange and various. He was accused of merchanting pornography, of advocating free love, of flirting with socialism and even anarchism. When the war came on, the discovery was made that he had a German name, and this became the basis of a fresh onslaught. One gallant professor, furloughed from the Creel press bureau for the purpose, had at him in a gallant manner and hinted that he ought to be put down by the police. As the Ku Klux Klan arose he became the chief butt of the new Ku Klux kriticism. What will be tomorrow's bugaboo? Whatever it is, the floggers of sophomores will see in it only Dreiser in a new false face.

So far as I know, Dreiser has never made a formal reply to these uproars or any other effort to still them. Why, indeed, should he? They have served to increase his trade far more effectively than the encomiums of his advocates— even more effectively than the idiotic enterprises of the Comstocks. For the first charge of the campus Taines and Brandeses synchronized almost perfectly with the appearance of rebellion against them in their own flocks, and so Dreiser became by rebound a sort of hero to the younger generation. That was in 1900, and the younger generation is now grown up. But its enthusiasms and aversions continue to be potent in our letters, and as the professors have gone down Dreiser has gone up.

The way was opened for him, in fact, by events in which he had no part at all, not even as a far from innocent bystander—to wit, the events of the electric 90s. The war of that decade opened in England, but was soon transferred to the United States. In both countries it was essentially a revolt against academic authority—against the dull, hollow dignity of pedants who continued to teach the Hawthornes and Emersons and were anesthetic to the new literature that was coming to flower all around them. It was a revolt more ardent than judicious, and in England its heroes were such discordant men as Pater, Wilde, and Ibsen. In America, after some imitative wabbling, the spotlights concentrated upon Dreiser. He was young, he was (academically speaking) a barbarian; he was bold, and he was the victim of injustice (from the timorous published aforesaid). So the scepter was shoved into his hands.

The attack upon him during the late war served him almost as well. It was made by poltroons, and so it only gave fresh enthusiasm to his customers. The war, indeed, ruined all the literary patriots. The art of letters demobilized almost as quickly as the art of money-lending and so left them high and dry. It would be curious to make a list of the more florid of them: Owen Wister, Robert W. Chambers, Irvin Cobb, and so on. Not one of them is taken seriously today. All the men who are talked about now were missing when roll was called by Dr. Creel: I point to Cabell, Sinclair Lewis, Eugene O'Neill—and Dreiser.

Well, what is there in Dreiser that justifies all this good luck? What has he done that is of solid worth? It seems to me he has done a lot, both as writer and as man. He has written at least two novels of the first rank, perhaps the best ever done by an American. He has written many shorter pieces of a rare and superlative excellence. He has thrown out idea after idea that is now the common property of all of us. But, best of all, he has shown resolution, fortitude, high and unshakable purpose. Best of all, he has stuck to his guns heroically, regardless of the stink bombs hurled by embattled birchmen, regardless of the Comstocks, regardless of alarmed publishers, regardless of the lures that have been set—many of them by his friends—to turn him from his goal.

In many ways his first novel, *Sister Carrie*, remains his best, despite its grossly incompetent design. What gave it instant distinction when it came out, and what keeps glow and vitality in it today, is simply its discovery of lowly and miserable folk as human beings—its artful and eloquent evocation of the tragedy of the poor. There had been, of course, novels about poor people before, even in America. But in practically all of them the approach had been from the outside and in a lofty manner. Either the poor were sentimentalized in the manner of the Sunday school books, or they were fondled like pet dogs or amusing children, in the manner of Dickens. Dreiser viewed them seriously—and realistically. Somehow, he got beneath their skins. Somehow, he made them real.

No wonder *Sister Carrie* was talked of! It was something quite new in the federal union, and certainly not too familiar in the rest of the world. It was the ancient story of the seduced village maiden, purged of all its commonplace pecksniffery and sentimentality, and elevated to the dignity of tragedy. The thing had a fine and high earnestness in it and a gusto that no sensitive reader could escape and a texture that belonged to it and to no other book. Reading it was a profound emotional experience. I doubt that many of the pious critics who denounced it ever read it, but you may be sure it was read by all the beginning novelists of the time, for its influence began to be felt within a year or two and remains in full tide today. The whole course of the American novel was changed by that one book. At a single stroke the genteel tradition was disposed of and novel-writing became a serious business in America, to be approached honestly and humbly.

Dreiser himself has written no better, though *Jennie Gerhardt*, which followed after eleven years, is obviously sounder in design, and in *The Titan* there is greater variety and color. But though he has not surpassed his first effort, he has certainly done no discredit to it; for the principles that it set forth have been adhered to in all his later work. I know of no other novelist, indeed, who has stuck to his ideas more resolutely. He knows more today than he knew in 1900, both of the tricks of his trade and of life itself, but he still sees the world as he saw it then. The philosophical speculations of his later years are no more, at bottom, than deductions from *Sister Carrie*. And his autobiographical volumes no more than show the scaffolding for it.

Dreiser's defect as a novelist lies in his lack of superficial charm. He is quite unable to be ingratiating as, say, Sinclair Lewis is ingratiating. There is little humor in him, and that little is grotesque and harsh. He is, again, curiously insensitive to the music of words; it would be difficult to imagine a literate man with less sense of style. He seems, indeed, to have an almost pathological preference for the trite phrase, the banal word. The consequence of all this is that he seems a bit uncouth to readers accustomed to the easy facilities and ingenuities of a clever generation. Every young novelist who comes down from Princeton or Yale writes better than Dreiser does.

But Beethoven also lacked charm, and yet he still lives. For he had something more important: he knew how to be poignant. Dreiser has it, too. His writing is slipshod, he maneuvers clumsily, he often seems to grope in darkness— and yet at the end there is always that effect of somber drama, that profound appeal to the feelings. To read him unmoved is to confess that there is nothing moving in the eternal tragedy of man. His books are not to be attempted lightly, as a diversion for a rainy afternoon. They call for a serious mood. When that mood is brought to them they yield something far more memorable and enduring than charm. *(March 15, 1925)*

OF MARK TWAIN's long awaited autobiography, the first
two volumes of which were lately published, the less said
the better. The old boy, especially in his last years, was a
highly adept press agent. He knew how to get himself
stared at and talked about. Like Wagner, Tolstoi, Oscar
Wilde, Anatole France, and George Bernard Shaw, he was a
great artist, but also a great mountebank. Thus his autobiography was not written under a bushel. On the contrary, it
was written in the glare of ten thousand spotlights, with
bands playing and the gallery packed full of reporters. The
news went delicately forth that the work was stuffed with
dynamite—that its publication after the author's death
would stagger humanity. Now he is dead and the first part
of it is published. It turns out to be flabby and harmless
stuff—so flabby, indeed, that the literary pedagogues are all
praising it lavishly.

But though his post-mortem bomb turns out to be a
squib, the fact will not down that Mark, taking him up and
down, fore and aft, remains the greatest artist in letters that
this immense and immaculate republic has yet produced.
His stature increases year by year, as considered judgment
measures him with his predecessors and contemporaries.
That he once trembled in the presence of Longfellow and
Whittier becomes a sort of standard joke, to be told to
sophomores on rainy days. That he envied Howells, and
even Holmes and Aldrich, passes out of respectable legend
into a sort of Apocrypha, though it is true. He had, so we
hear from Van Wyck Brooks, an inferiority complex, and
was henpecked by his wife, a militant Puritan. But wife and
complex, after all, were not enough to spoil him. The body

of his work remains. It comprises at least half a dozen books of the first rank—books clearly above anything that Irving or Cooper ever wrote, and fully the equals of anything done by Hawthorne or Emerson. It includes, beside, one book in a rank all its own, to wit, *Huckleberry Finn*. We have produced absolutely nothing to put alongside *Huckleberry Finn*, or to offer it even the feeblest challenge. In the whole range of the English novel, indeed, there are not five books to put alongside it.

Mark lived to be seventy-five, and passed his last thirty years on the front pages of the newspapers, but it is a curious and lamentable fact that he died with his inferiority complex in full blast, and only the slightest, most diffident suspicion that he belonged at the first table. The case, so far as I can recall, is without parallel; great artists are modest almost as seldom as they are faithful to their wives. A few months before he died there appeared an essay upon his work that gave him intense pleasure. The author was Professor William Lyon Phelps of Yale, and the essay was without evasions; it hailed Mark triumphantly as one of the major glories of the national letters. No wonder he was pleased! It was the first time that any American critic of academic dignity had admitted openly that he was an artist at all!

That was in 1910. I was myself so astounded and delighted by Phelps' accolade that I undertook a somewhat laborious inquiry into the history of Mark Twain's criticism, especially on the pedagogical side. That is to say, I examined all the treatises on American literature current in the federal union between 1870 and 1900—all the books in common use in schools and colleges. I found that, without a single exception, the learned authors had dismissed Mark

as a clown—a fellow belonging to the lodge of Petroleum V.
Nasby and Bill Nye. A few allowed that, as clowns went, he
had some merit, but the majority held their praises, and devoted themselves to lamenting that he was so often vulgar.
Such was the best critical opinion of his contemporaries.
Was Howells an exception? Perhaps. But only in the sense
that Emerson was an exception in the case of Whitman—
that is, he was an exception with prudent reservations.
Howells, who loved Mark sincerely as a man, spent many
years trying to tame him! It was as if the pastor of the First
Baptist church of Naumburg had tried to tame Nietzsche!

Even more than Whitman, indeed, Mark remains a
colossal monument to the imbecility of pedagogues. Whitman is now taught in all the colleges, and Mark is mentioned with respect. But if any literary tutor had so much
as mentioned *Leaves of Grass* in 1855 or *Huckleberry Finn*
thirty years later, the very elms of the campus would have
burst into flames. It takes a generation to penetrate such
skulls. In 1960 or thereabouts the heirs and assigns of the
current birchmen will be making their first shy exploration
of Cabell and Dreiser.

Fortunately, the fate of books does not depend upon
the suffrages of academic critics, else *The Golden Legend*
would be read today and *Leaves of Grass* would be forgotten. *Huckleberry Finn* gains nothing by the fact that they
now cease to sniff at it. The generation of boys to which I
belonged discovered it before their teachers had heard of it,
and have cherished it ever since—cherished it far more, indeed, than they have ever cherished any of the books com-
mended to their notice in school. It is, I believe, not only
the greatest work of the imagination yet produced in
America; it is the one most likely to endure. For there is in it

every quality that makes for permanent fame. It is a profound study of a people and an age, and yet it is transparently simply. It is full of high romance, and yet it is baldly true. It has a superb artfulness in every line, and yet it carries a disarming air of the casual, almost of the impromptu.

Mark himself never knew what a masterpiece he had created. To the end of his days he spoke of *Tom Sawyer* as if it were the equal of *Huckleberry Finn*; he preferred *Joan of Arc* to either, and apparently also *A Connecticut Yankee*. He wrote *Huck* unwillingly, and as a sort of chore. He put it aside three or four times to work on other books. More than once he was at the point of abandoning it altogether. In the end, tiring of it, he brought it to what he thought was an abrupt and ineffective finish. A worse critic, poor fellow, than even his critics! When he came to the last word of *Huck* he had written his ticket to immortality. Into it he had got Everyboy—and Everyboy is with us always, and is always the same age.

I incline to think, indeed, that it will outlast many works now vastly esteemed, including even *Leaves of Grass*. Surely I am not one to decry Whitman, but in the midst of the enthusiasm that his clanging dithyrambs evoke there should still be calm enough to remember that, after all, he was mistaken—that his vision had no more genuine substance than the dreams of a Marx or a Bryan. He emitted his barbaric yawps when democracy seemed to be at the top of the world; it has been going downhill ever since, and in another century or two the world may forget it altogether. Read in cold blood, his most eloquent lines take on a childish foolishness today. The America that he saw was purely imaginary, even in his own day; on some near tomorrow it may be downright unlawful! His verse, I believe, will not

survive that change, for, though men do not ask of poetry
that it tell them what is true, they at least demand that it
tell them what they may hope. It is now a penal offense in
nineteen American states to hope for what is in *Leaves of
Grass*.

Emerson, whom Mark always thought of as a good
Buddhist thinks of the Dalai Lama, is already passing into
the shadows, at all events in his own country. His ringing
individualism, it must be obvious, is now out of fashion;
mouthed today it takes on the quality of mere academic
prattling. No genuine American believes in it any more,
least of all the literary tutors who pretend to carry on the
Emerson tradition. Emerson left deep marks upon Europe;
you will find his ideas in the writings of such diverse men
as Carlyle and Nietzsche; he was the first American to ship
the gold of thought eastward. But in the United States he
long ago ceased to have any ponderable influence, and today he is a living presence only to the tutors aforesaid (who
try to show that he was the original 100 per cent American!)
and to the half-wits who dally with what is called the New
Thought. His weakness lay in his inexperience, his naïveté.
He had a sharp eye, but when he looked out of his window
he saw only a respectable Puritan village, with the grass
carefully cut and every one in bed by 9 p.m.

Mark had seen the wide, wide world. He had lived vari-
ously and inordinately. He was full of gusto. *The Conduct
of Life* is all very well—but *Huckleberry Finn* is alive!
(*February 8, 1925*)

ROBERT LOUIS STEVENSON

THE STEVENSON literature, for long consisting chiefly of lyrical gush, shows signs of late of taking on a greater dignity and accuracy. Two new biographies are now in the bookshops, and both move a long way in that direction. One is by Miss Rosaline Masson and the other by John A. Steuart. The former is largely devoted to defending and rehabilitating old Thomas Stevenson, the father of Louis and for many years a hobgoblin to the Stevensonians. The latter concerns itself more steadily with the private history of Louis himself, and especially with his early days in Edinburgh.

Neither work is wholly satisfactory. Miss Masson states the case for old Thomas so eloquently that she makes herself forget (though the reader is not apt to) that he was, after all, a hard boiled Calvinist, and that living with him, in consequence, must have been pretty dreadful, despite his occasional sentimentalities. And Mr. Steuart, for all his scientific frenzy, writes so badly, and intrudes himself into his narrative so absurdly, that he is very hard to read.

Room thus remains for a biographer better than either—one able to see Louis without illusion, and yet able to get something of his great charm on paper. He was surely not the towering genius that his worshipers have tried to make him, nor was he the chaste and peerless hero; but there was, nevertheless, a fine talent in him and a dauntless and hearty courage, and so he remains very attractive, if not exactly edifying. His life, I believe, was more interesting than his books. He was the first poet in history ever to realize the dreams of the whole fraternity. He revolted against Philistinism, and he won. From his earliest goatish days in Edinburgh to his last years on his South Sea isle, watering his banyan trees and consorting with cannibal kings, he led his own life. Wherever he went, there a perfect Greenwich Village went with him.

Regarding his books, alas, there is some doubt. They are esteemed this side idolatry by many, but those who most esteem are not otherwise notable for the higher judiciousness. His most ardent customers, I often suspect, are persons who seldom read any other author; in their dithyrambs there is often more than a suspicion of the naïve enthusiasm which goes with too much devotion to a single handsome library set.

Was he really a great essayist? I doubt it; his essays, in the main, are thin, conventional, and full of affectation. Was he a poet? I doubt it again; he wrote, perhaps, three poems worth remembering; the rest were drivel. Was he, then, a romancer of the blood royal, the heir to Scott and Dumas? I doubt it doubly and triply; had he lived twenty years longer he might have made the grade, but as it was he never got beyond the first experimental rushes. What remains of him that is genuinely solid and first class? Perhaps two short stories. Perhaps the better part of one romance. Perhaps the epitaph that he wrote for himself. Here Stevenson scored superbly. But elsewhere he mainly failed.

Mr. Steuart, in his biography, shows some of the causes of that constant failure. The trouble with Stevenson was, in brief, that he never achieved a manner of his own until just before his death. All his early work was badly imitative, and he had such poor taste that he often imitated ninth-rate models. And in the work of his maturity, though he played the ape less sedulously, that habit of imitation survived. He changed his style two or three times a year. His point of view shifted like the winds. First this model and then that one seduced him. It was not until after he got to Samoa, and was thrown upon his own, that he began to work things out for himself. And then, with *Weir of Hermiston* half done, he died.

The man, in truth, was very long coming to discretion; he was a small boy on a lark almost to the end. Mr. Steuart gives a truly depressing picture of his early days in Edinburgh; it does more to make one sympathize with old Thomas than all of Miss Masson's defense. Louis burst out of a Christian home to wallow with the swine. He frequented the lowest pubs of the town; he caroused day and night with blacklegs male and female; on one great occasion he scared his father half to death by proposing to marry a damsel of the pave.

Worse, these proceedings were not carried on in the sober, regretful manner natural to a Scot on the loose. The fellow insisted upon playing the zany as well as the profligate. He wore battered hats, with his long greasy hair sticking through their vents; he bought himself velvet coats and loud checked pantaloons; he refused to carry the umbrella that is the badge of a respectable Edinburgher; he made ribald songs, bawled them, and threw his legs in the air. His model was not Bobby Burns, decently asleep in a cow stable; he patterned himself after François Villon, mad with red wine, armed with a butcher knife, and fugitive from the police.

Try to imagine the effect on his father. The old man was not merely ordinarily respectable; he was probably the most respectable citizen ever heard of in Edinburgh. He was an important state official; his wife, Louis' mother, was the daughter of an eminent Presbyterian divine; the family had money, and the family home, by the simple device of walling up the windows, might have served admirably as a tomb for John Calvin himself. Picture to yourself the feeling of old Thomas when he discovered that his only son was a common jest upon the public streets—that bad boys followed him when he was in his cups, bombarding him with cobblestones, dead cats, and derisive epigrams. It was almost as if old John Coolidge had discovered young Cal upon a soapbox, preaching the dictatorship of the proletariat.

But Louis was to go even further. When his father remonstrated he fled to Paris, and there indulged himself in the lamentable recreations which now engage our own émigré literati. He learned the dreadful taste of *vin ordinaire*; he frequented studios and accompanied painters upon their sinister excursions; finally he settled down at Barbizon, sleeping all day and gabbling all night. It was there, as every one knows, that he met the grass widow Osbourne, and there that he definitely cut himself off from the Scots race and became a wanderer up and down the back alleys of the world.

His pursuit of the grass widow across the Atlantic and then across the continent to the Pacific is too familiar to need rehearsal; it has made him more admirers, especially in the finishing schools, than any of his actual books. There is now a monument to him in San Francisco, hard by the city jail, but while he trod the adjacent streets he almost starved. Illness overtook him, too; he was more dead than alive for a year, and never, indeed, quite recovered his health. The grass widow nursed him, and, when her husband had been disposed of, married him. The rest was relatively easy sailing. American magazines began to buy his stuff. He toured the health resorts, most of them expensive. He bought a yacht and sailed for the South Seas. And there he died.

Today his grave above Apia is the chief object of interest, as the guidebooks say, between Honolulu and Sydney. Great steamships full of male and female Babbitts stop there on their way around the world. Speeches are made by Kiwanians with the gift, and traveling pastors pray for the salvation of Tusitala. He is widely regarded as a safe author. In all his books there is no voluptuousness. His murders lack the barbaric goriness of Joseph Conrad's. His heroes eschew the wine cup—save, of course, Villon—and have no truck with other men's wives. He is read and praised by Clayton Hamilton, the critics of chautauqua, and the National Association of Teachers of English.

Well, that, too, is destiny. But hardly the one visioned for the picturesque Louis by the incandescent Stevensonians of, say, twenty years ago. Then the word went round that he was secure in Valhalla—that a niche was his forevermore among the great romancers. Some added that he had also another niche: among the immortal essayists. Others added yet a third: among the poets. I doubt that any such notions prevail today, save among the rhetoricians and pedagogues aforesaid. Just after the century dawned there appeared an apparition that took the thoughts of all other connoisseurs from *Treasure Island* and even from "Lodgings for the Night" and "The Sire de Maletroit's Door." It was the apparition of Joseph Conrad.

(December 14, 1924)

BEETHOVEN stands almost alone among the great artists, first, in that his greatness was recognized almost from the moment he began to write, and, second, in that it has never been questioned by any reputable body of opinion since his death. This second fact is even more remarkable than the first. Very few of the immortal creators have escaped periods of neglect and contumely. Shakespeare, as every one knows, was regarded as a second rater during part of the eighteenth century, and various imbeciles set themselves to the job of editing and improving him. Even Bach had his twilight, and it took a Mendelssohn to rescue him. But only fools have ever questioned the mightiness of Beethoven—and not many fools.

True enough some of his music heard today sounds a trifle old-fashioned. But that is the fault of the orchestra he wrote for rather than of the man himself. His C minor symphony, I believe, ought to be rescored by some one familiar with the larger and more resilient orchestra of today, say Richard Strauss. The colossal first movement, in the concert hall, is always a bit ineffective; the music never sounds quite as tremendous as it looks in score. But scored for the orchestra of *Till Eulenspiegel* or *Tod und Verklärung* it would be overwhelming. The stuff is actually there.

Beethoven himself, when he came to the roaring last movement of the C minor, tried to reinforce the every day orchestra of his time by adding a piccolo, a contrabassoon, and three additional trombones. But he lacked tubas and he lacked many other things, and even the trombone in 1807 was not understood as it is today. Would a composer of 1927, writing the C minor, confine himself to two kettle

drums and keep them banging away during a whole movement at C and G? It is surely not probable.

There is thus a certain thinness to the modern ear in
some of the greatest of old Ludwig's masterpieces as they
are heard in the concert hall, but there is no hint of it in the
actual structure of his music. He thought on a large scale,
and he had the skill necessary to execute his grandiose ideas.
The first movement of the Eroica is a monument to one of
the most gigantic intellectual feats ever performed by man.
In it Beethoven set the tone of music for almost a century,
and to this day it has never been surpassed within its own
field, not even by Brahms—not even, indeed, by Beethoven
himself. It is a creative work of the very first caliber, and in
every sense.

It was not conjured up, of course, out of free air—as
many too facile music sniffers, including the present humble subscriber, have often alleged. Its roots are actually to
be found in the Second symphony—a work curiously under-
esteemed and, hence, seldom heard. But between the Second and the Eroica there was still a tremendous leap, and
Beethoven could never have made it without the aid of
genius of the highest order. The first movement, as every
one knows, shocked and amazed Vienna when it was first
played: there were loud yells for mercy from the gallery. It
no longer shocks any one, but when the clowning of the
Stravinskys and Scriabines is forgotten it will begin to
amaze again. For there is in it that complete perfection of
design which belongs only to immortal masterpieces. It
might be written differently, but it could not be written
better.

In the smaller forms, with an instrument at hand that
was better organized and understood than the orchestra of

his time, Beethoven wrote works that remain unsurpassed to this day. For example, there are his later string quartets. No one has ever made the string quartet speak with a nobler voice. Beethoven found it chattering amiably—and going a round of easy emotions. He taught it how to be eloquent, and how to sing the siren's song. In those last quartets, even more than in the symphonies, there is the heavy charge of personal emotion which was, perhaps after all, Beethoven's greatest legacy to music. He found it gay, charming, brave, aphrodisiacal, devotional, even dignified; he made it tragic.

The man, of course, had the defects of his qualities. Compared to such a lordly, soaring *improvisateur* as Schubert—unquestionably the most gifted natural genius ever heard of in any art—he was laborious, and even a bit heavy footed. The thing vaguely called inspiration seldom gave him much help. His notebooks show by what ghastly struggles he devised his melodies—many of them still banal after he had sweated over them for months and years. It was not often in his life that a lovely tune popped into his head, all ready for use. Only too often even his hardest heavings failed to produce one and he had to go into action with nothing save a vagrant phrase.

But what he made of those phrases is the measure of his genius. He had scarcely stated them before they began to throw out sub-phrases, and in a short while, by devices that remain as marvelous today as they were when he first launched them upon the world, he had built up a structure of such intricate complexity, and yet of such transparent clarity and essential simplicity, that the effect was staggering. It was impossible to misunderstand him, and it was impossible to resist being moved by him. He knew how to enchant the mind, and he knew also how to search the heart.

No man before him, not even Bach, had ever surpassed his mastery of the materials of music. And no man following him, save only Wagner and Brahms, has ever offered him serious challenge.

To his melodic sterility add his immense moodiness and the tale of his deficiencies is told. His emotions at their highest flight were almost godlike; he gave music a sort of Alpine grandeur. But such feelings were more than even a Beethoven could bear for long, and so he sometimes slid from them into trivial and trashy moods, as a Rotarian, turning from the cruel demands of Service, takes refuge in golf, spitballs, and bawdy songs to keep his heart from busting. Beethoven invented the musical obscenity: he showed how the canon could be converted into a ribald limerick. And he wrote a great deal of sheer drivel for the publishers. But he never put any of it into the music of his first line. That first line ran a whole county beyond any first line that had gone before it, and not many men have so much as approached it since 1827.

In the life of such a man there is much fodder for the ironist, but there is also a great deal for the optimist. After all, a race of quadrupeds that can produce such creatures must have some solid worth in it, and there is more proof of that worth in the fact that it cherishes them. Beethoven, to be sure, has never been the great hero that Valentino was, or John L. Sullivan, or Adelina Patti. He has never been worshiped like Robert E. Lee, or Bismarck, or Roosevelt. But I don't believe that any prudent man would want to trade his fame for that of any of these darlings, for it is infinitely wider dispersed than theirs, and it will last a great deal longer.

He is dead now a hundred years and yet he remains as

alive today as if he still tramped his garden at Mödling,
damning his nephew and pondering his gnarled and asth-
matiç tunes. The great masses of mankind perhaps remain
unaware of him, but there is no civilized man who is wholly
unresponsive to his touch, or who doubts that he was one
of the greatest men that the human race has produced. During the last week the press of the world has printed ten
thousand articles upon his life and work, and in all the languages spoken by enlightened men. His anniversary has
been celebrated in all the great cities on earth; millions have
heard him speak and responded to his thoughts. He has
been remembered and given a full measure of devotion not
only by these crowds but also by countless lonely men and
women in the cultural wastes of Serbia, Nicaragua, Ontario,
Delaware, Madagascar, and Mississippi. Dead a century,
and his bones long rotted and blown away, he has come
back with the comfort and solace of an old and well loved
friend—nay, of a god. It is a fate that the captains and king
may well envy. Not many of them will outlast the grandson
of the chief cook at Ehrenbreitstein.

(*March 27, 1927*)

THE MUSIC OF THE AMERICAN NEGRO

THE FIRST BOOK of Negro songs ever published was brought
out by the Rev. G. D. Pike of the American Missionary association in 1872, and by 1892 its various editions had run
to a total sale of 130,000 copies. But Pike was an uplifter,
not a musician, and so his collection of the Negro spirituals,

which were then called jubilee songs, was little more than a crude source book. All the bold and peculiar harmonies of the colored singer were lost. Pike had apparently intrusted the arrangement of his specimens to some manufacturers of Methodist hymns. Some of the best of them were thus converted into the sort of garbage that is heard at Billy Sunday revivals.

It was not until 1914, when the late Henry Edward Krehbiel, music critic of the *New York Tribune,* published his *Afro-American Folk Songs,* that Negro songs got any intelligent examination. Krehbiel was a German pedant of the dullest type (though he became a violent American patriot during the world war), but he at least had some knowledge of music, and so his study was a valuable one. Its defects lay in the incompleteness of his knowledge. He had to get nine-tenths of his songs at second hand, and not infrequently they reached him in a mutilated—or, worse still, in a clumsily embellished—state.

The gaps in his work are now admirably filled by James Weldon Johnson in *The Book of American Negro Spirituals.* Mr. Johnson, himself a colored man, has gathered all his material from original sources. He grew up in the south, he was interested in music from his earliest years, and with his brother, J. Rosamond Johnson, he was mainly responsible for the rise of what has since come to be known as jazz. But the Johnsons are by no means mere jazzhounds. On the contrary, they are both educated musicians. Thus their book is one of solid dignity and value. James Weldon Johnson discusses in a long preface the origin and nature of the spirituals, and J. Rosamond presents scores of them in his own arrangements.

The spirituals probably had a complex ancestry and are

mulatto rather than Negro. All the original slaves brought in was a series of rhythms—many of them superb, but few of them accompanied by what Caucasians would recognize as melody. The Africans, to be sure, had tunes, but they were tunes of the vague, wandering sort that all other savages affect. They lacked what white musicians call form. There was no rhythm of structure under their rhythm of phrase, and so they could not convey that sense of design, that feeling of completion, which characterizes civilized melody.

But, as I say, the rhythms of the Negro were superb, and so all that was needed to make good songs was their reinforcement with melody. That melody, it is highly probable, came from the campmeeting, and at some time not earlier than the end of the eighteenth century. The whites in the south made no effort to educate their slaves in the arts, but they were greatly interested, after the first tours of Francis Wesley, in saving their souls, and that salvation was chiefly attempted, for obvious reasons, out of doors. There arose the campmeeting—and the campmeeting was a place of sturdy and even vociferous song. The Negroes memorized what they heard and then adapted it to their native rhythms. Thus spirituals were born.

The purely Negro contribution to them—good rhythm—was the more important part, and by far. To this day Methodist hymns seem banal to musicians because they lack variety of rhythm; nine-tenths of them bang along in the same depressing sing-song. But the spirituals are full of rhythms of the utmost delicacy, and when they are sung properly—not by white frauds or by high toned dephlogisticated Negroes from Boston, but by black singers from the real south—they give immense pleasure to lovers of music. Beethoven would have delighted in them, and Brahms, had he ever heard them, would have borrowed them for his uses—as, indeed, Dvořák did after him.

The Negroes, having started with Methodist hymns and improved them by joining them to decent rhythms, went a couple of steps farther. First, they improved them as mere melodies. That is, they displaced their obvious cadences with cadences of a greater piquancy and relieved their monotony with bold modulations. Some of these modulations, as Mr. Krehbiel demonstrated in his book, went back to Africa. Savages know nothing of the modes—or keys—that white men use. They see nothing wrong about inserting a glaring B flat or C sharp into the key of C major. They did this in many of the spirituals, and sometimes the effect was extraordinarily brilliant and thrilling.

Second, they improved the harmonics of the hymns, and for much the same reason. That is, they wandered into "errors" because they knew no better—and the errors turned out to be lush and lovely. The history of civilized music during the last two generations, indeed, has been largely a history of the discovery and adoption of such errors. When white musicians began to put them into music there were bitter protests from all the pedants, but now many of them have become quite orthodox, and music that is bare of them begins to seem bald and insipid. The Negroes were using some of them all the while. They were satisfactory to the African ear long before the Caucasian ear learned to tolerate them.

As Mr. Johnson shows, the Negro is a harmonist far more than he is a melodist. He doesn't care much for tunes; the things that interest him are harmonies and rhythms. Let a crowd of colored fellows begin to sing any current song, however banal, and they will presently give it a new interest and dignity by introducing strange and often entrancing harmonies into it. They seem to have a natural talent for that sort of thing. A gang of white boys, attempting song together, will usually sing in unison, or stick to a few safe harmonies of the barber shop variety, but darkies almost always plunge out into deeper waters, and not infrequently, in the midst of harsh discords, they produce effects of extraordinary beauty.

The spirituals are commonly called folk songs, and so the notion is abroad that they sprang full blown out of the folk—that they were written not by individuals, but by whole groups. This is nonsense. In that sense, indeed, there is no such thing as a folk song. Folk songs are written, like all other songs, by individuals. All the folk have to do with them is to choose the ones that are to survive. Sometimes, true enough, repetition introduces changes into them, but those changes are not important. The basic song belongs to one bard, and to him alone.

Mr. Johnson tells of such a bard he knew as a boy in the south, of the same surname as his own, but no relative— one "Singing" Johnson. Every southerner knows another. These minnesingers usually traveled about, singing for their keep. When they struck a new neighborhood they would make songs to fit what was going on in it—the advent of a new and powerful preacher, the conversion of a notorious sinner, a great flood or fire, the hanging of the local daredevil. Most of those songs died in infancy, but a few always survived. The best of the survivors in the campmeeting category are the spirituals that every one knows today.

Ah, that we could discover the authors of some of them! What genius went to waste among the pre-confederate fundamentalists! But did it go to waste? Perhaps not. Only its possessors were lost. The black unknown who wrote "Swing Low, Sweet Chariot," "Deep River," and "Roll, Jordan, Roll"—for I suspect that one bard wrote all three—left a heritage to his country that few white men have ever surpassed. He was one of the greatest poets we have ever produced, and he came so near to being our greatest musician that I hesitate to look for a match for him. There should be a monument to him in the south. He was worth a whole herd of Timrods.

(November 15, 1925)

ON REALISM

ONE OF THE strangest delusions of criticism is to be found in the notion that there is such a thing as realism—that is, realism grounded on objective fact in the same way that a scientific monograph, say, or the report of a law trial, is grounded upon objective fact. Nothing of the sort is imaginable. The arts do not and cannot deal with reality, for the moment they begin to do so they cease to be arts. Their function is something quite different, and even antagonistic. It is not to photograph the world, but to edit and improve the world. It is not to embrace the whole, but to select and exhibit the salient part. It is not to echo life, but to show a way to escape from life.

But perhaps I succumb to phrases. What I mean to

say, in plain language, is that no genuine artist would paint a picture if he were completely satisfied with the thing he depicts. His dissatisfaction is precisely what makes him an artist: he is moved by a yearning to put in something or take out something, to make a comment, to frame a gloss upon the word of God—or, as it is usually put, to express himself. And the measure of his virtue as an artist lies in that contribution, not in what he takes bodily from nature. If what he has to say is novel and charming, then he is a good artist. If what he has to say is trite and dull, then he is a bad one. The first and last thing is what he has to say.

Certainly all this should be obvious, but for some reason or other it seems to be not so. I have read of late a long essay on James Joyce's *Ulysses*, praising it in high, astounding terms as a complete and exact record of a day in the life of its people. It is, of course, nothing of the sort. At least nine-tenths of its materials came, not out of the Bloom family, but out of James Joyce. Even the celebrated unspoken monologue of Marion at the end is his, not hers. There are long sections of it that even the professional psychologists, who are singularly naïve, must detect as false— that is, false for Marion, false for a woman of her position, perhaps even false for any woman. But they are not false for Joyce.

Some years ago I enjoyed the somewhat laborious honor of reading in manuscript a new novel by a well known American novelist greatly esteemed for his fidelity to the metaphysical bugaboo known as the truth. It was, in more than one way, a work of high merit, but it had a number of obvious defects. One was a painful superabundance of irrelevant detail. Another was an excess of detail of a sort likely to arouse the libido of the Comstocks, and so get the book a bad name. I called this last blemish to the attention of the author, pointing especially to a scene depicting what has since come to be called a petting party. At once he rose to high dudgeon.

"You are," he roared, "a —— —— ——. You are asking me to make my story false. It is like asking a woman to cut off the ears of her child. What you object to actually happened. It had to happen. It was inevitable. I defy you to describe a petting party without mentioning it."

I did not accept the challenge, but proceeded by a more indirect route. That is to say, I described the same petting party in different terms. I included all the details that my eminent friend had included, but then went on to include some details of my own. The first brought him up.

"But you can't——" he began, in some agitation.

"Did it happen?" I demanded. "Am I going outside the record?"

He retreated behind indignation, and I proceeded. My second canto drove him out of the room. But while I was in the midst of my fifth or sixth he returned and proposed peace.

"You are quite right," he said. "It is impossible to tell it all. I thought I was doing it, but I see now that I really wasn't. Every passage you have objected to comes out."

But this was going too far, and so I protested in turn.

"Not at all," I said. "If they are true to you, then they stay in. It is your book, not mine. It doesn't represent objective reality; it represents your reaction to reality. Did those passages seem sound and inevitable when you wrote them? Then they stay in."

So they stayed in, and the Comstocks duly raided the book.

Thus argument, as usual, led only to contradiction, enmity and disaster. On another such occasion the consequences were less deplorable. I have another friend, a distinguished anatomical artist, whose drawings are celebrated for their precise and merciless fidelity to nature. He paints landscapes quite as well as livers and lights, but in the same way. He is strongly against the new movement in painting, and believes that it is the artist's highest duty to present the object depicted exactly as it stands.

One day I told this gentleman that I'd like to have a specimen of his work, and he presented me forthwith with a truly marvelous drawing. It represented, he told me, a kidney in the last stages of some dreadful disease, and was to be reproduced in a forthcoming medical work. Knowing nothing of kidneys, I could admire it as a work of art, and as such it seemed to me to be magnificent. So greatly did I esteem it that I had it framed and hung it in my office, that visiting customers might share my pleasure in it.

The first visitor to see it was a critic of painting. He anchored himself before it and gazed at it for ten minutes.

"How do you like it?" I asked at length.

"It is superb," he said. "Leonardo himself was not a better draftsman. You have a masterpiece. Where did you get it?"

"Do you know what it represents?" I asked.

"No," said the critic. "Who cares what it represents? It may be whatever you choose to call it. All it represents to me is a first rate draftsman. The fellow can draw. And he has something to say."

Whereupon, in the manner of art critics, my friend proceeded to a disquisition unintelligible to me. But one thing, at least, I understood: that this master realist had not fetched him by realism.

In so far as it has any meaning at all, indeed, realism simply means the opposite of consciously false. Daisy Ashford's *The Young Visiters* was brilliantly realistic, and in the best sense, though it was full of palpable absurdities. But Daisy did not intend them to be absurdities. She felt them as truths, and so she was a realist. The world she depicted was authentically the world that she saw. And what she added to it represented exactly her private view of the way it might be made better and more charming.

In this sense—the only true sense—all novelists of any merit whatsoever are realists. Joseph Conrad was, though he dealt habitually with strange people and unfamiliar situations, often near the border line of the fantastic. Anatole France was, though he more than once crossed the line. Realism is simply intellectual honesty in the artist. The realist yields nothing to what is manifestly not true, however alluring. He makes no compromise with popular sentimentality and illusion. He avoids the false inference as well as the bogus fact. He respects his materials as he respects himself.

But all that certainly doesn't make him a photographer. In the world as he sees it there are facts that lie outside him and facts that lie within, and they are of equal importance. It is his contribution that converts a dead external reality into a living inner experience, and conveys his own emotion to the reader. If that emotion of his is common and shoddy, then what he writes will be common and shoddy, but if it has dignity in it, and some echo of the eternal tragedy of man, then he will produce a genuine work of art. What ails most of the so-called realists, particularly in this great republic, is simply that they are inferior men. They see only what is visible to an ice wagon driver. They bring to it only the emotional responses of a trolley conductor.

(*August 15, 1926*)

VIEW OF LITERARY GENTS

MY TRADE forces me into constant association with persons of literary skill and aspiration, male and female, foreign and domestic. I can only report, after a quarter of a century of commerce with them, that I find them, in the main, very dull, and that I greatly prefer the society of Babbitts. Is this heresy? If so, I can only offer my sincere regrets. The words are wrung from me, not by any desire to be unpleasant, but simply by a lifelong and incurable affection for what, for want of a better name, is called the truth.

It may be true in other countries, though I doubt it, that literary endeavor is a gesture toward the stars, but it is seldom so, I believe, in this great imperial republic. Nine-tenths of the literary gents I know are hotter for the dollar than any Babbitt ever heard of. Their talk is not about what they write, but about what they get for it. Not infrequently they get a great deal. I know a number who make more annually than honest bank presidents, even than Christian bank presidents. A few probably top the incomes of railroad purchasing agents and nose-and-throat specialists, and come close to the incomes of realtors, lawyers, and bootleggers. They practice a profitable trade.

And no wonder, for they pursue it in the most assiduously literate country in Christendom. Our people, perhaps, seldom read anything that is good, but they at least read— day and night, weekdays and Sundays. We have so many magazines of more than 500,000 circulation that a list of them would fill this column. We have at least a dozen above 1,000,000. These magazines have immense advertising revenues, and are thus prosperous. They can pay high prices for manuscripts. The business of supplying such manuscripts has made a whole herd of authors rich.

I do not object to their wealth; I simply report its lamentable effects upon them and upon the aspirants who strive to imitate them. For those effects go down to the lowest levels. The schools of short story writing all respond to them. The neophyte seldom shows any yearning to discharge ideas, to express himself, to tackle and master a difficult enterprise. He shows only a desire to get money in what seems to him to be an easy way. He hears that Harold Balderdash, writing a short story in 48 hours, receives $2,000 for it. It is this news that lures him from his stool in the lime and cement warehouse.

Such is the typical young literatus of the republic: a fellow with a great itch to write and publish, but nothing in particular to say. He is no more an artist than a movie actor is an artist; he is simply a lazy young man. That laziness clings to him when, by the providence of God, he is disappointed in his chief ambition—that is, when the expected dollars do not roll in. The bankrupt literary tradesman then turns revolutionist. He discovers a way of writing poetry that is quicker and easier than the way followed by Swinburne. He invents a form of short story that requires no form, and no content save a sophomoric obscenity.

The Greenwich Villagers, in their day, have all waited in the ante-chambers of the *Saturday Evening Post*. Turned away, they pour their indignation into doggerel and denounce Thomas Hardy as a numskull. Some add that he is in the pay of international finance.

So at the bottom, as at the top. Short cuts, quick sales, easy profits—it is all very American. Do we gabble about efficiency? Then the explanation is to be sought in the backwash of Freudism. Nowhere else on earth is genuine competence so rare. The average American plumber cannot plumb; the average American cook cannot cook; the average American literary gent has nothing to say, and says it with rubber stamps. Of the 10,000 short stories that are printed in American magazines every year—bought and paid for, often lavishly—not a score belongs to literature in any rational sense, and not half a dozen are remembered a year after their publication.

But I was speaking of the literati as persons. They suffer, I believe, from two things. The first is what I have just described; their general fraudulence. They are not, taking one with another, artists at all, but simply artisans. What, in a genuine artist, might be a pardonable and even charming eccentricity, becomes in a manufacturer of pot boilers a mere irritating affectation. One somehow resents the pretensions of a man who is for sale.

The other defect of literary gents among us springs out of the fact that their position, in the republic, is insecure—that they have no public dignity. It is no longer honorable *per se* to be engaged in travails of the spirit, as it used to be in the New England of the Aufklärung; it is honorable only if it pays. I believe that the fact discourages many aspirants who, if they went on, might come to something. They are blasted in their tender years, and so literature loses them. Too sensitive to sit below the salt, they join the hearty, red blooded he-men who feast above it, admired by the national gallery.

It is, indeed, not surprising that the majority of college graduates, once headed as a matter of course for the grove of Athene, now go into business—that Harvard now turns out ten times as many bond salesmen every year as metaphysicians and martyrs. Business, in America, offers higher rewards than any other human enterprise, not only in money, but also in dignity. Thus it tends to attract the best brains of the country.

Is Kiwanis idiotic? The answer is that Kiwanis no more represents business than Greenwich Village represents literature. On the higher levels its bilge does not flow—and on those higher levels, as I have hinted, there are shrewder fellows, and more amusing, than ever you will find in the Authors' club. These fellows, by the strict canons of ethnology, are Babbitts, but it seems to me they are responsible, nevertheless, for everything that makes life in the United States tolerable. One finds, in their company, excellent wines and liquors, and one seldom hears any cant.

I don't believe this is a healthy state of affairs. I believe business should be left to commonplace and insensitive minds, and that men of genuine originality, and hence of genuine charm, should be sucked automatically into enterprises of a greater complexity and subtlety. It is done in more ancient countries; it has been done from remote antiquity under civilizations that have aged in the wood, and so got free from fusel oil. But it is not yet done in these states. Only an overwhelming natural impulse—perhaps complicated by insanity—can urge an American into the writing of fugues or epics. The pull is toward the investment security business.

That pull, yielded to, leads to high rewards. The successful business man among us—and only the sheer imbecile, in such times as these, is not successful—enjoys the public respect and adulation that elsewhere bathe only bishops and generals of artillery. He is treated with dignity in the newspapers, even when he appears in combat with his wife's lover. His opinion is sought upon all public questions, including the esthetic. In the stews and wine shops he receives the attention that, in old Vienna, used to be given to Beethoven. He enjoys an aristocratic immunity to most forms of judicial process. He wears the Légion d'Honneur, is an LL.D. of Yale, and is received cordially at the White House.

The literary gent, however worthy, scales no such heights under our kultur. Only one President since the birth of the republic has ever welcomed men of letters at the White House, and that one, the sainted Roosevelt, judged them by their theological orthodoxy and the hair upon their chests. A few colored poets were added to make the first pages; that was all. The literati thus wander about somewhat disconsolately among us, and tend to become morose and dull. If they enjoy the princely fees of the train boy magazines, they are simply third rate business men—successful, perhaps, but without the larger vision. If they happen to be genuine artists—and now and then it does happen—they are as lonely as life insurance solicitors at a convention of Seventh Day Adventists. Such sorrows do not make for Gemütlichkeit. There is much more of it in the pants business.

(November 29, 1925)

THE AVALANCHE OF BOOKS

THE OTHER DAY there came to me a package of books from a well known American publishing house. It was one of six or eight that arrived that day, but by chance I opened it first, presently I was examining its contents: five new novels, all of them by authors unknown to me. Being in a lazy mood, and disinclined to literary composition, I spent the whole afternoon looking through them. What I found, not to put too fine a point upon it, was simply bilge. In the whole quintet there was not the slightest sign of anything even remotely describable as literary skill or passion. The five authors were only lucky bunglers who had somehow managed to get their drivel printed.

Why are such books published? On what theory do reputable publishers go to all the elaborate trouble of getting them set up, printing them, binding them, encasing them in gaudy slipcovers, advertising them voluptuously, and burdening the book stores with them? Who reads them? Who, having ordinary sanity and taste, *could* read them? I often wonder. For they come out in an endless stream, hailed, whooped up, and then suddenly forgotten. Six months after publication they have disappeared completely. Who stands the loss? And why?

It is commonly believed that the authors pay for their publication, but that, I am convinced, is true very seldom. Not many American publishers of any dignity ever print books on that basis. A few third-raters do it—they are known in the trade as lemon squeezers—but they do not seem to prosper: it is too easy to get books published by reputable publishers, and at their expense. The firm that issued the five novels was of that character. It has many books of great importance on its list. It publishes authors of international celebrity. And yet it also published that depressing rubbish!

If this firm were singular, its hospitality to such rubbish might be set down to an aberration of its constituent Barabbases, but the fact is that practically all of the leading American publishers show the same weakness. Their lists are crowded with second and third rate books and they advertise some of them in a way almost worthy of a new cure for halitosis. There seems to be a race among them to find out which can publish the most books, and every contestant appears to be willing to call anything within covers a book in order to win. An author of honest purposes and dignified achievement finds himself cheek by jowl on his publisher's list with bogus geniuses just out of high school and all sorts of dull hacks and cheap jacks. Every imprint known to American readers during the last dozen years has appreciably diminished in value, and some have diminished so much that they are now of scarcely any value at all.

I assume that the general prosperity of the book trade is partly to blame. The business of publishing since the war has been very good. Americans are reading far more books than they ever did before and paying higher prices for them. More, they are reading over wider fields. There was a time, and it was not long ago, when the only American best sellers were novels, but now it is not at all uncommon for a book of history or biography, or even a treatise on psychology or philosophy, to reach a huge sale. And, as sales have increased, book stores have multiplied, so that there are now a dozen where there used to be only one.

Thus it is easy for the publishers' drummers to take orders—far easier than it was before the war. If each book store in the country takes only five copies of a new book— and if it is sufficiently advertised they will certainly average more than five—there is already a good sale. If the book has a good press some of them will reorder instantly—and thereafter it is a pretty gamble. Every American publisher playing that game has rolled up now and then heavy winnings. So all of them keep on playing.

But there are too many players sitting in and too many chips on the table. With such immense numbers of new books coming out not one in ten can have a genuinely successful sale—that is, a sale profitable alike to the publisher, to the author, and to the book seller. Only too often the first orders are never repeated—and never worked off upon the public. Every book seller in the country has his shelves crowded with such failures. He contemplates them gloomily for a while, and then, with more and more new books crowding upon him, he tries to force the publisher to take them back. If he succeeds, the publisher faces a heavy loss. If he fails, he himself faces a heavy loss.

Such losses of late have been so numerous that a great many American publishers find their profits cut very seriously and a great many American book sellers are close to bankruptcy. Some time ago, indeed, a distinguished American publisher told me that he knew of not more than a score of book stores in the whole country, excluding department stores, that were indubitably solvent. The rest are hanging on by their eyebrows, accumulating more and more formidable inventories and demanding heavier and heavier discounts on new books. They are drowned in unsalable stock. They had to lay it in in order to show a wide assortment to their customers and meet the competition of their rivals. And now it drags them down.

It is the sheer multiplicity of new books that is mainly to blame. So many come out every month that a book seller who pretends to carry a comprehensive stock must buy far more than he can sell. He has no means of determining in advance which of the newcomers will be successes and which will be flops. So in order to have all of the former in hand when the demand comes he buys great stacks of the latter—and presently he finds his shelves overloaded and his takings insufficient to meet his incoming bills. Hence the dreadfully long credits that he demands. And hence his endless struggle for larger and larger discounts.

Most American publishers of any standing have made money during the last few years, but not many, I suspect, have made as much as they ought to have made on their turnover. As fast as their returns come in they are invested in more books—which means that they are put into cold storage and remain unproductive for from six months to two years. Thus publishing begins to require more working capital than any other comparable business, and one really bad season would be sufficient to put more than one very prosperous house into difficulties.

The way out, it seems to me, is for the publishers to abandon their present wild yearning to fatten their lists and go back to publishing only books that have a sound reason for being and are reasonably certain to have profitable sales. The current gambling is ruining the book sellers by loading them down with unsalable stock and imperiling the publishers themselves by tying up their capital. Who gains by it? The reading public? The reading public gains only the unhappy knowledge that honorable imprints are no longer worth as much as they used to be. The only real gainers are the bad authors. They get very little money, but their vanity is satisfied, and so the number of them tends to increase steadily.

The question whether a given manuscript is of sound merit and worth publishing is seldom hard to answer. Publishers' readers do not make many mistakes in that direction; the tales of rejected masterpieces that go 'round are tales only. A dozen years ago I offered free of charge to find a publisher for any genuinely good manuscript that was sent to me. About five hundred came in, but only one of them was good: I found a publisher for it within twenty-four hours. The present swamping of the book stores is caused by gambling in half good, quarter good, and no good ones. A piece of rubbish is printed with a great hullabaloo because it somehow resembles, or is thought to resemble, a book that made a success last season. The book sellers buy it, put it on their shelves—and then begin to contemplate the unpleasant business of getting enough money to pay for it. The publishers could save them by refusing to print such stuff. Unless they do so, and very shortly, they will get the whole trade into trouble.

(December 25, 1927)

IV. RELIGION, ETHICS, AND SCIENCE
※

Two of Mencken's major works, Treatise on the Gods *and* Treatise on Right and Wrong, *were the result of an intense and lifelong interest in theology and ethics.*

Both are recommended to readers who would pursue further ideas hinted at in this section.

An immense amount of research went into Treatise on the Gods, *which sold well but met with a chilly reception from the critics.*

This critical failure was a disappointment that Mencken felt keenly even in his twilight years. In a discussion of his books a few months before he died, he said he still thought it one of his best.

Written when his mature style was at its peak, the volume is an exposition of the development and psychology of religion colored with Menckenian atheism.

Essays touching on science are included here because the author based much of his religious skepticism on the premise that science is incompatible with theology. Consequently, he frequently mentioned one while discussing the other.

121

FUNDAMENTALISM: DIVINE AND SECULAR

THOSE OPTIMISTS who plan to put down fundamentalism by educating *Homo boobiens* are on all fours, it seems to me, with that simpleton of fable who sought to lift himself over a stile by pulling at his boot straps. *Homo boobiens* is a fundamentalist for the precise reason that he is uneducated. That is to say, he is quite unable to grasp the complex evidences upon which the civilized minority bases its heresies, and so he seeks refuge in the sublime simplicities of revelation. Is Genesis incredible? Does it go counter to the known facts? Perhaps. But do not forget to add that it is divinely simple—that even a Tennessee judge can understand it.

Perhaps the process is a bit clearer on another plane: I choose that of medicine. As every one knows, scientific medicine has made more progress since the middle of the last century than it had made in the fifty centuries preceding. Today it is rapidly divesting itself of what remain of its old superstitions; it is becoming scientific in the exact sense, and year by year its practical efficacy, its capacity to cure disease, is greater. Yet in this very time of its greatest progress it is confronted by ever increasing hordes of quacks. The very day that news of insulin is in the newspapers *Homo boobiens* seeks treatment for his diabetes from a chiropractor.

Why? The reason seems to me to be simple. When an ignorant man goes to a doctor he wants not only treatment but also enlightenment and consolation. He wants to know what is the matter with him and how it is to be cured. Now try to imagine a medical man explaining to him the nature of diabetes and the action of insulin. If you can imagine it, then you have an imagination indeed. The whole thing is inordinately complex. The explanation must be itself explained. To get to the bottom of it, to understand it in any true sense, is a sheer impossibility to a man not specially trained, and that training may be given only to men of unusual intelligence. But any moron can understand the explanation of the chiropractor. It is idiotic but, like most things that are idiotic, it is also beautifully simple. So the moron grasps it—and cherishes it.

Something of the same sort goes on in the department of divinity. The clodhopper's objection to the hypothesis of evolution is not primarily that it is heathenish: that, indeed, is only an afterthought. His primary objection is that it is complicated and unintelligible—in the late Martyr Bryan's phrase, that it is "stuff and nonsense." In order to understand it a man must have a sound grounding in all the natural sciences; he must bring to the business an immense and intricate knowledge. And in order to get that grounding he must have a mind capable of taking it in.

Obviously, such minds are not common—that is, viewing the population as a whole. In the cities, where the sharpest fellows congregate, they may run to four or five per cent of the total, but in the back reaches of the land, where the population has been degenerating for generations, they are probably far below one per cent. The fact was brilliantly on display at the late trial of the infidel Scopes at Dayton, Tenn. What impressed me most, watching that trial through long sweaty days, was the honest bewilderment of the assembled yokels. They simply could not understand the thing that Scopes was accused of teaching. Its veriest elements were as far beyond their comprehension as the music of Bach or the theory of least squares.

Nor was it only the obvious peasants who showed that

pathetic puzzlement. The judge on the bench was plainly flabbergasted. His questions were those of a man completely ignorant and, what is more, of one completely unable to learn. When Darrow attempted to explain the A B C of the evolutionary hypothesis to him he sat there with his mouth open, blinking his eyes uneasily. The thing was beyond his powers, and so he quite naturally concluded that it was senseless and against God. An explanation of the nature and causes of diabetes would have dismayed and alarmed him in exactly the same manner.

The central difficulty lies in the fact that all of the sciences have made such great progress during the last century that they have got quite beyond the reach of the average man. There was a time when this was not so. Even down to the end of the eighteenth century any man of ordinary intelligence could understand every scientific concept in good repute, even in astronomy. In medicine the thing was quite simple. Read the memoirs and biographies of the period—for example, Boswell's *Johnson*—and you will find every sick man disputing with his doctor as an equal, and often driving the good man into an uncomfortable corner.

But with the dawn of the nineteenth century all that began to change. Chemistry slowly took on the character of an exact science; physics, stimulated by the discovery of electricity, made vast and rapid progress; geology began to stand on its own legs; biology was born. More important, the sciences began to interchange facts and ideas; it was no longer possible for a zoölogist, say, to be ignorant of chemistry, or for a pathologist to neglect physics. There followed an era of synthesis, culminating dramatically in Darwin's publication of *The Origin of Species*, and science was reborn. Simultaneously it threw off all its old diffidence, its ancient subservience to general opinion, and especially to theological opinion. The earliest scientists of the new order had to step very softly; the whole world was yet a sort of Tennessee. But the later revolutionists promulgated their heresies boldly, and met the ensuing uproar bravely. In England it was Huxley who led them; in every civilized country there was another like him. When the battle was over science was free at last, for the first time in the history of man. Since then no scientist coming upon new knowledge in his laboratory or in the field has had to pause before announcing it to sound out the bishop.

This freedom, as every one knows, has immensely increased what may be called the momentum of scientific research. Discoveries have followed one another at a rapid pace, and some of them have been of the first importance. There is scarcely a science that has not been completely revolutionized since 1860, and to the old ones many new ones have been added. Thus the body of scientific knowledge has grown immensely, and as it has grown it has taken an ever greater and greater complexity. No man of today could hope to sweep the whole field of the sciences, as many men did so lately as 1850. And no man can take in all that even one science has to say without long and difficult training, and a special aptitude for that sort of knowledge.

Meanwhile, man in general has lagged far behind. He remains, indeed, precisely where he was when all this tremendous advance began. His mind is simple; his talents are few. In the days when the sciences themselves were simple, he could be made, perhaps, to understand their elements— in other words, he was educable. But today the thing is quite beyond him. No conceivable training could convert an ice wagon driver into a pathologist or a hill billy into a

mathematical physicist. But the former may become a chiropractor and the latter may become a rustic judge. And there
we are.

The fundamental fallacy is the assumption that all this
is not true—that *Homo sapiens* is still capable of grasping
anything and everything that goes on in the world. It is an
imbecility, and hence dear to pedagogues. They are responsible, at bottom, for fundamentalism. Half-educated themselves, they have sought to crowd an impossible education
upon their victims. The young moron in the village high
school must be taught geology, paleontology, biology—all
completely incomprehensible to him, and both incomprehensible and sinister to his pa. No wonder his pa sounds the
fire alarm, rushes to the village tabernacle, and appeals for
succor to the Lord God Jehovah!
(*September 20, 1925*)

THE REV. CLERGY

THE EASIEST WAY to get a reputation as a liar is to tell the
truth. It is an ancient platitude, but still hale and hearty.
There was a new proof of it very lately, when Sinclair Lewis
published his *Elmer Gantry*. All the Gantrys of the land
rose up as one man to denounce the book as a libel upon the
cloth and its author as a scoundrel. Yet that book remains
fundamentally true. Lewis does not argue in it that *all* evangelical clergymen are like his grotesque hero; he merely ar-
gues that such men exist. Who, having any first-hand knowl-

edge of holy men, and being free to speak frankly, will deny it? Certainly not I.

In this department, I believe, I may pretend to a certain expertness, or, at all events, to rather more learning than is common. For the reverend clergy, as representatives of the most ancient profession known to man, have always interested me greatly, and I have devoted no little of my time, since laying off the follies of youth, to studying their ideas and searching their psyches. There is too much tendency, in the modern age, to dismiss them as anachronisms. This, I am convinced, is a grievous error, and I have not been guilty of it. They are still important men, and they will remain so for long ages. So I have striven diligently to load up with knowledge of them, and to try to understand them.

Well, it is my firm conviction, after all this labor, that Elmer Gantry is a true and palpable hit. He is not only possible; he is even typical. There is, in almost every American town, an evangelical pastor who approximates him quite as closely as any real American boy ever approximates Huckleberry Finn. He may not be exactly duplicated, of course, anywhere, but he is duplicated at least in part well nigh everywhere. For all Lewis' portrait of him says, reading it aright, is that the clergy of the hell fire sects, taking one with another, are not what is called gentlemen—that they come, in the main, out of the humbler orders of the people, and carry the peculiar weaknesses of their class into the sacred office. This is not merely true; it is obvious.

But there is no need to get into a lather of excitement and indignation over the fact. For all I know to the contrary, it may be better to have them so than to have them otherwise. I am inclined, in truth, to believe firmly that it is. It is precious easy, as the history of the world has often demonstrated, to so refine a clergy that it quite loses contact with the flock it is told off to serve. When that happens the church becomes a mere parasite, without rational purpose or usefulness. The doctrines it teaches may continue to be highly virtuous, and may even increase greatly in plausibility and beauty, but they can have no more effect upon the masses of men than the sonorous blather of university philosophers.

I am not arguing here that the ideas propagated by the Gantrys of this great republic are true. As a matter of fact, I question many of them, and have often put my questioning into harsh and even ribald terms. But I believe that they are ideas suitable to the intellectual habits and limitations of the people they are aimed at, and that, whether they are true or false, they at least urge those people to what is commonly regarded as better living. Is that urge always translated into overt acts? I don't know, and it is not important. The main point is that the urge itself is implanted. The devices used are often absurd, and sometimes almost insane, but it would certainly be going too far to say that they are wholly ineffective.

Their effectiveness, indeed, is probably quite as great as that of the devices of any other religious system. For no religion, it must be plain, ever succeeds in transforming its votaries completely, save perhaps in the case of isolated saints. In even the most subtle and rational there is an enormous gap between the teaching and the practice. It must be thus so long as mankind is what it is—and the fact is always as plain among the clergy as in the flock. Gantry is thus no libel; he is simply the projection of an undeniable fact. And in the character of his peculiar weaknesses, it seems to me, he beautifully exemplifies the special deficiencies of the theological scheme he stands for and of the class from which he springs.

The theological scheme labors under the difficulty of having to make itself comprehensible to men and women of elemental minds, lacking in even the most ordinary information and quite incapable of any sort of thought save the simplest. The fact robs it at once of the mystical elements which enter so largely into all other religious systems and reduces it to a series of bald syllogisms, most of them palpably unsound in premises. Its logic has the childish naïveté of that of a political orator, a newspaper editorial writer, or a chiropractor. In proportion as it stampedes the groundlings it dismays the learned.

But it must be kept on that level in order that it may be grasped at all, and so the business of propagating it can only be carried on by men with a special gift for nonsense. Either they are innocents themselves, and hence anaesthetic to dubious evidence and confused reasoning, or they are romantic cynics like Gantry, full of a conviction that a good end justifies any means. I don't think that many of them are hypocrites. Gantry himself is surely not one. He is simply a man who estimates syllogisms, not by their premises but by their conclusions, and logicians by their success, not by their professional correctness and private virtue.

Educated beyond a certain point, such men tend to revolt against the oversimplified dogmas of their primary faith. But not many of them are so educated. There is within their communion a deep-seated and powerful feeling, almost an instinct, that the business is dangerous. So part of their function as ecclesiastics is to combat certain sorts of knowledge with every resource at their command, and in the more remote and isolated parts of the country they commonly succeed. In some places, indeed, they have resorted to the ancient ecclesiastical device of calling in the secular arm to aid them, and there the astounding spectacle is presented of teachers being punished for teaching what every civilized human being is supposed to know.

But this endeavor, in a country wherein communications remain comparatively free, grows increasingly difficult. What the young cannot acquire officially they pick up by bootlegging, and their eagerness for it augments in proportion to the difficulty of getting at it. Its effect upon them, from the standpoint of the dominant theology, is plainly disastrous. They may not abandon that theology formally; even *in petto* they may retain a sentimental affection for it. But its hold upon them is loosened; they no longer feel any urge to propagate it. Thus recruiting for the sacred office becomes difficult, and even impossible, in this relatively enlightened class, and candidates for the cloth must be sought on those lower levels where the density of Gantrys is higher.

The fact explains both the curious ignorance of the great majority of evangelical clergymen—an ignorance often shocking to the observer who makes any contact with them —and their weakness for the devices of quackery. It is not the graduate of the Yale law school who becomes a shyster; it is the poor fellow whose equipment is barely sufficient to make him a lawyer at all. And it is not the young doctor from the Harvard medical school who becomes a quack, but the alumnus of the college that is only one jump ahead of the police. So among holy men. The easier the way to the pulpit and the heavier the burdens upon genuine knowledge, the larger the production of Gantrys.

I am no constructive critic, and hence do not propose a remedy. No doubt nature will achieve an effective one, given time enough. For the tides of human progress are obviously running against the whole Gantry hocus-pocus. It is no more possible to dam them up by law than it would be to dam up the tides of the sea. Soon or late they must overwhelm even the Bible belt. When that time comes the Gantry type of pastor will find his flock laughing at him, not only when he is clowning, but also and more especially when he is in deadly earnest. Thus he will either have to take on the enlightenment and intellectual integrity of the higher varieties of holy clerk, now the chief objects of his scorn, or abandon the ghostly trade altogether.

(*April 24, 1927*)

COUSIN JOCKO

The late William Jennings Bryan, LL.D., always had one great advantage in controversy: he was never burdened with an understanding of his opponent's case. His talents, indeed, were always far more homiletical than dialectical; he was at his best, not in argument, but in denunciation. The fact made itself felt brilliantly during his last great combat with the evolutionists. Whenever he stated their doctrines he stated them inaccurately, and whenever he undertook to refute them he resorted to nonsense. His mind was of the sort that is simply unable to grasp scientific facts. They fevered him as flies fever a bull, and he got rid of them by lashing his tail.

Unfortunately, some of his scientific antagonists played into his hands by trying idiotically to perfume their own case. Of such sort were all the more fatuous reconcilers of science and religion, led by Professor Henry Fairfield Osborn, Sc.D., D.Sc., LL.D., Ph.D. And of the same sort were the professors who hastened to assure the booboisie that Darwinism, after all, did not mean that man had descended from the monkey. These earnest gentlemen, I believe, went a great deal too far. They admitted too much, and so played into Bryan's hands. And by the same token they gave an air of dubiousness and uncertainty to the doctrines they ostensibly defended.

There is, in point of fact, no possibility of reconciling science and religion—that is, religion of the sort preached to the peasantry by Bryan. If the one is sound, then the other is bilge. He himself, for all his ignorance, was well aware of the fact. When the biblical narrative collided with a known fact he instantly rejected the known fact. I myself, with my own ears, heard him argue violently against the notion that man is a mammal. To maintain that such "religious" ideas can be reconciled with science is to maintain that the Volstead act can be reconciled with the bill of rights. The two things are not only different; they are squarely and eternally antagonistic.

The yokels that Bryan preyed upon, when they thought of the evolutionary hypothesis at all, thought of it as the doctrine that their own grandfathers were gorillas. They could not grasp the concept of great spaces of time; moreover, most of them had seen their grandfathers—and so the plausibility of the notion made them shiver. Bryan took advantage of the fact. Discreetly disregarding their grandfathers, he based his case upon their grandmothers, thus appealing powerfully to their chivalry. They responded by whooping for Genesis, in which Eve, though she is depicted as a somewhat loose woman, is at least 100 per cent human.

The professors of scientific apologetics responded by attempting an elaborate and none too convincing explanation. It was no longer contended, they said, that man was descended directly from the monkey; all that was argued was that man and monkey, in some remote past, had a common ancestor. The remoteness of that past was sufficient to make the connection aseptic. It ran to hundreds of thousands, millions, perhaps, even billions, of years. Long before the civil war, even before the revolution, the separation was complete. It was rammed home, so to speak, by man's acquirement of a soul—no doubt in early biblical days.

This explanation, I believe, failed to fool the fundamentalists, and I see no reason why it should fool any one else. Its defect was that it simply begged the question. What difference did it make whether man was descended from a monkey, or from some remote ancestor of all the monkeys —a more primitive and hence obviously more unappetizing quadruped than any monkey ever heard of? All the scientists accomplished by their nonsense was to make the fundamentalists even more skittish than they had been before. Some of the harder hearted of them had begun to be reconciled to the notion that their grandfathers had tails and lived in cages. But when they began to hear talk of remoter ancestors it made them think of skunks, rats, pigs, and such abhorrent creatures, and so they shivered again, and resumed their whooping for Bryan.

The truth is that the biological relationship between man and monkey, whatever the precise lines of descent, is quite as close as even the most frantic fundamentalist ever accused scientists of believing, and that increasing knowledge tends to make it appear closer and closer. I turn, for example, to the latest authoritative work upon the subject, *The Morphology and Evolution of the Apes and Man*, by Dr. Charles F. Sonntag of University College, London, and point to page 255. There Dr. Sonntag announces the pleasing news that the blood of man and that of the higher apes is chemically almost identical.

This is an accurate and an extremely subtle test. In its more refined forms it is sufficiently delicate to differentiate between one man and another. As between man and, say, the horse or the dog it is infallible. A horse's blood or a dog's blood can never be mistaken for the blood of a man. But when one comes to the higher apes the test begins to grow unreliable. The blood of a common organ grinder's monkey (*Cebus capichinus*) is easily differentiated from man's, but that of the baboons begins to show similarities, and that of the gibbons, chimpanzees, orangutans, and gorillas is so nearly identical that one begins to sympathize with the shivering of the fundamentalists.

Such proofs of extremely close relationship—and there are others—make all questions of descent seem academic. Whether man is a glorified grandson of the ape, or the ape is a degenerate man, or the two are descendants of a common ancestor—this problem, perhaps, will never be solved. Nor is it important. The important thing is that ape and man are biological cousins and as closely related as duck and canary bird. The anatomical and physiological differences between them are mainly trivial; the likenesses are innumerable and profound. Shave a gorilla and it would be almost impossible, at twenty paces, to distinguish him from a heavyweight champion of the world. Skin a chimpanzee, and it would take an autopsy to prove he was not a theologian.

Dr. Sonntag's investigations into the physical makeup of the primates have been admirably supplemented of late by elaborate studies of their mental powers. This work has been done chiefly by Dr. Wolfgang Köhler of the University of Berlin, who spent four years at Teneriffe, in Canary Islands, studying a collection of chimpanzees gathered there. But important additions to the knowledge thus gained have been made by Dr. Robert M. Yerkes of Yale, who worked at Quinta Palatino, Cuba, where Mme. Rosalia Abreu has an immense collection of all sorts of monkeys—the largest, indeed, in the world. Dr. Köhler's conclusions are printed in a book called *The Mentality of Apes*, and Dr. Yerkes' in three volumes: *The Mental Life of Monkeys and Apes, Chimpanzee Intelligence and Its Vocal Expression*, and *Almost Human*.

What these investigations demonstrate, in brief, is that all the higher apes actually think, and that their thinking process differs very little, if at all, from that of the lower orders of man. A gorilla, true enough, cannot write poetry and neither can it grasp such a concept as that of Americanization or that of relativity, but is fully equal to all of the thinking that a subway guard, a bass drummer, or a chiropractor has to do, and if it could only speak English it could be made into a competent train conductor or congressman in thirty days.

In some ways, indeed, it is measurably more clever than many men. It cannot be fooled as easily; it does not waste so much time doing useless things. If it desires, for example, to get a banana, hung out of reach, it proceeds to the business with a singleness of purpose and a fertility of resource that, in a traffic policeman, would seem almost pathological. There are no fundamentalists among the primates. They believe nothing that is not demonstrable. When they confront a fact they recognize it instantly, and turn it to their uses with admirable readiness. There are liars among them, but no idealists.

(*November 8, 1925*)

JACQUERIE

THE FUNDAMENTALISTS say that God is on their side. It is a somewhat blatant and cocksure way of stating an indubitable fact. I believe that, in the long run, they will win—that is, in all those areas where they carry on serious war. What is more, I believe that they deserve to win. For what they revolt against, essentially, is not a Great Truth, as some of their enemies allege, but one of the worst of human delusions. That is the delusion that mankind, in the mass, is intelligent and capable of learning—that all men may be educated, if only energy enough be applied to the business. Who actually believes it? Only hopeless romantics. The evidence supporting it, so far as I can make out, is exactly on all fours with the evidence that Jonah swallowed the whale.

Why are the bucolic fundamentalists so hot against the hypothesis of organic evolution? Is it because the thing is in contempt of Holy Writ? Then why are they not equally hot against the doctrine that the earth is a sphere and circles around the sun? Isn't that in contempt of Holy Writ also?

I can discern no difference between hypothesis and doctrine, save that the former is less positive and uncompromising and hence less heretical than the latter. Yet the fundamentalists everywhere, save perhaps in Matteawan, N.Y., and Dayton, Tenn., admit freely that the earth goes round the sun. Why?

The easy answer is that the Copernican astronomy offers no affront to man—that it does not invade human dignity as the Darwinian zoölogy invades it. But that answer, I believe, does not really answer, for it is not the dignity of *Homo sapiens* that fundamentalists appear to be concerned about, but the dignity of the Bible. They care nothing, in fact, for the dignity of man. In the case of their opponents, they categorically deny that it exists. Mr. Darrow, to them, is not merely a chimpanzee; he is a pig (*Sus scrofa*), a jackal (*Canis aureus*), and a rat (*Mus rattus*). I have heard their pastors call him all of these things. And I have heard them call the late Mr. Darwin a viper (*Viper berus*).

Nay, it is not any tenderness for man that makes them gag at what they call Darwinism; it is simply the fact that Darwinism is beyond their comprehension. It is based upon a series of observations that lie outside their experience; it involves deductions that violate their customary habits of thought. The man who would understand it must not only have an education differing enormously from theirs; he must also have a natural equipment differing enormously from theirs. Unable to grasp the veriest elements of the evolutionary hypothesis, they dismiss it as occult, insane, and against God. In precisely the same way they dismiss the music of Beethoven as occult, insane, and against God.

Here I do not speculate idly. For months past I have been devoting my leisure to a study of the principal denominational papers of the fundamentalist sect. I have read, I suppose, at least a hundred formal refutations of Darwinism. I have read, too, a great many books and pamphlets against it, some by eminent divines. What I get out of my depressing studies is simply the firm conviction that not a single fundamentalist in the United States has the slightest notion as to what Darwinism is. Every one of them proves in every line he prints that he is ignorant of the elements of biology. And every one proves, by his own hot and grotesque words, that he is incapable of learning.

In these earnest and consecrated men, indeed, one encounters a special type of mind, and it differs radically—and, I believe, incurably—from the type that is fitted for taking in scientific facts. It cannot follow a chain of evidence dispassionately; it is forever running off into emotional irrelevances. What it sees, looking at an objective fact, is not at all what intelligent men see, but a mass of ectoplasms and poltergeists, many of them theological and all of them imaginary. They divert it instantly from the object, and it lacks the capacity to work its way back. Reading these fundamentalist accounts of what men of science believe is exactly like reading a standpat Republican account of what a Socialist believes.

But much worse; much more astonishing. The standpat Republican, however much he may distort and garble the Socialist's delusions, is at least capable of comprehending them; they do not take him outside the boundaries of the world he knows. But the fundamentalist, tackling the natural sciences, crosses that frontier almost instantly, and is quickly lost in a maze that baffles and enrages him. Everything he sees is strange and incomprehensible. Fleeing back, he reports that it is of the devil.

This intellectual helplessness is marked in the rustic pastors who do most of the ranting against the crimes of science, but it is also obvious in the most high toned of the fundamentalists. They show plainly that the baldest A B C of biology is Choctaw to them. They read the words without coming into even the remotest contact with the underlying ideas. Nature simply did not plan their minds for such uses. So the more assiduously they apply themselves to their studies, the more frantic they become. All the fundamental concepts of science elude them, and eluding them, enrage them.

For example, the concept of time in the geological sense—of thousands, hundreds of thousands and millions of years. The yokels at Dayton, Tenn., trying to grasp it, publicly proclaimed their failure. They could go back, in thought, a few generations, or even a dozen generations, but beyond that they couldn't go at all. So they kept on thinking of their actual grandmothers as gorillas in the adjacent trees, and thus thinking, they dismissed the whole evolutionary hypothesis as an absurdity. It was not so much that they objected to it on filial grounds as that they objected to it on logical grounds. Within the range of their intelligence it simply could not be imagined. They laughed, therefore, at the scientists and gave three cheers for the late William Jennings Bryan.

What is constantly overlooked is that fundamentalism is not a phenomenon of theology alone—that its manifestations are visible in almost every department of human life and thought, especially in democratic states. The progress of knowledge has simply gone beyond the capacity of the inferior half of mankind to take it in. The laborious schoolmarm, attempting to ram it into the unyielding heads of morons, only too often ends by demonstrating that she can't grasp it herself.

Thus one observes, in all fields, a series of attempts at evasion—or, perhaps, more accurately, of simplification. The moron, unable to comprehend what is set before him, seeks surcease from the struggle in something that is easier. Biology is inordinately complicated and confusing. Genesis is beautifully simple and plain; ergo, Genesis is true and biology comes from hell. Again, modern pathology is complex and full of snares—and chiropractic is so clear and neat that even an ice wagon driver can take it in; ergo, it is superior to the science of Virchow, and the ice wagon driver is superior as a scientist.

On the political plane this simplification is always going on; it is perhaps the salient phenomenon of democracy. The problems that confront a modern state are so difficult that they daunt even men specially trained to deal with them. To the general they are as unintelligible as the non-Euclidian geometry. The common man is not only unable to solve them; he is unable even to imagine them. When their solution is laid upon him, he makes an easy and characteristic escape from his tortures. That is to say, he translates them into terms of simple emotion. What was a matter of weighing elusive and shifting evidence thus becomes a simple and exhilarating matter of chasing a bugaboo. That chase is led by a hero who is also an ignoramus. The crusade of the fundamentalists is led by heroes of precisely the same kidney. What they are against is simply what is beyond their intelligence. They are against it, not because they see any actual error in it, but because thinking about it at all fevers and dismays their minds.

(*January 3, 1926*)

MAN AS A MAMMAL

Is it only a coincidence that the rise of fundamentalist fury in the Bible belt has been simultaneous with great advances in the study of the genealogy and biology of man—that is, of man as a mammal? I begin to suspect that there may be some relation of cause and effect here. A generation ago, or even a decade ago, there lingered certain reasonable doubts about the participation of *Homo sapiens* in the general evolutionary process. In more than one way he seemed to stand apart from it. But now those doubts are all gone. No competent biologist cherishes them any longer. Man is now proved overwhelmingly and unanswerably to be a mammal like any other mammal, and his relations to his lowly kinsmen, the *Simiidae*, have been made so plain that they must be accepted as scientific facts, of precisely the same order of authority as the fact that the earth revolves around the sun.

Their theological opponents, facing them, are thus unable to dispose of them by logical and evidential means, and have to resort to legal means. They try, by statute, to conceal them from the young, for they are well aware that the young, hearing them, would accept them. The device is dishonest, and in the long run, I believe, it will fail. What the schoolma'm is forbidden to teach in Tennessee and Mississippi will be bootlegged in by her pupils themselves. They will discuss biology because it is under an official ban, just as they discuss sex because it is under a ban. And, discussing it, they will infallibly learn something about it.

I allude, of course, to the more intelligent minority of them. The rest, in the future as in the past, will simply serve as clinical material to prove the truth of the evolutionary theory. There are, no doubt, still plenty of fundamentalists in Mississippi who believe that the earth is flat and that a horse hair put into a bottle of water will turn into a snake. Not a few of them, I take it, are clergymen. But such morons, it must be manifest, do not count in the cosmic process. What they believe no more binds the human race than what tadpoles believe.

As I have said, there has been of late a great increase in our knowledge of the early history of man and of his biological relationship to other animals. The Paleolithic caves in southern France and other parts of Europe have been explored by competent and industrious men, and a vast mass of new facts about our remote forefathers has been brought to light. These facts were admirably set forth four years ago by Dr. Henry Fairfield Osborn, in a book called *Men of the Old Stone Age*. It was so charmingly written that it made a popular success, but it was confined, unfortunately, to a relatively narrow area, and I believe that a better survey of the whole field is to be found in *Human Origins*, by George Grant MacCurdy, and *Fossil Man*, by Marcellin Boule, published in Edinburgh.

The former is a work of the highest scholarship, and covers the field thoroughly. It has a large number of excellent illustrations, some of them in color, and there are elaborate lists of the prehistoric monuments. But the Boule book, which is translated from the French, is probably better for the general reader. It tells the story of prehistoric man in a delightfully easy and entertaining fashion, and yet without any sacrifice of scientific precision. Professor Boule, who is director of the Institut de Paléontologie Humaine at Paris, is familiar at first hand with all the relics of early man that have been found in France and Spain. More, he is not a narrow specialist, but a man of wide and varied interests, and the fact shows itself in his writing.

All these are relatively large works. The reader who wants something less elaborate will find it in *The Evolution of Man*, a book written by six eminent scholars under the editorship of Dr. George Alfred Baitsell. It covers the whole field in remarkably small space, and at the end of it there is a useful bibliography of other works on the same subject.

To the fundamentalist, of course, evolution means simply the doctrine that man has descended directly from the ape, and is still the ape's close cousin. Just how much truth is in this notion will be found set forth at length, and very interestingly, in *The Pedigree of the Human Race*, by Professor Harris Hawthorne Wilder of Smith College. Dr. Wilder, who is a zoölogist, goes back to the first appearance of mammals in the world, and shows, step by step, how they have developed. Coming to the *Anthropoidea*, to which suborder man belongs, he discusses the likenesses and differences between its various members at great length, and with the full knowledge of a specialist.

He is inclined to think that man stands far closer to the great tailless apes of the Eastern Hemisphere than even the most heretical Modernists have assumed, and that, in fact, it is a zoölogical absurdity to separate him from the *Simiidae*. The differences between the two, he says, are so small and unimportant that if they were noted among related animals of any other sub-order no competent zoölogist would dream of dividing them into two families. But that is by no means saying, of course, that even the most primitive fundamentalist had an actual gorilla for a grandfather. Man and the apes, descending from a common ancestor, separated far back in Miocene times hundreds of thousands of years ago. The earliest known man was already unmistakably a man.

Dr. Wilder devotes several very instructive chapters to the existing races of *Homo sapiens*. The most thoroughly typical man, he says, is not the white man, but the native Australian. He straddles the peak of normalcy. The white man, in fact, departs considerably from the norm, but not so much so as the black, who, if variability were the only criterion, might be called the most advanced of men. Dr. Wilder believes that the blacks are descended from whites, or, at all events, that they had common ancestors in relatively recent times. Another shock for the Mississippi fundamentalists!

Of books upon man as a living organism, realistically considered, there have been many of late. One of the best is a small volume called *The Human Body*, by Dr. Arthur Keith, in the excellent Home University Library. It is inexpensive, and yet comprehensive. Another, on a somewhat larger scale, is *Man, the Animal*, by Dr. W. M. Smallwood of Harvard, and yet another, devoted especially to the mind of man, is *What Is Man?* by Dr. J. Arthur Thomson. To these should be added, perhaps, Dr. George W. Crile's new book, A *Bipolar Theory of Living Processes*, though the reader without a considerable acquaintance with biology, chemistry, and physics will find it difficult.

But perhaps the most interesting of all the new books are those devoted to the study of the apes. Until a few years ago nothing worthy of scientific consideration was known about their behavior, but now they have been investigated very elaborately, and there has piled up a vast mass of evidence that their mental processes, though naturally primitive, are indistinguishable from those of man. The most readable of such books is *Almost Human*, by Robert M. Yerkes of Yale; the most thorough is *The Mentality of Apes*, by Dr. Wolfgang Köhler of Berlin. To them, for readers desiring to go further into the subject, should be added *The Morphology and Evolution of the Apes and Man*, by Dr. Charles F. Sonntag of London, and *Chimpanzee Intelligence and Its Vocal Expression*, by Dr. Yerkes and Dr. Blanche W. Learned.

All the books that I have mentioned are readily accessible, and most of them should be comprehensible to any reader of average education and intelligence. They are in all public libraries, or ought to be. Taken together, they offer such a terrific refutation of the fundamentalist blather that it is difficult to imagine any sane man entertaining it further. They prove absolutely that man is an animal like any other animal; that he descends like the rest of them from the primeval mammals of the Mesozoic; that he and the apes had common ancestors in the Eocene, and that in body and mind he is closely and unmistakably related to the apes today. Are these facts unpleasant? Unpleasant or not, they are nevertheless facts.

(August 29, 1926)

HAVELOCK ELLIS

IT IS a curious fact, and not without its dark humors, that Havelock Ellis had passed his 67th birthday before the first book about him was published. For the chances seem to be very good that he will be remembered as long as any other Englishman of his generation, and perhaps far longer than any save a corporal's guard. Such a man, one would think, would be a great deal discussed and written of. But it has not been so. I have read him constantly since the 90s, when his first book, *The New Spirit*, was new, and I have had certain polite contacts with him for ten years, but until Dr. Isaac Goldberg's excellent "biographical and critical survey" of him came into my hands, a month or two back, I knew little more about him, as a man, than I knew about the Grand Lama of Tibet.

Goldberg's book, in a way, explains why this should have been so. It shows Ellis as a man almost fabulously careless of the usual fruits of fame. He seems to have absolutely no desire to make a stir in the world. No man that I know of has done more, in his time, for the liberation of the human mind, and yet no man has done less to press his own ideas. When, in 1897, the first volume of his great work, *Studies in the Psychology of Sex*, was suppressed by the English comstocks, he accepted the fiat without resistance, and kept on with his labor quite unruffled. The six volumes, by a delightful irony, are now published in the United States, but in England they are still under the ban, and Ellis, so far as I know, has never made any effort to have it lifted.

His admirers at home, I suspect, were eager to challenge the comstocks and make a martyr of him. If so, he gave them no aid and comfort himself. The job that he had planned was still ahead of him, and he kept at it serenely. To this day the generality of Englishmen seem to know little about him. His celebrity is greatest on the continent, and he has had his largest influence, perhaps, in the United States.

Ellis' inquiries into the psychology of sex constitute but a small part of his life work, and in his own view, perhaps, they are less important than other things he has done, but it is probable that he will be remembered for them long after some of his other enterprises are forgotten. They had the astounding effect of breaking down one of the oldest and most rigid taboos known to man. When he published his first volume the subject of sex was never mentioned save with ribaldry: the almost universal view of it was the Abraham Lincoln view. When his sixth was done the thing had become respectable, and the book shops of the world swarmed with treatises upon it. More, its study had become scientific.

That change is sometimes ascribed to Freud, but I don't think that Freud had half so much to do with it as Ellis. The defect of Freud was that he concerned himself almost exclusively with the pathology of sex—that is, with such manifestations of it as were unusual and, to the average person, alarming and revolting. Ellis concentrated his attention upon what was normal. For the first time the every day manifestations of sex were examined calmly and scientifically, without bias or prejudice. For the first time the basic facts were disentangled from the ages old mesh of superstitions and false observation, and sexual phenomena were discussed like any other natural phenomena.

The effects of this inquiry were tremendous. Not only was a vast mass of new and valuable knowledge unearthed, but the fact was made plain that knowledge could be imparted decently, without pious snuffling and dishonest evasion. At one stroke the subject came out into the open, after unnumbered centuries in the shadows. Today, despite some lingering snarling by prudes, it is discussed frankly and honestly, and even the highest ecclesiastical dignitaries are found arguing that its elements should be imparted to the young. It seems to me that this is genuine progress. I don't contend that the discussion has solved any of the fundamental problems; on the contrary, I am convinced that most of them will forever remain insoluble. But when an ancient taboo is broken down something is gained that is more valuable than the solving of problems—and that something we owe to Ellis.

It is unfortunate that, in the United States at least, his services in this field have obscured his service in others. His writings on sex, in fact, constitute but a small part of the body of his work. What interests him more is not the specific problem, but the general attitude of mind. The thing he has flung himself against is the general human disinclination to take in new ideas; the utopia he has preached is a utopia of free spirits. His enemy is the unyielding prejudice, the immovable axiom. He sees life, not as a series of cowardly yieldings to rules, but as a gay and somewhat gaudy adventure, an endless experiment.

His first book, *The New Spirit*, was in form simply an eloquent protest against the boiled mutton complacency and stupidity of Victorian England. It was published at the very beginning of the revolutionary 90s, and all the younger men of that electric decade quarried it to good effect. In it was the first adequate essay in English upon the Zeus of the new movement, old Henrik Ibsen, and in it, too, were capital chapters on such earlier free spirits as Diderot, Heine, and Whitman. The thing he spoke for was "a quickening of the pulse of life"—in brief, Emerson all over again, with a new assurance borrowed from the physical sciences. Emerson sat in a grove, mooning over the emancipation of the human mind. Ellis saw and proved that this emancipation could be made real.

The New Spirit is now forgotten, but in its day, I believe, it had an immense influence. The young Englishmen of the 90s got more out of it than convenient facts; they got the new orientation that they needed. It threw out its ripples, too, upon the continent. The gladiators of the New Germany movement read it, and it was translated into French by Henry Bérenger, now French ambassador to the United States. Nor was it unheeded in the United States. I remember well the splash that it made, and the eager borrowing of its ideas.

In those days, I suspect, Ellis was himself somewhat uncertain about his path in life. Trained as a medical man, but an artist at bottom, he seems to have stood somewhat irresolute before the arts, especially literature, and the sciences. In these days of narrow specialization it may seem incredible, but it is a fact that at one time he was editing both the Mermaid Series of old English dramatists and the Contemporary Science Series—both of them works of the first importance. The former remains unchallenged to this day; to the latter Ellis contributed two books of his own, *The Criminal* and *Man and Woman*.

During the 90s and until near the end of the first decade of the new century, the sciences seemed to have first call upon him. It was in those years that he published his *Studies in the Psychology of Sex*, his *Study of British Genius*, and his *World of Dreams*. But after 1910 and especially after the beginning of the war he turned to the fine arts, and to the period since 1914 belongs his fine series of books upon the art of living: the three volumes of *Impressions and Comments*, and *Little Essays of Love and Virtue*, and *The Dance of Life*.

These volumes revealed a new Ellis. It was not so much that his ideas changed as that his manner changed. His earlier scientific books had displayed him as an adept at clear exposition, but their style was naturally somewhat barren and formal. But in the first volume of the *Impressions and Comments* he blossomed forth, almost surprisingly, as a master of colorful and eloquent English, a stylist in the best sense. What he had to say was still apposite and important, but even more important was the charming way in which he said it. The three volumes were widely read, and I daresay Ellis made friends in quarters where he had been long under suspicion.

So he stands at 67, still in full vigor and with plenty of work still ahead of him. He has fought a long and a good fight, and it has been for things worth while. I believe he'll not be soon forgotten.

(July 11, 1926)

ON EUGENICS

THE MORE I plow through the literature confected by the eugenists and their allies, the birth controllers, the more I am convinced that their great cause is mainly blather. Somehow, what they write so indignantly always reminds me of the music of certain of the so-called moderns, who wander around in a maze of tonalities without landing anywhere. In none of their books have I ever found a clear definition of the superiority they talk about so copiously. At one time they seem to identify it with high intelligence. At another time with character, i.e., moral stability, and yet another time with mere fame, i.e., luck. Was Napoleon I a superior man, as I am privately inclined to believe, along with many of the eugenists? Then so was Aaron Burr, if in less measure. Was Paul of Tarsus? Then so was Brigham Young. Were the Gracchi? Then so were Karl Marx and William Jennings Bryan.

This matter of superiority, indeed, presents cruel and ineradicable difficulties. If it is made to run with service to the human race the eugenist is soon mired, for many men held to be highly useful are obviously second rate, and leave third rate progeny behind them; for example, Gen. Grant. And if it is made to run with mere intellectual brilliance and originality the troubles that loom up are just as serious, for men of that rare quality are generally felt to be danger-ous, and sometimes they undoubtedly are. The case of Fried-rich Wilhelm Nietzsche is in point. I suppose that no ra-tional person today, not even an uncured Liberty Loan orator or dollar a year man, would argue seriously that Nietz-sche was inferior. On the contrary, his extraordinary gifts are unanimously admitted. But what of his value to the hu-man race? And what of his eugenic fitness?

It is not easy to answer these questions. Nietzsche, in fact, preached a gospel that, to most human beings, is un-bearable, and it will probably remain unbearable for cen-turies to come. Its adoption by Dr. Coolidge, by and with the advice and consent of the senate, would plunge this re-public into dreadful woe. And Nietzsche himself was a chronic invalid who died insane—the sort of wreck who, had he lived into our time, would have been a customer of chiropractors. Worse, he suffered from a malady of a scandalous nature, and of evil effects upon the sufferer's offspring. Was it good or bad luck for the world, eugenically speaking, that he was a bachelor?

But their vagueness about the exact nature of superiority is not the only thing that corrupts the fine fury of the eugenists. Even more dismaying is their gratuitous assumption that all of the socially useful and laudable qualities (whatever they may be) are the exclusive possession of one class of men, and that the other classes lack them altogether. This is plainly not true. All that may be truthfully said of such qualities is that they appear rather more frequently in one class than in another. But they are rare in all classes, and the difference in the frequency of their occurrence between this class and that one is not very great, and of little genuine importance.

If all the biologists in the United States were hanged tomorrow (as has been proposed by the Mississippi clergy) and their children with them, we'd probably still have a sufficiency of biologists in the next generation. There might not be as many as we have today, but there would be enough. They would come out of the families of bricklayers and politicians, bootleggers and bond salesmen. Some of them, indeed, might even come out of the families of Mississippi ecclesiastics. For the supply of such men, like the supply of synthetic gin, always tends to run with the demand. Whenever the supply is short the demand almost automatically augments it.

Every one knows that this is true on the lower levels. Before baseball was invented there were no Ty Cobbs and Babe Ruths; now they appear in an apparently endless series. Before the Wright brothers made their first flight there were no men skilled at aviation; now there are multitudes of highly competent experts. The eugenists forget that the same thing happens on the higher levels. Whenever the world has stood in absolute need of a genius he has appeared. And though it is true that he has usually come out of the better half of humanity, it is also true that he has sometimes come out of the worst half. Beethoven was the grandson of a cook and the son of a drunkard, and Lincoln's forebears for many generations were nobodies.

The fact is that the difference between the better sort of human beings and the lesser sort, biologically speaking, is very slight. There may be, at the very top, a small class of people whose blood is preponderantly superior and distinguished, and there may be, at the bottom, another class whose blood is almost wholly debased, but both are very small. The folks between are all pretty much alike. The baron has a great deal of peasant blood in him and the peasant has some blood that is blue. The natural sinfulness of man is enough to make sure of that. No man in this world can ever be quite certain that he is the actual great-great-grandson of the great-great-grandfather whose memory he venerates.

Thus when the relatively superior and distinguished class ceases to be fecund (a phenomenon now visible everywhere in the world) natural selection comes to the rescue by selecting out and promoting individuals from the classes below. These individuals are probably just as sound in blood as any one in the class they enter. Their sound blood has been concealed, perhaps for generations, but it has been there all the time. If Abraham Lincoln's ancestry were known with any certainty it would probably be found to run back to manifestly able and distinguished men. There are many more such hidden family trees in the folk.

The eugenists simply overlook them. They are also singularly blind to many familiar biological phenomena—for example, the appearance of mutations or sports. It is not likely that a commonplace family will produce a genius, but nevertheless it is by no means impossible: the thing has probably happened more than once. They forget, too, the influence of environment in human society. Mere environment, to be sure, cannot produce a genius, but it can certainly help him enormously after he is born. If a potential Wagner were born to a Greek bootblack in Toledo, O., tomorrow, the chances of his coming to fruition and fame would be at least even. But if he were born an Arab in the Libyan desert or to a fundamentalist in Rhea county, Tenn., the chances are that he would be a total loss.

The eugenists constantly make the false assumption that a healthy degree of human progress demands a large supply of first rate men. Here they succumb to the modern craze for mass production. Because a hundred policemen, or garbage men, or bootleggers are manifestly better than one, they conclude absurdly that a hundred Beethovens would be better than one. But this is not true. The actual value of a genius often lies in his singularity. If there had been a hundred Beethovens the music of all of them would be very little known today, and so its civilizing effect would be appreciably less than it is.

The number of first rate men necessary to make a high civilization is really very small. If the United States could produce one Shakespeare or Newton or Bach or Michelangelo or Vesalius a century it would be doing better than any nation has ever done in history. Such culture as we have is due to a group of men so small that all of them alive at one time could be hauled in a single Pullman train. Once I went through *Who's Who in America*, hunting for the really first rate men among its 27,000 names—that is, for the men who had really done something unique and difficult, and of value to the human race. I found 200. The rest of the 27,000 were simply respectable blanks.

An overproduction of geniuses, indeed, would be very dangerous, for though they make for progress they also tend to disturb the peace. Imagine a country housing 100 head of Aristotles! It would be as unhappy as a city housing 100 head of Jesse Jameses. Even quasi-geniuses are a great burden upon society. There are in the United States today 1,500 professional philosophers—that is, men who make their livings at the trade. The country would be far better off if all save two or three of them were driving taxicabs or serving with the Rum Fleet.

(*May 15, 1927*)

HUMAN MONOGAMY

SOME TIME AGO, while I was lolling in the great Christian city of Los Angeles, studying its contributions to the progress of the human race, a gentleman representing one of the press associations called me up and told me that a lady named Mrs. Anna Garlin Spencer was raging through the south denouncing me as a foe to monogamy. The news, I confess, shocked me excessively. For years and years I had been defending monogamy with the utmost heat and eloquence; even in the far-off days when I was a Young Intellectual I was in favor of it. Yet here was a gifted woman, of mature years and noted for her sagacity, who so far misunderstood me that she accused me of a foul assault upon her own case.

As I say, I was shocked, but it would be going too far to say that I was surprised. The older I live the more I am convinced that the capacity of the human mind to take in ideas easily and accurately—and even of the highly polished mind—is strictly limited and conditioned, no doubt, by the will of God. Yell "Water!" and the majority of his images will translate it instantly as "Fire!" Say "black" and you will be put down as saying "white." Since my earliest infancy I have been a Tory in politics, and ever since I acquired the art and science of prose composition I have supported and celebrated the Tory cause; nevertheless, the Red chasers who now haunt the land classify me as a radical, and some time ago I was damned as such on the floor of congress.

The other day, more strangely still, I found my name on a list of pacifists. Worse, it had been put there by persons who were pacifists themselves. By what process are such errors arrived at? It is hard to make out. For years I have argued in favor of war as the most charming of sports, both to the player and the spectator, and not six months ago I printed a long and rhetorical article demanding that another grand combat to save democracy be started at once, and that it be made bloodier than the last one. Many pacifists read this article. I know, for I received protests from them. But within half a year they were putting me down as one of them!

As for monogamy, I believe that it is one of the few institutions of civilization that stand in accord with the fundamental instincts of *Homo sapiens*. I do not argue that all men, under civilization, are monogamists; I simply argue that they *would* be if they could cast off the influences which now pull them in the other direction. What makes them wander, nine times out of ten, is no more than the public expectation that they *will* wander. That public expectation, I regret to have to add, is often supported and encouraged by their wives. The female sex, as every one knows, has a great talent for martyrdom; a woman loves to suffer, as a man loves to boast. The easiest way to attain to this martyrdom, in the experience of the average woman, is for her to suspect and accuse her husband John of bootleg doings with the red haired widow around the corner.

Is John actually innocent? I believe he is, at least when the uproar begins. His transactions with the widow, in the normal case, have been confined to a few shy leers, mainly esthetic in character. But once he is accused, it quickly becomes a psychological impossibility for him to deny his guilt. His wife, by her revilings, is crediting him with an enterprise that makes him somehow romantic, both in her sight and in his own. He has become, of a sudden, a devil of a fellow. His friends flatter him by punching him in the ribs; his wife's mother flatters him even more by recoiling from him in horror. Soon it is as impossible for him to confess the humiliating truth as it would be for an American Legion commander to confess publicly that he served through the late war in the kitchen police.

Nature, said Oscar Wilde, always imitates art. The fact is never so plain as in the field of human conduct. All of us, in the long run, do what we are expected to do. It is the immemorial theory of women, born of their craving for martyrdom, that all men are liars and scoundrels. It is likewise their immemorial theory that all men are slovens. Neither theory is sound in fact. The overwhelming majority of normal men are both neat and virtuous. But thousands of them are driven into lamentable wickedness, as thousands are driven into dropping ashes on the parlor carpet, by the expectation of their wives that they should do such things.

The normal man is a monogamist for plain reasons. Amorous enterprise is painful to him. It takes up too much of his time; it exposes him to humiliating reverses; it is too expensive; it is dangerous. Once he has collared one woman he thanks God that his days of hazard and alarm are at an end—that he has come into safe waters at last. His vanity is caressed by the thought that he has a monopoly of her— that she has chosen him above all other men. He feels safe and secure; she has done her worst and can do no more. She is his; ergo, she is superior. Contemplating her, so long as she is not downright revolting, fills him with ease and satisfaction, like contemplating a policeman, a fireman, or a bottle of pre-war Scotch.

No such ease and satisfaction is to be found in the society of extralegal charmers, save, perhaps, by the man whose thirst for danger approaches the pathological. The normal Christian man finds them disquieting. Their very willingness to be amiable to him is proof enough to him that they are also amiable to other men. Even when he knows positively that a given one is true to him today he harbors a sneaking fear that she may change her mind tomorrow. In other words, such women do not qualify as property. They may encourage a transient and feeble vanity, but they do not encourage pride.

Pride lies dormant, indeed, until it is aroused by connubial suspicions. The first accusation fills the poor fellow with a strange but agreeable glow; he has become, it appears, a devil of a fellow. The subsequent proceedings complete his undoing. He can't reform and recant save in terms of humiliation. So he goes on leaping through the seventh hoop in order to prove to the world—and above all, to himself—that he is not a slave in chains. His wife has not lost him; she has chased him out.

His natural tendency toward monogamy, I believe, is instinctive and sound like all other instinctive things. Monogamy is by no means a human invention. It runs back to the higher apes, and even to the lower apes—the forebears of the fundamentalists of today. Polygamy came in relatively late, and was forced upon the race by accidents of history, as every one must know who has studied the chronicles of the Mormons. When it is practiced willingly it is only by men of aberrant character. The normal man no more wants two wives than he wants two watches or two noses.

Some of the more obvious advantages of monogamy I have already rehearsed. But there are other and more subtle ones. In marriage, as in every other human relation of a permanent and intimate character, the most important of all elements is mutual confidence. It is not sufficient for the partner A to be sure that B is not deceiving him; he must also know that he is not deceiving B. Once his conscience is not clear on that point his sense of security turns into an agony of apprehension, and thereafter he is skittish and unhappy. Trust is something that cannot be monkeyed with. There can be no compromise with it. Either it is absolute or it is nothing.

For these reasons—and I could nominate many more —I have praised and encouraged monogamy for long years.

It has, to be sure, its discomforts. It puts a burden upon honor—and honor, in a materialistic society, gets so little exercise otherwise that it is apt to be feeble. But, human beings being what they are, I think it works—all the man eating suffragettes and other such fanatics to the contrary notwithstanding. The happiest men I know are strict monogamists. The unhappiest are men who continue into middle age the natural exploratory adventuring of youth. Their wives, wrapped in the robes of martyrdom, are often happy. But they themselves are sad.

(*January 16, 1927*)

ANOTHER LONG–AWAITED BOOK

SINCE PHILIP DORMER STANHOPE, Earl of Chesterfield, published his celebrated letters to his morganatic son, in 1744, there has been no adequate book, in English, of advice to young men. I say adequate, and the adjective tells the whole story. There is not, of course, a college president, or a boss Y.M.C.A. secretary, or an uplifting preacher in the United States who has not written such a book, but all of them are alike filled with bilge. They depict and advocate a life that no normal young man wants to live, or could live without ruin if he wanted to. They are full of Sunday school platitudes and Boy Scout snuffling. If they were swallowed by the youth of today the republic of tomorrow would be a nation of idiots.

I point to the obvious example of the volumes of so-called sex hygiene. If there is anything in them save pious balderdash then I have yet to encounter it—and in the pursuit of my dismal duties as a critic of letters and ideas I have read literally hundreds of them. All of them are devoted to promoting the absurd and immoral idea that the sexual instinct is somehow degrading and against God—that whenever a young man feels it welling within him it is time for him to send for a physician and perhaps even for a policeman. If he is moved to kiss his girl he is in grave peril. If he yields to the devil and actually necks her he is already halfway to hell.

What could be worse rubbish? The sole effect of it, assuming it to be believed, is to send the young reader into manhood full of preposterous fears and shames and to shut him off from one of the chief sources of human happiness. For life without sex might be safer, but it would be unbearably dull. There would be very little hazard in it and even less joy. It is the sex instinct that makes women seem beautiful, which they are only once in a blue moon, and men seem wise and brave, which they never are at all. Throttle it, denaturize it, take it away, and human existence would be reduced to the prosaic, laborious, boresome, imbecile level of life in an ant hill.

But it is not when they address young men as males but when they address them as citizens that the current authors of such books achieve their worst nonsense. The absurd cult of Service, invented by swindlers to conceal their knaveries, is hymned eloquently in all of them. The chief aim and purpose of civilized man in the world, it appears, is to Do Good. In other words, his chief duty is to harass and persecute his neighbors. If he shirks it, then he is a bad citizen, and will go to hell along with the draft dodgers, tax evaders, atheists, and bachelors.

It seems to me that this highly dubious doctrine is re-

sponsible for much of the uneasiness and unhappiness that
are visible in the United States today, despite the growing
wealth of the country. Accepting it gravely, the American
people have converted themselves into a race of nuisances.
It is no longer possible, making a new acquaintance, to put
any reasonable trust in his common decency. If he is not a
policeman in disguise he is very apt to be a propagandist,
without disguise, which is even worse. The country swarms
with such bores, and the chief aim of the current instruction in the duties of the citizen seems to be to make more
of them.

No argument, I take it, is needed to show that this is
an evil tendency. The happiness of men in the world depends very largely upon their confidence in one another—
in A's belief that B is well disposed toward him and will do
nothing intentionally to make him uncomfortable. But the
whole purpose of the uplift is to make other people uncomfortable. It searches relentlessly for men who are having a
pleasant time according to their lights and tries to put them
in jail, or, still worse, to stir up their conscience. In other
words, it tries to make them unhappy. It is an engine for
the dissemination of the disagreeable. Seeking ostensibly to
increase the number of good citizens, it only increases the
number of bad ones.

But the young, it is argued, must be schooled in public
spirit, else they will all become highwaymen, just as they
must be schooled in virtue, else they will all become de-
bauchees. That argument, in various mellifluous forms, is
constantly heard. It constitutes the fundamental postulate
of such organizations as the Y.M.C.A. and the Boy Scouts.
To question it becomes a sort of indecorum and is commonly represented as a questioning of public spirit and vir-

tue themselves. Nevertheless, it remains nonsensical. There is not the slightest evidence that the normal young American, deprived of his books of civics, would take to the highroads, or that, deprived of his books of sex hygiene, he would set up practice as a roué.

The young come into the world, indeed, with a great deal of innate decency. It is their inheritance from the immemorial dead who fashioned and gave a direction to the delicate and complicated organism known as human society. That organism arose out of mutual good will, out of tolerance and charity, out of the civilizing tendency to live and let live. It emerged from the level of savagery by yielding to that tendency. The savage is preëminently his brother's keeper. He knows precisely what his brother ought to do in every situation and is full of indignation when it is not done. But the civilized man has doubts, and life under civilization is thus more comfortable than it is in a Tennessee or an African kraal.

If the young are to be instructed at all it seems to me that they ought to be instructed in the high human value of this toleration. They should be taught what they learn by experience in the schoolyard: that human beings differ enormously, one from the other, and that it is stupid and imprudent for A to try to change B. They should be taught that mutual confidence and good will are worth all the laws ever heard of, ghostly or secular, and that one man who minds his own business is more valuable to the world than 10,000 cocksure moralists. This teaching, I fear, is being neglected in the United States. We are hearing—and especially the young are hearing—far too much about brummagem utopias and far too little about the actual workings of the confusing but not unpleasant world we live in.

I know of no course in honor in any American Sunday school, yet it must be plain that human relations, when they are profitable and agreeable, are based upon honor much oftener than they are based upon morals. It is immoral, in every rational meaning of the word, to violate the Volstead act, and it is moral to give the Polizei aid against any one who does so. But what is the practical answer of decent men to those facts? Their practical answer is that such giving of aid is dishonorable. The law does not punish it; it rewards it. But it is punished swiftly and relentlessly by civilized public opinion.

My contention, in brief, is that there is room for a book showing why this is so—for a book of advice to young men setting forth, not what some ancient hypocrite of a college president or Y.M.C.A. secretary thinks would be nice, but what is regarded as nice by the overwhelming majority of intelligent and reputable men. In other words, there is room for a book of inductive ethics, based upon the actual practices of civilized society. Such a book, in the department of sexual conduct, would differ enormously from the present banal manuals. It would denounce as ignoble many of the acts they advocate and it would give its approval to others that they ban. And in the wider field of the relations between man and man it would differ from them even more radically. It would have little to say about ideals, but a great deal about realities.

Most boys admire their fathers and take their notions from them in this department. The boy who has a father who is a genuinely civilized man needs no advice from outside experts. Common decency will be in him when he grows up. He will not be afraid of women and he will not try to make over men. But vast herds of American fathers, succumbing to the Service buncombe, have ceased to be safe guides for their sons. Their practice is misleading and their counsel is dangerous. Thus the way opens for a counselor less credulous and more sagacious. Thus a vast market shows itself for the sort of book I have been trying to describe.

(September 12, 1926)

HOLY WRIT

PURSUING, of late, advanced researches into theological pathology, I have had the sad duty of reading certain "new," "modern," "American," and "idiomatic" translations of the New Testament, including those of the Rev. MM. Weymouth, Moffatt, Goodspeed, and Ballantine. All of these translators, I believe, are pious and righteous men, and every one of them undertook his task with the sole object of making Holy Writ more intelligible to the plain people, and hence more persuasive and precious. But I can only report professionally as a theologian that all of them, in my judgment, will go to hell for their pains.

And richly deserve the singeings there in store for them. For all they accomplish, in putting the original Greek into familiar English, is to put it into English so flabby and preposterous that all the beauty is gone out of it. Consider, for example, the sonorous and magnificent line in the Lord's Prayer—thus in the authorized version: "Give us this day our daily bread." Well, this is what it becomes in the Weymouth version: "Give us today our bread for the day." And this in the Goodspeed version: "Give us today bread for the day." And this in the Ballantine version: "Our bread for the coming day give us today." And this in the Moffatt version: "Give us today our bread for the morrow."

Could vandalism go further? It is almost like arranging Schubert's serenade as a waltz for the bagpipes. All the loveliness is squeezed out of the line. Its ancient charm and eloquence vanish into thin air: it ceases to be a prayer and becomes a mere demand. And is there any compensating gain in clarity? Is an error in the authorized version rectified? Certainly not. As a matter of fact, the four experts simply introduce confusion and obfuscation into what was formerly crystal clear. Two of them make it appear that the bread asked for is wanted at once; the other two say that it will not be needed until tomorrow.

I turn to the book of John, and to an episode that most latter day preachers of the Word delicately avoid: the episode of the woman taken in adultery. It is unpleasant reading for vice crusaders, prohibitionists, and other such wowsers, for it sets forth, in succinct and highly dramatic form, the basic principles of the Christianity actually preached by Christ. You recall, no doubt, the great speech that confounds the scribes and Pharisees, eager to put the woman to death: "He that is without sin among you, let him first cast a stone at her." But perhaps you have forgotten the superb dialogue that follows, between Christ and the woman —the most stupendous scene in all drama, sacred or profane. I quote it from the authorized version:

When Jesus had lifted up Himself, and saw none but the woman, He said unto her, Woman, where are those thine accusers? Hath no man condemned thee?

She said, No man, Lord. And Jesus said unto her, Neither do I condemn thee; go, and sin no more.

Well, what do the modernizers make of this austere and colossal beauty, this masterpiece of simple and lovely English, as it was of Greek? Goodspeed, more discreet than the rest, omits it altogether: I can't find it in his version of John. But Weymouth tackles it boldly, and with this almost unbelievable result:

Then standing up, Jesus spoke to her. "Woman," He said, "Where are they? Has no one condemned you?" "No one, Sir," she replied. "And I do not condemn you either," said Jesus. "Go, and from this time do not sin any more."

Imagine it! "No one, Sir"! And "do not sin any more"! But Ballantine, as impossible as it may seem, is still worse:

Jesus raised himself up and said to her, "Woman, where are they? Has no one sentenced you?" She said, "No one, Sir." Jesus said, "Neither do I sentence you. Go. From now on sin no more."

And Moffatt, with a herculean effort, manages to be worse than Ballantine:

Raising Himself, Jesus said to her, "Woman, where are they? Has no one condemned you?" She said, "No one, Sir." Jesus said, "Neither do I; be off, and never sin again."

Give your eye to that "be off." And then ask yourself if a million centuries in hell will be enough for that translator!

All of these dreadful perversions of incomparable beauty, as I have already said, are full of good intentions: they show enough, indeed, to pave hell from the Torquemada monument to the Avenue of Revivalists. What ails them is simply a gross misunderstanding, on the part of their rev. perpetrators, of the nature of religious feeling. These worthy gentlemen all seem to think that it is a product of ratiocination—that it arises out of logic and evidence, like the belief, say, that two and two make four. It does nothing of the sort. It begins, not as a series of ideas, but as a mystery, and it remains a mystery to the end. Religion is most potent to sway the mind, indeed, when the evidences of its objective truth are most vague and unconvincing—when it is apprehended, not as fact at all, but as sheer poetry, the very negation of fact.

The success of Christianity in the world, I believe, is due largely, if not chiefly, to the unmatchable beauty, as poetry, of its sacred books. It is hard to think of any other oriental religion that is not logically more plausible and persuasive, but no one of them has a sacred literature even remotely to be compared, for simple loveliness, to that of the decadent Judaism which, alone among them, has conquered the west. There are single Psalms that have ten times more beauty in them than the whole literature of Brahminism, ancient and modern; in the story of the Christ Child there is more poetry than was ever heard of in Greece and Rome. It is precisely this profound and disarming poetry, this irresistibly beautiful evocation of the unattainable and ever to be desired, that give Christianity its continued strength in the modern world, despite the gradual destruction of two-thirds of its objective evidences.

Poetry does not fetch a man by convincing him; it fetches him by robbing him of the wish to be convinced—by lulling the censor within him and so giving free rein to his deepest emotions. Few Americans of the present day, I take it—that is, few of the more enlightened sort—accept the story of the Christ Child in all literalness. It violates their notions of the probable; in part, at least, it seems to them to be plainly fanciful. But that man must be a dull clod indeed who is not moved by it, and never catches himself wishing a bit wistfully that such things could really be. It is, of all the stories ever devised by man, enormously the most beautiful. Whoever reduced it to words, conquered, by that stroke, the whole civilized world.

But poetry is a fragile flower, and will not bear transplanting. Forced into the harsh forms of prose all its charm is gone; it becomes simply nonsense. This is true of great poetry as well as of poetry that is not great, as every fresh attempt at a prose translation of the Odyssey bears witness. It is preëminently true of the poetry which makes up the sacred books of Christianity. Try it with any of the Psalms, with the Sermon on the Mount, with the story of the Nativity, with the roaring strophes of Revelation. The thing becomes, in the speech of every day, a mere absurdity. It is not only not moving; it is, only too often, perilously close to being laughable.

So all such "modern" versions of the New Testament as those of MM. Goodspeed, Ballantine, Moffatt, and Weymouth are bound to be botches. They reduce the narrative to a series of syllogisms, and so make it banal. The fundamentalists, in their different way, do the same violence upon it. Trying to make it literal and impeccable, like a stock report, they succeed only in making it preposterous.

(July 18, 1926)

V. POLITICS, GOVERNMENT, JURISPRUDENCE

❦

Mencken's talent for dissecting frauds equipped him well for reporting on politics, a rich field for one seeking stuffed shirts to deflate.

A study of his political writings for the Baltimore Sun-papers shows that he wrote infrequently in terms of partisan party theories, Democrats v. Republicans. But he was constantly captivated by the individual.

Gerald L. K. Smith, Dr. Francis E. Townsend, "Sockless" Jerry Simpson, and what he called other "glittering fish" were a source of unending fascination to him.

The doctrines a politician profeoood wore of only passing interest; what Mencken looked for was the savage struggle for individual political success, the cunning with which a man destroyed his opponents.

This sharp focus on the human element led to many essays delightful for their insight. But the resulting blind spot for currents in political thought made Mencken the world's worst prophet.

He thought that Hoover might be re-elected. He stumped cheerfully for Alfred M. Landon in 1936 (the Maine-and-Vermont year), and in 1924 filed from the Democratic party convention a story which announced: "John W. Davis will never be nominated."

Only minutes after the story was dropped on the copy
desk of the Baltimore Sun, *the convention selected Davis.*
Unembarrassed, Mencken quipped to a colleague: "I
hope those idiots have sense enough to drop the negative."

THE UNITED STATES SENATE

LIKE ALL the other more refined and elegant clubs of this
great nation the United States senate has been vastly damaged by prohibition. Not, of course, that it has actually
gone dry. I do not frequent it personally, but I am told by
reliable agents that its members, wet and dry, still manage
to lave their whistles when the need arises. The senate, in
its earliest days, was full of three bottle men, and its traditions have been somewhat bibulous ever since. One of the
most accomplished guzzlers that Washington has seen in
modern times served in it until very recently. He was an
honest man, drunk or sober, and always voted wet.

The senate has been ruined by the preposterous frauds,
chiefly from the south and middle west, who drink wet and
vote dry. Obviously, they are not gentlemen, and equally obviously a club which gives them all the rights of membership
is not an agreeable resort for men who are. Worse, they
constitute a majority, and so the whole place takes its tone
from them. I do not object to teetotalers. On the contrary,
I have a high respect for them, as for men capable of a feat
that is inordinately difficult under prohibition, and, in my
judgment, against the law of God. But how any one can be

polite to a scoundrel who sobs for prohibition with a jug in his pocket is quite beyond my imagination. I'd as lief be polite to a prohibition agent, to a Y.M.C.A. secretary, or to a hangman.

In private life, one treats such swine to the boot tip, literally if they are encountered *a cappella*, and metaphorically if they are accompanied by their friends. But a senator cannot kick another senator. It is not only a high crime and misdemeanor, it is also unclubby. He must treat even a wet dry courteously, and listen to him. It is my contention that no man can stoop to such revolting hypocrisies without doing grave damage to his immortal soul. He becomes, like the wet dry, a fraud. The whole senate, of late, is sicklied o'er with the pale cast of fraudulence. Its best days are behind it.

Not, of course, that it lacks able and interesting men, even today. The two Reeds, from Missouri and Pennsylvania, are certainly not lacking in ability. The Reed of Pittsburgh, just past 45 and in the full bloom of vigor, is the perfect model of a high toned corporation lawyer—suave, alert, well informed, easy in manner, very sure of himself. He rose as the tail of the Mellon kite, but he will be heard of later on, I believe, on his own account. The great crater left by the translation of Penrose to the celestial pastures still yawns tragically. The Curtises and Smoots rattle around in it like Cal in the White House. It will have a new tenant, I predict, toward the end of Senator Reed's first term, and it will be comfortably filled by the middle of his second.

The other Reed, of Kansas City, gets vastly less attention than he deserves from the Washington correspondents. He is an incorrigible independent, and hence beyond their imaginations. They are all sturdy regulars, and of both parties: the man they most admire is the perfect stalwart. One cannot spend all morning drenching Mr. Coolidge with vas-eline and cologne water, and then rise to Senator Reed in the afternoon. He has all of the qualities that pessimists say have gone out of our public men. He is an adept and highly successful politician, and yet he is the complete antithesis of the party hack. No more formidable debater has been heard in the senate in recent years. He is a master of the art of thinking on his legs—and he thinks in terms of 16 inch shells.

The senate half of the *Congressional Record* would be as dull, without Reed, as the house half. When he horns into a debate, if only to ask a casual question, the whole at-mosphere changes. What was, perhaps, only a series of flat-ulent recitations becomes at once a clash of ideas and wills. Tender senators take to the cloakrooms, and leave him to his sanguinary hunting. Once he achieved the curious feat of making a colleague burst into tears on the floor. In the bat-tle over the egregious Charles Beecher Warren he achieved the still more curious feat of knocking out the senate major-ity and the President of the United States.

But such men are now rare in the senate, and their number, I believe, tends to diminish, chiefly because of the seventeenth amendment. Direct elections fill the chamber with mountebanks of the type of Magnus Johnson, the Min-nesota professional yokel, and Capper, the Kansas profes-sional Christian. It is easy for boob bumpers, trained in the rustic chautauquas, to get in, but it is very hard for men of any genuine dignity. And the seats that the boob bumpers fail to grab fall to hack politicians of the school of Watson of Indiana and Weller of Maryland.

The most independent and useful senators, some one was lately observing, now come from the less populous states. Borah of Idaho and Walsh of Montana are examples. One reason is that their constituents are usually far off, and so cannot march upon Washington and waste their time. Another is that they have fewer constituents to think of, and hence fewer factions to placate. An eastern senator, if he comes from a large state, has to devote at least two-thirds of his time to purely political business. Even the late Henry Cabot Lodge, for all his lofty mien, was an assiduous job getter, and always had half an hour for visitors from Massachusetts. The Pennsylvania senators, during a republican administration, and the Virginia senators, when the Democrats are in power, are literally overwhelmed. Only recently Senator Pepper of Pennsylvania was so rattled by the demand for jobs that he fell into the dreadful obscenity of denouncing the titular head of his party.

The ambassadors of the states west of the Mississippi escape most of this nuisance, and so they are able to give their attention to statecraft, and when they happen to be intelligent, they attain to proficiency at its practice, and get upon the first pages. Both of the senate floor leaders come from the transpontine regions. Some day you will be reading a great deal about the senators from Hawaii and Alaska.

The senate, as I have said, has been spoiled as a club by prohibition—and by the direct election of senators. Certainly it must be depressing for a man of any intelligence to have to associate, day in and day out, with a rabble of Anti-Saloon league marionettes and cow state John Baptists. There was far better society in the old time saloons of Washington; there is better society, even today, among the colored intellectuals of the town. But the charm of the upper chamber still lingers, and it is easy to see why.

A United States senator, once he is sworn in, is almost the only genuinely free man left among us. Unlike a representative, he doesn't have to start his campaign for reëlection at once; he has a term of six years and may take his ease for four of them. Unlike a member of the cabinet, he is not responsible to any one, and need not give an account of himself. And unlike a President or a justice of the Supreme court, he is under no obligation to work on days when he feels like loafing.

For six long years he is completely his own man, free to say whatever he pleases and do whatever he pleases. If he offends the high and mighty, the high and mighty must grin and bear it. If he jumps the party traces, it takes a long while to punish him. If, tiring of the great affairs of state, he wants a holiday, he is free to take it. There is no way to gag a senator—that is, no way that is certain to work. A representative, under the present rules, is no more than a private in a regiment, with no rights that the officers are bound to respect. But a senator is an officer himself, and of field rank. He must be attended to. It is dangerous, even for other senators, to use him roughly. He can bite.

Thus, gentlemen who like that sort of power continue to put their names on the senate waiting list, despite all the cow state John Baptists, and all the hack politicians, and all the Anti-Saloon league lickspittles. They hope, I daresay, for better days. The senate chamber is the only place where such hopes may be still entertained. At the other end of the capitol there is only Egyptian night.

(*February 7, 1926*)

THE NATIONAL CONVENTIONS

THE NEWS that the town boomers and cheer leaders of the great city of San Francisco are laying plans to get one or both of the national conventions next year will fall gratefully upon the ears of all the persons—whether candidates for the presidency or pickpockets, newspaper correspondents or bootleggers—who attended the Democratic convention there in 1920. For that convention lingers in American political history as the only genuinely charming one ever held. It was not merely bearable; it was delightful. Most of the ladies and gentlemen in attendance had to travel at least two thousand miles to reach the hall. They went damning the national committee for putting them to so much trouble and expense. They came home shouting glad hosannas.

I have been a steady customer of national conventions since the opening of the present glorious century, and in that time have missed very few of them. All save the one at San Francisco have been abominable. I hesitate to choose the worst, but perhaps that distinction belongs to the one held in my native Baltimore, in the Maryland Free State, in 1912. The weather was hellishly hot, the very meager hotels of the town were intolerably overcrowded, and the convention hall was in a remote and inconvenient place, with wretched transportation facilities. The Baltimore boosters spent $150,000 to wrest the convention from the other cities that wanted it—and made so many bitter enemies for the town that tourists steer clear of it to this day despite its tremendous wetness.

I never meet an old time newspaper correspondent, in fact, that he doesn't mention his sufferings during the pro-

ceedings and condole with me for having to live in so hot
and miserable a place. I have long given up trying to convince such complainants that it is sometimes cool there,
just as I have given up trying to convince them that it now
has plenty of taxicabs and at low rates. They think they
know better—and by hard personal experience. The Washington correspondents, who were all present, are afraid of
Baltimore to this day, though it is but forty miles from
Washington and usually much more comfortable. When
one of them is ordered there to track down a United States
senator on a jag he makes his will and kisses his children
good-bye.

I estimate that that convention cost Baltimore, in addition to the $150,000 that the national committee de-
manded, at least $150,000,000 in good will. It was almost
as costly as the great fire of 1904, and it is proving harder to
live down. Most other cities that entertain national conventions fare just as badly. The weather is almost always hot,
the hotels are overcrowded, and there is, in consequence,
immense discomfort for every one in attendance. So the
delegates, alternates, correspondents, and other victims go
home full of bile, and the result is a bath of advertising
comparable to that going with an epidemic of smallpox.

The Coolidge convention of 1924 almost ruined Cleveland, though the weather, by some freak, was mild. What
graveled the visitors was the lack of decent refreshment.
Ohio, at that time, was in the grip of the Anti-Saloon
league, and all the dry blacklegs were concentrated in
Cleveland. They did their work so well that even the local
newspaper reporters had to go on the water wagon. Law
enforcement in America, in fact, probably reached its peak
there during those miserable ten days. Long before Dr.

Coolidge was nominated at least a third of the delegates
had gone home in disgust.

I did not suffer myself, for I had Christian friends in
the town, but the news of the drought reached certain other
friends at Windsor, Ontario, and they hastily loaded a small
yacht with bottled beer and set off to the rescue. Unluckily,
there were heavy seas on Lake Erie and they made very poor
time, and when they reached the Cleveland breakwater they
found that they had consumed exactly half of their cargo.
In fear that if they landed what was left they would themselves suffer on the return journey, they decided to return
at once. Later they telegraphed me their apologies from
Windsor, saying that they had arrived with but thirty-five
bottles of beer. I got none whatever, and have had a prejudice against Cleveland—and, in fact, against the whole state
of Ohio—to this day, though, as I have said, the Christian
people of the town did what they could for me.

Chicago, on account of its size and central location, has
probably had more national conventions than any other
city. I recall attending three there—all of them intensely uncomfortable. The last was in 1920: it was the convention
that nominated the martyred Harding. It was held in a hall
with a glass ceiling, and during the afternoons the heat
therein was quite unbearable. That heat, indeed, had more
to do with the nomination of Dr. Harding than all the
machinations of the George Harveys, Tom Lamonts, and
other such eminent men. The delegates, reaching Saturday
morning, gave notice that they refused to stay into the next
week, and so the leaders had to find a safe vacuum and
break the deadlock. Thus Dr. Harding was raised to the
purple.

New York has had but one national convention in

modern times, and there is not much chance that it will
have another. That one, as every one knows, was three years
ago, and it lasted three weeks. The hotels of the town certainly did no profiteering—a curse almost everywhere else
at such times—but the high scale of metropolitan living,
combined with the long duration of the convention, broke
most of the rural delegates, and many of them had to send
home for funds. In some of the southern states public sub-
scriptions for them were opened. Even so, hundreds deserted, and when Dr. Davis was nominated at last it was
mainly by alternates and alternates of alternates. One state
delegation, in fact, was reduced to a single alternate and
half a dozen of his lady friends. Another delegate, at the
end, represented two whole states.

That was the worst national convention within my
recollection—the most tiresome and the most uncomfortable. Fortunately, the town booticians were alive to their
duty, and so the suffering of the delegates was a shade less
than it might have been. But many of the southern Ku
Kluxers, having been warned by their pastors against the
diabolical ways of Tammany, were afraid to drink what was
on tap, and when the white mule that they had brought
with them was exhausted they began to fall like flies.

In San Francisco, in 1920, no such lamentable scenes
were witnessed. The weather was cool, a bit foggy and
damp, and inexpressibly exhilarating. The hall was a noble
structure—clean, beautiful, and well ordered. The hotels
handled the crowds without the slightest discomfort or
confusion. There was no profiteering. The town wowsers
were somehow squelched during the session, and the delegates were offered very sporty entertainment, including
cock fights. Best of all, there was plenty of sound liquor,

and a great deal of it was supplied gratuitously by communal agencies. Not a single delegate lost his life, either by thirst or by wood alcohol—a record unique in the history of national conventions.

That was the most charming convention ever heard of. The delegates simply refused to quarrel: life in that hospitable and beautiful town was too delightful. Instead, they fell into one another's arms. One afternoon the proceedings were suspended and there was a dance on the convention floor. No one was ever drunk, but every one was always happy, in every sense of the world. The magical San Francisco fog made the cheeks of the girls as rosy as cherries. I saw delegates kissing and hugging lady delegates, and even suffragettes—women who had not been approached with such insults for twenty years. I myself, after a swallow of bourbon, embraced a sob sister forty-six years of age.

San Francisco, I hear, is still wet. If so, its boosters would do well to let the fact be delicately known. For the statesmen who attend national conventions don't want to be lured to another Cleveland: one dry convention is enough. All of them, as their party platforms will show next year, are in favor of law enforcement, and many of them are eminent as drys. But when the band strikes up and they find themselves safely away from home they like to sin a little. In twenty-seven years of national conventions I have encountered but one dry who would actually refuse a drink. His name deserves to be recorded upon the rolls of fame in letters of imperishable brass. He was the Hon. William Jennings Bryan, LL.D.

(*May 8, 1927*)

ALL THE GREAT boons and usufructs that, in the advance notices, were to have flowed out of prohibition have apparently gone a-glimmering, and even the professional prohibitionists on dark days doubt their reality. But there is one benefit issuing from the attempt to enforce the Volstead act that has genuine substance, and so, though it was unpremediated, it ought not to be overlooked. In brief, it is this: that the American people have been cured of their old superstitious reverence for law—that they have even got rid of some of their old faith in government. Is the change deplorable? Then it is better to be foolish than to be wise.

The light began to dawn, I believe, at the precise moment when the prohibitionists ceased arguing that prohibition would cure all the sorrows of the world, and began arguing that it ought to be submitted to simply because it was the law—in other words, at the moment when they introduced the doctrine of law enforcement. That doctrine, it soon became obvious, had little foundation in logic; it was almost purely mystical. What it amounted to was a denial that the citizens of a free state had any natural and inalienable rights at all. If, by whatever chicanery, a law was passed ordering them to cut off their children's ears, then they were bound to obey. If, by the same chicanery, a law was passed forbidding them to wash the same ears, they were equally bound to obey.

It needed little gift for ratiocination to penetrate to the absurdity of this doctrine. Or to grasp the fact of its extreme antiquity. Even a moron could see it was simply the ancient dogma of the king's divine right in a new false face.

It could not be disentangled from the concept of the citizen as a mere subject. Above him stood an occult something called the government, a force distinct from the people and superior to them. Did the people, under democracy, create it and give it the breath of life? Then, once created, it was nevertheless distinct from them and superior to them. They were forbidden to resist it. By the more extreme prohibitionists they were forbidden even to denounce it.

I incline to believe that these disagreeable facts, gradually oozing into the communal mind, did far more to undermine prohibition and bring it to its present parlous estate than any of its objective failures, disastrous though they plainly were. The plain people suddenly began to see that a vast machine for oppressing them had been fabricated, and that once it got into full working order they would have a dreadful time escaping from it. More, they began to look behind the machine to the force operating it—that is, to the potent and inscrutable power called the government. And what they saw was simply a gang of men—men exactly like themselves—men, in many cases, inferior to themselves.

The resultant disillusion was probably unpleasant, but it would be going too far, I think, to call it insalubrious. At one harsh wrench the American people got rid of one of their oldest superstitions—one of the cardinal articles of their national voodooism—to wit, the notion that government is an abstract, an impersonal force, a thing of laws. It is no such thing, and never has been. Government is a thing of men—and under democracy of men palpably inferior and ignominious. Knowing this is very useful. It was not knowing it that exposed the people of America to prohibition.

A long time must elapse, of course, before the lesson

soaks in. When no antidote is within reach, the frantic patient is apt to swallow more of the same poison. In the same way the subjects of this great empire, cozened by mountebanks, turn to fresh mountebanks for relief. But they have at least come to suspect that they face mountebanks, and not heroes. The old haloes fall off. Government reveals itself, not as a benign and supermortal power, devoted disinterestedly to the public good, but as a mere camorra of rogues and vagabonds, devoted wholly to their own advantage. On one side stands the dry congressman, wet inside and eager to be wetter. On the other stands the prohibition agent, with his hand out. And in the center stands the ermined judge, judicially tearing up the bill of rights to roll cigarettes.

Such is government, scientifically viewed. Such are the evangelists of law enforcement. I preach no holy war against them. I know of no way, in fact, to get rid of them. But it seems to me there is great advantage in seeing them, at last, exactly as they are—that it is a good and valuable thing to pull them out of their old disguises. Suppose we can't get rid of them at all, now or hereafter? *Soit!* But we may at least avoid the disastrous error of mistaking them for benefactors. We may at least cease mistaking their witless and oppressive orders for divine commands.

Do I exaggerate the stupidity and obliquity of these gentlemen? I think not. Turn to the governors of the American states: there are forty-eight of them. How many show any genuine competence and professional dignity, any honest desire to perform their duties honestly and well, any actual courage, independence and integrity? Certainly not a dozen. Well, then, how many are at the other end of the scale—how many are limber and ignoble Jenkinses, willing and eager to do anything to hold their jobs, to get better jobs—how many have been wet once, became dry, and are now getting damp again? Certainly twice as many. And what will you find in the middle? You will find vacuums, nonentities, blobs.

Turn to the national house of representatives. It consists of nearly 500 men. Of them perhaps forty are of such dignity that it may be said of them that they cannot be bought—not even with votes. Of the forty perhaps a dozen have genuine intelligence. What of the rest? They are absolutely indistinguishable, gathered in plenary session, from a convention of garage keepers. They leap at the word of command, peering this way and that. When there is no command they lie docilely, like dogs upon a hearth rug. It makes little difference where the command comes from: if it is sharp enough, they leap.

The chamber of these abject ciphers is the shrine of government among us. Their absurd proceedings, sufficiently prolonged, result in the enactment of what is called law, and that law we are asked to revere as something almost sacred. Flouting it is not only a breach of decorum; it is an act of treason. If, run amok by fanatics, they decided that we should all wear green neckties, it would become a patriotic duty to wear green neckties. If, run back by other fanatics, they banned green and prescribed red, we should have to change to red.

But isn't law necessary? Of course, it is: who denies it? But it is necessary only when it is necessary. The rest is only insult and oppression, and the citizen is under no more obligation to submit to it than he is to submit to any other insult or oppression. Say I am ill and send for a doctor. He prescribes a dose of Glauber's salts, and I take it without question, for the general experience of man is in favor of it. Moreover, I believe the doctor to be an honest man. But suppose he prescribed, in addition to the Glauber's salts, ten grains of strychnine, a pound of tenpenny nails, and a quart of ground glass? And suppose he pulled out a revolver and ordered me to get his prescription down on penalty of death, and then, having me conveniently stuck up, proceeded to empty my pockets?

This, under the name of government, is what goes on every day. We need laws for certain essential purposes, and we select men to make them for us. Sufficiently urged, they do it. But then they go on to enterprises of their own. They make laws that rob us, laws that annoy and oppress us, laws that deprive us of capital and inalienable rights. They do all this, not mistakenly, but for their private advantage. They forget your business and mine completely, and devote themselves gloriously to their own. And then they try to convince us that what is theirs is really ours—and order us to jail when we protest.

Law enforcement? Go tell it to the marines!

(January 10, 1926)

BLACKMAIL MADE EASY

THE BRITISH SOCIETY OF AUTHORS, tiring of pouring out its treasure in the defense of members falsely accused of plagiarism, has come to an agreement with Lloyds, whereby, for a small fee, authors may take out insurance against the charge. This insurance is precisely analogous to that which physicians carry against suits for malpractice. Unluckily, the underwriters of the United States do not offer such policies, and so the authors of the republic remain exposed to embarrassing actions, costly when won, and ruinous when lost.

That the risk is serious is shown by the experience of certain American dramatists. There is among them a man who has been the defendant in at least six such suits, and in one, if my memory does not err, an idiotic jury gave a verdict against him, though his innocence was plain enough. There is another who has been haled into court twice, both times on evidence such as not even a spiritualist or a Mississippi congressman would have taken seriously. The first time, though he was completely exonerated of plagiarism, the costs of the defense almost bankrupted him. The second action is still pending. I have read the play he is accused of having plagiarized. It is no more like his own work than a wart is like the Jungfrau.

The defense in any such case is always difficult. If the complainant can show any resemblance at all between his work and the defendant's—and usually, of course, he can—the defendant is in a tight place, for he must prove either that his own work was written before the defendant's or that both were preceded by some very similar work, done by a third party. The first proof is often impossible, and the second, at best, involves certain unpleasant embarrassments. Thus the man accused is commonly thrown upon the common sense of the judge and jury, and not infrequently he finds to his dismay that this is a slender reed, indeed. Judges, as every one knows, only too often become mere law machines, bending everything to their archaic rules, and juries, in a battle between a successful man and a failure, are very prone to give a solatium to the failure.

More often than not, perhaps, the plaintiff is honestly convinced that his property has been cabbaged. It is always hard for any of us to grasp the fact that our ideas may have occurred also to other men. Moreover, the lower ranks of authorship are full of nuts, and their aberration commonly takes the form of a violent belief in their own unparalleled genius. But what is so easy for honest fools is just as easy for blackmailers. In many of the accusations of plagiarism that have been made in late years, in England and America, there has been nothing save a yearning to get a whack at what seemed to be very opulent royalties.

This effort to get money by threats and intimidations has gone so far in the department of movie scenarios that most of the movie producing companies now refuse absolutely to read manuscripts sent in by strangers. Most of them take truly elaborate precautions. When a manuscript comes in, and the address of the sender is on the envelope, it is returned unopened, and with it goes a printed notice that it has not been read. At the same time entry of the sender's name and address is made in a record book, with the date, and this entry is formally authenticated by the person in charge of incoming mail.

Despite all this machinery claims are made to the so called ideas in almost every film, and not infrequently they are backed up by suits for heavy damages. Inasmuch as these ideas, in the main, descend to us from Neanderthal man, it is often quite impossible for a given movie author to prove that he invented what he is accused of having stolen. So he must hunt for it in the literature of the past, and thus prove that, if he lifted it himself, so also did the man claiming it. Defending such suits has familiarized the solicitors of the movie folk with all the popular literature back to the earliest written records. There is one lawyer in Los Angeles who is said to have memorized Joe Miller's Jest-Book, the Gesta Romanorum, the whole Deadwood Dick series of dime novels, and all the evidence taken in all the English divorce cases since adultery was first prohibited.

Here, it seems to me, our civil procedure is defective, for it permits any lunatic or blackmailer or malicious person to enter suit for damages against any one else, with or without probable cause, and under cover of that suit he may make allegations of an extremely damaging nature, and expose his victim to heavy and unescapable expense. In criminal cases the law is far more jealous of the rights of the accused. He cannot be put on trial on anybody's mere say-so, with or without reason. Before he may be haled into court at all, his accusers must first convince a grand jury that there is a plausible case against him. If the grand jury is not convinced, then he goes unmolested, and at no expense to himself. And if, after his accusers have convinced the grand jury and he has been brought to trial and acquitted by a petit jury, those responsible for his troubles may be sued for damages.

In other words, it is of the essence of the criminal law that one accusing another must have reasonable grounds for his accusations, and that these grounds must be convincing to two separate juries of unbiased men, to say nothing of the judge. But under our civil procedure the first jury is omitted. Being in a mood of constructive criticism, I hereby propose that the omission be rectified. That is, I propose that there be a sort of grand jury in the civil courts as there is in the criminal courts, and that no suit be put down for trial until, when, as, and if this jury has been convinced that there is a probable cause for action in it.

I propose, in fact, nothing new. No less a tribunal than the Supreme court of the United States lately set up such a jury. It is composed, true enough, of the learned judges themselves, but nevertheless it functions as a grand jury rather than as a court. In the old days practically any litigant, if he had the money, could drag his case up to the Supreme court, and so harass and maybe wear out his opponent. But now, save in a few special cases, he must first convince the court that he has a probable cause for appealing to it. If he so convinces it, it issues a writ of certiorari, and the case comes up. But if he fails, then he is denied any further hearing, and the decision of the lower court must stand.

A great many civil actions, including especially those involving charges of moral turpitude—to which class plagiarism suits belong—are probably fomented by shyster lawyers who know that the average man, rather than stand cross-examination about his private and professional acts, will commonly pay substantial damages. In view of this fact it has been proposed more than once that lawyers maintaining such actions, when they are defied and beaten, be disbarred. But it seems to me that this is a poor way to get at relief and reform, for a lawyer facing any such penalty would naturally hesitate to take a case involving the slightest doubt, and that would deprive many perfectly honest and honorable litigants of decent legal advice.

My own scheme, I believe, is much better. It would not involve any great expense. The existing grand jury is one of the cheapest agencies of government that we have, and one of the most efficient. In many jurisdictions it cuts down the criminal actions by at least a third, and in some it goes beyond that. Its members serve for very small fees, and, hearing only *ex parte* testimony, they frequently get through dozens of cases in a day. A grand jury in the civil courts might function just as cheaply and effectively. It could hear the plaintiff's case briefly, and determine if there were any merit in it. If it found this to be the case, it could return a paper analogous to a true bill, and so put down the case for trial. And if it were unconvinced, it could shut off further proceedings, and so prevent a great deal of dishonest and costly litigation.

My natural gifts as a jurisconsult are unsupported by formal researches; in consequence, it may be that I propose a legal impossibility, or, worse still, that what I propose is already in effect in one of the constituent states of the federal union. But I throw it overboard without pausing to seek counsel from the learned. If it is bad, then let it go the way of the Wilson idealism. If it is good—*soli Deo gloria!* (*March 6, 1927*)

A LONG-FELT WANT

WHO WILL DO a textbook of the art and science of politics under democracy—that is, of practical politics, of the politics of job getting and boob bumping? Surely there is a long-felt want here. The politician, as every one knows, is one of the most opulent and puissant professional men in practice among us, and every year his subtle craft attracts a larger number of eager practitioners. Yet one searches the

libraries in vain for a book expounding its principles. There
are texts of scientific salesmanship, of osteopathy, of sanitary plumbing, even of the art of the evangelist, but there is
none of politics.

I do not forget two that go half way: *The Great Game
of Politics*, by Frank R. Kent, and *Behind the Scenes in
Politics*, by some one anonymous—both published two years
ago. Mr. Kent describes what may be called the machinery
of politics with great skill; the constitution of parties, the
structure of party discipline, the organization of precinct,
district, state, and nation. And the nameless one—obviously
a practical man, of hard experience in national campaigns—
shows by plentiful examples how little principles and party
lines really count—how great is the advantage of the skilled
professional, no matter which side he stands on.

But both of these experts keep away from the funda-
mentals. They prove abundantly that a sound knowledge of
mob psychology is the chief asset of the politician, but they
do not state clearly what he ought to know. Does he get
farther by slapping backs and haw-hawing, like Jim Watson
of Indiana, or by maintaining an aloof and superior reserve,
like the late Henry Cabot Lodge? Does it profit him more
to be thought shrewd or to be thought honest? Here are
practical and important questions. Both Kent and the
anonymous sense them, but do not elucidate them.

The author of the textbook I bawl for, if it is ever
written, will get a great deal of valuable matter, I believe,
out of the existing texts of scientific salesmanship, mental
mastery, and so on. Their single aim is to teach the student
how to make *Homo boobiens* do what he doesn't want to
do—in fact, what it is plainly to his interest to avoid doing.
They show how to get at him by appealing to his weak-

nesses. Is he vain? Then he can be fetched by flattery, not too delicate. Is he timorous? Then he is nailed by searching out his fears—of halitosis, of pyorrhea, of gallstones, of dying bankrupt, of losing his wife's love.

Much the same problem confronts the practical politician. It is his business to convince the mob (a) that it is confronted by some grave danger, some dreadful menace to its peace and security, and (b) that he can save it. Both premise and conclusion are usually manifestly false. The horrors that politicians talk of are mainly imaginary. They gabble darkly of famine, oppression, slavery; the reality is seldom worse than a transient inconvenience. And the remedies they hawk all belong to quackery. Only once in a blue moon, indeed, are the ills of mankind curable by purely political means. When they are disposed of it is usually by an economic process, and when it is not by an economic process it is by an undiluted act of God.

But the plain people always believe otherwise. They trust to the vote, the palladium of their liberties. They believe the way to get more money for less work is to turn A out and B in. When the scheme fails, they turn to C. When C is caught in flagrante they go back to A or B. This, in brief, is the process of politics under democracy. It is the aim of every politician to be today's savior. If the mob is not already scared, he must scare it by the devices of his ancient and wily art. And once it is scared, he must convince it that he can succor and secure it.

For this art some men have a great natural talent. There was, for example, the late Col. Roosevelt. He radiated bugaboos as a New Thoughter radiates optimism. At least once a month, until the advances of age overcame him, he started a new one—and then set the mob to howling for him by pursuing and scotching it. Most of these bugaboos, I believe were without substance, and few of those that were real were actually scotched. Nevertheless, Roosevelt knew how to make the hunt seem genuine, and even perilous, and so he had the mob with him so long as he kept his health.

It must be plain that, even among professional politicians of the first eminence, skill of so high an order is rather rare. Most of them fail quite as often as they succeed; in fact, half of them have to fail every time in order that the other half may win. In this struggle that practitioner goes farthest whose victories outnumber his defeats—that is, whose skill is measurably above the general.

How does he acquire such skill? As things stand, he must either be born with it or get it by the costly method of trial and error. What I contend is that, assuming him to be literate, he would be helped vastly by a sensible textbook upon the fundamental principles of his art. Such books, I believe, have helped salesmen; their use has greatly increased the sales of automobiles, 8 per cent bonds, and endowment insurance. A good one would help politicians, too.

No actual politician, of course, could write it. Politics is pussyfooting; the adept guards its secrets jealously. But there is no reason why the job should not be done by an intelligent psychologist. The materials are surely not esoteric. They are spread through all the political biographies of the times; they are on the public records; they are in the files of newspapers. What is needed is simply a scientific analysis of them, with a deduction of the underlying principles. A laborious job, and difficult, but far from impossible.

I incline to think that those underlying principles, when they are unearthed at last, will turn out to be few and simple. In other words, the most successful politician, taking one year with another, is the one who sticks most faithfully to a few well tried tricks. What worked last year will work again today, and yet again tomorrow. The worst disasters of politics are due to ventures outside the narrow circle. The ambitious politician, made imprudent by success, decides to be original. At the next ensuing plebiscite he is retired to the icehouse.

Only too often, I believe, that originality takes the form of overestimating the intelligence of the rabble. Soon or late almost every politician above the city boss level decides to make a bold appeal to the enlightenment of his lieges. It is a dreadful error, and not infrequently it is fatal. The beaches of politics, in fact, are strewn with the corpses of such logicians. They pass out under great suspicion. They have addled the public mind, and so caused public pain. The whisper goes around that they are radicals. Any idea, to the mob, is radical.

The professionals lower down never make such mistakes, and in consequence their season lasts far longer. The average city boss survives twenty mayors, a dozen governors, and six or eight Presidents. Why? Simply because he sticks to the tried and true stuff. His appeal is never to the imaginary intelligence of his customers; it is to their immemorial weaknesses. He plays upon their cupidity, their vanity, their ignorance—above all, upon their fears. He knows that uneasiness is their dominant mood—that the struggle for existence, even at best, falls just short of being too much for them. His trade is that of reassuring them. He makes life easier for them—or makes them believe that he has made it easier. He is safe so long as they cling to that pathetic delusion.

But here I begin to write the textbook aforesaid—and my unfitness for the task is only too apparent. I call upon some more competent professor to undertake it. It will be useful to the innumerable young men who aspire to service at the public trough—and it will offer an instructive and appalling picture of democracy in action.

(*October 18, 1925*)

VIVE LE ROI!

CONFIDENTIALLY I am no admirer of the Hon. Mr. Coolidge, twenty-ninth President of the United States, and if the news came tomorrow that he had resolved to retire in 1929 in order to become the vaudeville or radio czar or to take a stool in the office of J. P. Morgan & Co. I'd certainly not set up any blubbering. But candor compels me to say that some of his critics and opponents, especially within the bounds of his own party, fatigue me excessively. And they fatigue me particularly when they argue that his reëlection next year would amount to giving him a third term, and that he is under an obligation of duty and honor to refuse it.

This doctrine is pure nonsense. There is no such obligation either in law or in the punctilio. Its only rational basis lies in the fact that George Washington, having suffered two terms in the Swampshurst bungalow that then passed as a White House, declined a third. But what went on in Washington's time is surely no safe guide to what ought to be done today. Washington was a wine-bibber and ran a still. Washington, when he observed a pretty girl, gave public notice of the fact by manipulating his right eyebrow. Washington kept slaves. Washington was an officer and a gentleman.

Alive today, he would probably be in jail. In jail or not he'd certainly not be in the White House. No man of the class to which he belonged has inhabited that gloomy mansion since March 4, 1829, and there is no more chance that another will get there hereafter than there is that a blackamoor will get there. For weal or for woe, we have made men of his peculiar sort ineligible for the job, and with their physical presence, it seems to me, there has gone all need to respect their pruderies. To follow them part of the way and then shrink back would plainly be absurd. To follow them all the way would be to shock beyond endurance a populace that is convinced, if it is convinced of nothing else, that the habits of mind and life of gentlemen are somehow scandalous and dangerous.

It is easy enough in the present case to conjure up images of men who, in this way or that, would surpass Dr. Coolidge as First Chief of the Republic. As a matter of fact, such men exist in the flesh and a number of them aspire to the office. At least two of them are noticeably more handsome than Dr. Coolidge and several are probably wiser, at all events, in book learning. But these men have no more chance to beat him than I have to beat Gene Tunney. They are far too frank and honest; there is too much reasonable suspicion that, like Washington, they are gentlemen. If he is beaten at all it will have to be by a mountebank—by one who is both wet and dry, for the Interests and against them, a friend of the farmer who can yet carry the First assembly district of New York. In other words, it will have to be by one who is four times as bad as Dr. Coolidge, even estimating him at his worst.

Such men are not rare among us. The senate swarms with them, and all of them are willing. They govern most of our states. But I see no sound reason for accelerating the inevitable course of nature by shoving one of them into the White House in 1929. The gentleman there now, whatever his deficiencies, is at least endurable. He has carried himself in a respectable and decorous manner. He has avoided the carnalities that disgraced the country in Washington's day. Having avoided them, it seems to me that he is under no duty to regard the superstitions that went with them. If he wants a third term, and can get it, he will have as good title to it as Washington had to his distillery and his slaves.

As for me, I herewith withdraw in his favor and nominate him for a fourth term in 1932. Going further, I nominate him for a fifth term in 1936, and a sixth in 1940. In his last year he will be 68 years old. Well, Washington was 65 at the end of his second term and Jackson was 69. Taylor, had he lived, would have been 68, and the first Harrison would have been 72. The average span of life in Vermont is 114 years and men are on record who have held office there continuously for 95 years. In 1940 Dr. Coolidge will be merging into the prime of his manhood. Not until 1960 will he begin to age visibly.

This article is designed for printing in various far-flung states, some of which have extraordinarily harsh laws. For example, California, where it is now a felony to imagine a change in the constitution. I therefore refrain, on the advice of counsel, from proposing that the Hon. Mr. Coolidge be made king, but if it were certainly lawful I'd probably do it.

After all, why not? The prejudice against kings is as absurd
and archaic as the old prejudice against exposing the female
patella. Seven years ago every educated American was full
of fears of synthetic gin; today even the judiciary guzzle it.
I think we'd get used to a king just as quickly.

As a matter of fact, the instincts of the human race run
in favor of monarchy, and they always have. Our own history is full of proofs of it. In 1787, when the constitution
was being formulated, a considerable number of the delegates were in favor of setting up a king instead of a President, and in 1789, when Washington began his first term,
the movement was formally revived. For many days the
First congress debated a motion to give him the title of his
highness—an obvious attempt to insert the opening wedge—
and that motion came very near being carried. In 1797, as
every one knows, there was a widespread demand that
Washington accept a third term, and behind it was a plain
hope that he would also proceed to a fourth and a fifth.
Jackson faced the same demand in 1836, and Lincoln, had
he lived, would have faced it in 1868.

More, there has always been a visible tendency to make
the presidency hereditary. John Adams' son, John Quincy,
was elected in 1824, and William Henry Harrison's grandson, Benjamin, in 1888. Lincoln's son, Robert, was a formidable candidate in two campaigns. Grant's son, Fred, was
mentioned more than once, and so was Garfield's son,
Jimmy. The son of Roosevelt, Teddy Jr., has been a candidate since the age of 11 and will undoubtedly make a noise
hereafter. He is still under 40 and will not be 60 until 1947.

It must be plain from this that a President's son or
grandson runs an enormously greater chance of becoming

President himself than any other man. There were at least 3,000,000 eligible adult males in 1824, when John Quincy Adams was elected. He beat them all at odds of 3,000,000 to 1. There were nearly 15,000,000 in 1888, when Benjamin Harrison was elected. In 1908, when Jimmy Garfield was talked of, not more than 100 other men were talked of— 100 out of nearly 20,000,000. His advantage over the average man was thus as 200,000 is to 1. Today the active candidates include the 96 members of the senate, the 48 state governors, and perhaps 50 others—say 200 in all. Young Teddy is among the 50. His advantage over the other 25,000,000 eligibles (disregarding women completely) is thus as 125,000 is to 1.

What the science of mathematics thus unearths is simply an ancient human instinct, too powerful to be upset by democratic rhetoric. Theoretically implacable enemies of the monarchical idea, the American people actually favor the crown prince by odds running from 125,000 to 3,000,-000 to 1. Is this instinct unsound? Not at all. John Quincy Adams made a very fair President, and so did Benjamin Harrison. Jimmy Garfield in 1908 would have been no worse than Dr. Taft, and Teddy Jr., had he succeeded to the purple on his father's death, would have been quite as good, in all probability, as the sainted Dr. Harding. Robert Lincoln for many years was chief counsel to the Pullman company and then its president. Was the Pullman company during those years run worse or better than the United States?

I am informed by an insurance actuary that Dr. Coolidge's chances of life, as a Vermont politician, are 41 years, three months, and five days. This will bring him to the year 1968, or the end of his twelfth term. Young John, in 1968, will be just short of 60 years old—the precise beginning of a Vermonter's mellow middle years. He is a young man of diligent habits and good taste. Ascending the throne in the course of nature, he would have 47 years of intensive training behind him. Try to compare him to Bryan at 36, fresh from the steppes—or to McAdoo at 64!

(*June 19, 1927*)

VI. EDUCATION, PHILOLOGY

As a recognized and respected student of the American language and its origins, Mencken was unique.

He had no degrees, not even university training of any sort. In writing The American Language and its supplements he departed widely from scholarly traditions by employing a racy style not unmixed with a little humor.

The resulting readability of his massive academic chore stands out like a champagne glass in a boiler factory when it is compared with other ponderous literature on the subject.

Mencken's interest in philology provides yet one more contradiction in a complex character. He thought pedagogues were bores, constantly assailed them, and all the while was exerting major efforts in what is certainly an esoteric field of academic endeavor.

Besides tracing the origins of American speech, Mencken further served the language by adding to it when its stock seemed to him inadequate.

He coined "smuthound" for censor, a word superbly suited for expectoration.

The word "wowser" he imported from Australia to de-

*scribe a kill-joy. Pronounced slowly, it does seem an excel-
lent example of onomatopoeia, embalming in a few gloomy
sounds the gray fervor of one "too niggardly of joy to allow
the other fellow time to do anything but pray."*

THE PEDAGOGUE'S UTOPIA

THE HISTORIANS of the future will probably tell their customers that in the second decade of the twentieth century
the *furor pedagogicus* reached its climax in the United
States and then began to decline. The very worst manifestations of that frenzy, I daresay, are still ahead of us, though
maybe not far off. Half the towns and villages of the country are going bankrupt building new public schools, and the
endowments of the great rolling mills of the so-called higher
learning are increasing steadily and immensely. What the
total annual cost of education has come to among us I don't
know precisely, and neither does any one else, for there are
large expenses that do not enter into the official figures, but
certainly it must be colossal. It goes far beyond the annual
cost of the army and navy, or of the police, or of the
churches; perhaps it even surpasses the annual bootlegging
bill.

The schoolmaster, in the days of my nonage, was still
a lowly and modest fellow. He operated in a bare and forbidding room, his garb was that of an evangelist in hard
luck, and his sole professional equipment consisted of a box
of chalk and a rattan. The theory then was that he was a

Spiritual Force, and hence needed no elaborate paraphernalia. His prototype was a mangy philosopher sitting on a log and passing the hat at the end of his lecture. But now he works in palaces that cover whole blocks and are fitted up with all the voluptuous lavishness of movie parlors. The average schoolhouse in America used to cost $300. Now it costs $500,000, and it will cost $1,000,000 tomorrow.

Meanwhile the schoolmaster himself has gone up the ladder. His emolument was once that of a diligent book-keeper or drug clerk; it is now that of a trust company vice president. His sister, the schoolma'm, used to get $15 a month and her board and lodging; her loftiest dream was to buy one good store dress a year and catch a husband in it. But now she goes to work in such gauds as Solomon's wives might have envied and her pay and allowances approximate those of a chorus girl.

Educational theory has kept pace with educational equipment and honoraria. Down to the end of the nineteenth century, at least in America, it was very simple, and even austere. The notion was that any one who knew anything could teach it, and that the better he knew it—and especially the better he loved it—the better he could teach it. The candidate for the birch had no need to perfect himself in the higher branches of human knowledge; if he could spell accurately and parse with fluency, and bound Afghanistan without hesitation, he was considered fit for his office.

But now even the most modest and obscure of schoolma'ms must take on such a load of intellectual baggage as would have bent the back of Sir Issac Newton. In order to insert even the elements of the new enlightenment into the cerebrums of her pupils she must be hep to all the secrets of psychology—a difficult subject at best, and, since Dr. Freud

horned into it, often vaguely pornographic. Her mathematical gifts in the old days were considered sufficient if she had
mastered the rule of three, but now even the differential
calculus is scarcely enough to get her through her maze of
graphs, curves, and statistical questionnaires. She must
know faunal biology and parliamentary law. She must be an
ethnologist, a psychiatrist, and an expert in criminal jurisprudence.

Her purely technical equipment has kept pace with the
improvement in her general culture. The pedagogical journals used to be full of pleasant poetry and edifying fairy
tales; they are now so heavy with scientific jargon that no
layman can hope to read them at all. All the operations of
teaching have been reduced to complicated mathematical
formulæ, full of Greek letters, modululi, derivatives, anti-
derivatives, infinitesimals, and solidi. Grammar is translated
into curves, sinuous and mysterious. The flag drill becomes
an equation, bristling with x's, ='s, and oo's.

Such is human progress in these last, gaudy, sunset days
of *Homo sapiens*. The lowly pedagogue, once a drudge on
the level of a milkman or a church organist, is now lifted to
professional parity with an orchestral conductor, a horse
doctor, or an osteopath. His trade, once so simple, has become occult, and as it has become occult it has naturally increased in dignity. It was formerly regarded as so easy that
any literate person could practice it, just as any literate person could run a newspaper. But now it is so recondite that
it lies wholly beyond the ken of the general, and even the
pedagogues themselves, to judge by their professional papers, seem to be convinced that at least two-thirds of their
number are unfit to pursue it.

Well, what is the net result of all this improvement? Is

pedagogy, as it is now encountered in the republic, any more efficient than it was a generation ago, before graphs and formulæ lifted it from a trade to a science? The pedagogues, I daresay, will instantly answer yes, and in proof thereof they will point to many impressive facts. Many a child of 10, whose father, at the same age, was scarcely able to bound Rhode Island, is now an expert in solfeggio and competent to act as chairman of a massmeeting. The little girls whose mothers ran aground upon long division know all about calories and vitamins. Their brothers have learned the principles of rotary and how to tie knots. All alike have mastered the hardest words in the tabloids.

But what of their general sense and information? What of their basic fitness to live in the world? Has it improved or has it not improved? I doubt that many fair observers would answer that it has. The new pedagogy has crammed the poor kids with showy knowledge, but it has plainly failed to make them any better as human beings than their fathers. At the high tide of its golden age, and in the country of its loftiest triumphs, the net product of all its sorceries is a proletariat distinguished mainly for its credulity, its fear of ideas, and its inability to think, and made up of individuals who tend to be as alike as peas in a can.

Here perhaps we have asked too much of the pedagogues. But what has been asked of them is surely no greater than what they have offered. The excuse for the immense expenditures that they demand is that, by some mysterious magic, they can turn the populace into something that it is not—that is, that they can turn sows' ears into purses. But can they really? All the evidence seems to show that they cannot. The American people, taking them in the mass, reveal not the slightest sign of growing more intelligent than they used to be. On the contrary, they reveal every sign of growing dumber and dumber as year chases year.

The public schools, in truth, have probably helped along that process a great deal more than they have hindered it. There was a time when, encountering a pupil whose capacity for taking in knowledge was obviously nil, they turned him out at once and let him go to work on an ash cart. But now they hold him and struggle with him, and the result is disastrous to the whole educational scheme. It is not that pupils of actual intelligence are held back to accommodate the dolts—for that difficulty is being surmounted—but that the struggle with the dolts consumes a large part of the energy of the general machine, and that its hopelessness promotes the concoction of high sounding but meaningless formulæ, fatal to all honest grappling with the problems of teaching.

These formulæ naturally tend to proceed from the lower strata to the higher. That which conceals the inevitable failure of pedagogy when it deals with morons is also useful in giving it a false profundity when it deals with children who are not morons. Here, perhaps, are the origins of the dreadful hocus-pocus which now fills all the pedagogical journals and textbooks. The old arm of the schoolma'm, so simple and so effective, has become transformed into a complicated and largely unintelligible necromancy, at which quacks are more apt and plausible than honest men. The first result is a vast and idiotic dissipation of the public funds. The second is the complete failure of the process to give help to those children who most need it and can best make use of it.

(May 1, 1927)

ON GOING TO COLLEGE

Up to a few years ago there was nothing more generally believed in the United States than that education, and especially education of the so-called higher variety, was a valuable thing, and worth any sacrifice of time or money. The notion had emanated, originally, from the Puritans of New England, who cherished it as they cherished their romantic belief in a hot and eternal hell. With the passage of the years it had permeated the whole country, and only a few forlorn iconoclasts challenged it. The study of books, it appeared, could transform any plowboy into a Lincoln, and, what was even more wonderful and alluring, into a successful dealer in high grade investment securities. After the late war, with money flowing freely, all the yokels of the land began sending their progeny to college.

The result was a great congestion in the halls of learning, and that congestion still continues. In some of the state universities there are so many students that merely keeping track of them enlists the services of whole hordes of bookkeepers, top sergeants, policemen, and adding machines. They cram the classrooms to suffocation, make the adjacent bootleggers rich, and drive the sweating professors frantic. There are not enough competent teachers in the country to handle them, and so a great many unprepared aspirants have had to be called in to help. These aspirants, I daresay, do the best they can, but certainly it is not much. While they are learning their trade, their pupils are learning nothing.

Some of the latter, more earnest than the average, now begin to protest. They complain that their time is wasted by pedagogical ignoramuses. In some colleges they publish stenographic reports of the lectures they are forced to listen to, seeking to show the world what bilge is in them. In others they denounce the faculty in their campus papers, and so get themselves expelled. Everywhere there seems to be a rising doubt about the efficacy and utility of the educational process. Every time I refer to pedagogues in this place I receive scores of letters from students, describing the imbecilities that oppress them, and fishing for support for their apparent theory that it would be wiser to quit college at once and go to work.

This theory, unfortunately, I find myself unable to support. For, despite the rise of skepticism on the subject, the theory that a college education is a valuable thing is still very widely held in America, and so long as it prevails the sagacious youngster will bend it to his uses. It may not be true, but that is no argument against it. The important thing is that it is believed. So long as it is believed the young man or woman who has been through college will have an advantage among us, and though that advantage may not run beyond the first few hurdles of life, it will remain of the utmost value there.

Nor is this belief entirely illusory. A college course, at worst, offers all the charms and benefits of a Wanderjahr: it is a sort of grand tour, and hence illuminating. The learned professors that the student encounters may be, in the great majority of cases, merely jackasses, but they at least differ from his father; they at least make him privy to notions and points of view that he has not encountered at home. He may not grasp those new points of view, or, grasping them, he may reject them, but at all events he has heard of them. Certain fragments of novel ideas will linger in his consciousness. He will never be again quite the innocent that his father is.

In this process his fellow students will often play a more important part than his professors, most of whom, perhaps, he will never apprehend save as vague shapes. Regimentation has gone far in the American college, but it can never go all the way. The campus bolshevik survives almost undimmed from Emerson's day. Is he quickly detected and expelled? Then it is not until he has spread his poisons— not until he has awakened hundreds of his fellows to the charm of heretical ideas and to the joys of passing them on. They go home, perhaps, resolved that the ancient faiths are safer and even better, but they go home somewhat changed. Even George F. Babbitt, with four years of college behind him, was never the complete Babbitt. In the midst of his gaudy certainties he had his interludes of doubt.

But the boys who now have doubts about college are not potential Babbitts: they are youngsters of more active and eager mind. Observing quickly that the great majority of their instructors are poor drudges who know little that is worth knowing and have small capacity to impart that little lucidly, and that at least nine-tenths of their campus brethren are numskulls doomed to be engulfed swiftly by Rotary, the Shrine, and the Klan—observing this, they often conclude that it would be far better to depart at once for Wall street, the coal regions, Park Row, or Hollywood.

Here, too, it seems to me, there is error. It lies in the assumption that what college has to teach all comes out of books, or may be imparted by instructors. This is not true. What college has to teach, in the main, is simply familiarity with the notions and habits of that vast and mysterious organism known as human society. The world that the student comes into is measurably larger than any world he has hitherto known, and for more complex. It is not quite the still larger world that he will enter later on, but it is nevertheless a great deal like it. It has its rulers and its ruled, its drudges and its men of privilege, its sharp fellows and its dummies. Is it, basically, a fraud? Then so is the world that encompasses it.

The discovery of the fraudulence, I believe, is one of the principal aims and achievements of true education, if not the first of them all. A man soundly fitted for life is not one who believes what he is told, as a schoolboy believes, but one trained in differentiating between the true and the false, and especially one trained in weighing and estimating authority. If the young man at college learns nothing else save the fact that many of the bigwigs of the college world are charlatans, and that position and attainments do not necessarily go together, then he has learned something of the utmost value. The tragedy of the world is that the great majority of human beings never learn it. If going to college can teach it, if only by the method of the horrible example, then going to college is worth while.

I believe that it is being taught in the American colleges today, and on an unprecedented scale. Swamped by hordes of unteachable students, with their faculties overworked and what they call their plants strained to the uttermost, they have been forced to throw their old standards overboard, and to take in all sorts of pedagogical amateurs and quacks. These quacks now essay to instruct the young of the land. What they try to teach is not learned and maybe is not worth learning, but what they are themselves is detected and remembered, and in that remembrance there are the rudiments, at least, of true education.

Moreover, they accomplish something else: they throw up in a brilliant light the merits of those of their colleagues who are genuinely men of learning. In the average American college, perhaps, there are not many of the latter, but in even the meanest college there are apt to be a few. The influence of such men upon the students is immensely salubrious and valuable. They make it plain to even the dullest that there are ends in this world quite as alluring as material success—that men of high character may and do pursue them, and gladly. They are standing answers to the whole rumble-bumble of American Babbittry.

If a boy emerges from college with an understanding of that point of view, so rare in America, and with a soundly cynical attitude toward the pretensions that fill the world with noise and confusion, he has gained quite enough, it seems to me, to compensate him for four years of his life. His increase in positive knowledge may not be great, but it is very likely to be great enough: two-thirds of the things that are taught in college, even when they are well taught, are not worth knowing. The main thing is to learn the difference between appearances and realities. That may be done, of course, anywhere, but it is probably best done, at least in the case of the average boy, in some institution which represents the world as little, and in which the experience of man on earth is fairly boiled down.

(October 9, 1927)

WHY THE SCIENCE of philology should be backward in the United States I don't know, but backward it is. We have produced very few philologians of any authority in any part of the field, and in the special area of the national speech we have produced almost none. The best existing grammars of English are not by Americans, but by Europeans: perhaps the best of them all is by a Dane. There is no native etymologist even remotely comparable to Ernest Weekly, the Englishman, and no writer on current usage to be mentioned in the same breath with H. W. Fowler. In the department of phonetics there is but one American book of value, and that one leans heavily upon the work of Daniel Jones, of the University of London.

There was a time when this inferiority was considerably less marked—when an American school of philology seemed to be getting upon its legs. But that was nearly three-quarters of a century ago, just as George P. Marsh and William Dwight Whitney returned from Europe, their veins running with enthusiasm for *Sprachwissenschaft*. Whitney, who survived until 1894, was the father of all the American philologians who now exist; the fact that they do him little credit cannot be laid at his door, for he labored magnificently and was always eager to help younger men. But his work won him many honors abroad, and he was given the Prussian order *Pour le Mérite* in succession to Carlyle. But he left no successors behind him.

Marsh was considerably less learned, but he did a great deal of invaluable pioneering. His *Lectures on the English Language*, first published in 1861, antedated Whitney's *Language and the Study of Language* and cleaned off much of the rubbish left by Noah Webster's ignorant speculations. He would have gone further had he not dispersed his energies over too wide a space: he was politician and diplomat as well as philologist.

In most departments of English in the American universities there are no philologists at all, but only dull drudges who devote themselves idiotically to hunting for typographical errors in the early editions of Chaucer or writing school texts. These drudges are responsible for the current theory that the rules of a living language are to be formulated by calling conferences of pedagogues, none of whom knows how to write. They belabor the poor boys and girls in the public schools with the nonsensical doctrine that *ain't* is an evil word, and with distinctions between *will* and *shall* that disappeared from the speech of the United States generations ago. The material that pours into their ears every day makes no impression upon them. They are simply too stupid to apprehend it.

Whole years go by without these pontifical dullards producing a single book, or even paper, of any interest or value upon the language that 110,000,000 people speak. If you doubt it go look through the files of the trade journals they write for, say, *Modern Language Notes*. Two or three years ago, in the hope of opening the way for a scientific and useful discussion of the living American tongue, Dr. Louise Pound, of the University of Nebraska, set up a monthly journal called *American Speech*. But the philologues have contributed little to it that has been worth reading. Their total contribution, indeed, would scarcely make one respectable article. The best philology visible in the journal has come from a Catholic priest and the best writing from a poet.

Two or three years ago announcement was made that a grand dictionary of American English was projected, with headquarters in Chicago. The question naturally arose where the projectors would find a native American competent to edit it. They presently answered that question very frankly by announcing the appointment of Dr. W. A. Craigie of Oxford. He came here, viewed the field, and was presently reported to be back in England. There he is now, apparently looking for help.

This scarcity of competent philologians in the United States becomes all the more remarkable when one remembers that the country fairly swarms with teachers of English, and that all of them are supposed to be grounded in the science of language. There are so many of them that they have a national organization almost comparable to the Elks or Knights of Columbus, and they hold formidable annual palavers, and promote what they call a Better Speech Week. All among them who are Ph.D's—and whole brigades and corps of them are—have studied Early English, Middle English, and Modern English, and are supposed to know at least the elements of comparative philology. But it is only once in a blue moon that any of them ever publishes anything above the level of a paper fit for reading before a women's club.

The books turned out by these vapid pedants are dreadful, indeed. You will search them for days without finding anything properly describable as an idea, and when you encounter one at last you will almost invariably discover that it is nonsensical. I have at various times reviewed such books in the public prints, and given extracts from them and summaries of their contents. Every time I have done so readers have written in to accuse me of inventing the rubbish I have printed. It seems incredible that men capable of such blowsy pedantries should hold important chairs in American colleges of any pretensions, but it remains a fact. Some of the worst of them are really very doggy, and now and then favor the general public with specimens of their learning. It always turns out to be identical with the learning issuing from country schoolma'ms.

In other languages the American showing is rather better, though in no department of philology does this country hold a place comparable to that of Germany, France, or England. But in the department of English there is almost a vacuum. The materials that lie under every philologue's nose are not being studied or even collected, and in order to get a dictionary of American English launched it has been necessary to import an expert from England.

So far I have been speaking of the philological side of the English faculty—that is, of those learned men who concern themselves with the English language rather than with English literature. Those who pursue the latter subject show rather more competence: they turn out, now and then, works as sound as Prof. John Livingston Lowes' *Convention and Revolt in Poetry*, or Prof. W. L. Cross' *Life of Laurence Sterne*. But even in this field the American *Gelehrte* are mainly of very low intellectual visibility. Nine-tenths of them spend their whole lives editing trashy school-texts, and trying to convince generations of helpless students that Washington Irving was a great writer and that James Branch Cabell is a bad one.

They were unanimously convinced, half a century ago, that Walt Whitman was a fraud, and so taught their victims. A bit later they ranked Mark Twain with Artemus Ward and Petroleum V. Nasby. When Frank Norris appeared they missed him, and soon afterward they missed Dreiser. Today they continue gloriously in their traditional imbecility. Only a short while ago a professor of English at one of the leading American universities was warning his customers that *The Spoon River Anthology* was not poetry —including, I assume, even "Ann Rutledge"! His colleagues in the other rolling mills devote themselves mainly to intensive studies of Crashaw's prosody and the sources of the lesser Elizabethan dramatists. The literature that is in being is beneath their notice.

It must cost a great deal of money to support these learned donkeys, for there are thousands of them, and the notion that American pedagogues are badly paid is full of folly, for they actually get a great deal more than men of comparable intelligence derive from other trades. Moreover, their work is light, they have long vacations, and they are pensioned when they become senile. Yet more, there is money to be made out of the ghastly text-books that they turn out so copiously. Whatever the annual cost, it is money wasted. Not one American college student out of ten, going through his four years, gets any sounder or more useful view of the national letters than he could get by reading the *War-Cry*. What he learns is not much, and that little is mainly not so. Next to the professors of "education," who are in a separate and fantastic class and really belong almost to fable, the professors of English are probably the worst incompetents in the whole academic gang.

(September 4, 1927)

BABEL

NOTHING more beautifully displays the imbecility of *Homo sapiens* than the diversity of his tongues. All dogs understand one another easily and at sight; a chow and a St. Bernard, meeting for the first time, fall into amicable discourse instantly, though one may have been born in Nanking and the other at Zermatt. It is the same with cats, horses, cows, bullfrogs, and ants, and even with human beings after death, as the news sent back from the spirit world by the late Valentino attests. But on the earthly plane men cling to their discordant and preposterous dialects, and so view one another with doubt and suspicion and work up hatreds and engage in wars.

It is almost impossible to get rid of the uneasiness that a strange language engenders. The man speaking it inevitably seems somewhat uncouth and idiotic, and there is a facile transition from the uncouth to the inimical. If Sacco and Vanzetti had been able to speak English fluently and correctly at the time of their trial the chances are very good that the jury would have laughed at some of the nonsensical "evidence" brought against them. They might, indeed, have been acquitted. But their woppish gargling was against them, and so they got short shrift. Now, having improved their seven years behind the bars by perfecting their English, they are treated far more politely and thousands are for them who were formerly against them.

No counter interest seems to be strong enough to neutralize this deep seated and almost instinctive linguistic hostility. The entente cordiale blew up on Flanders fields, with English and French soldiers ducking the same shells and jawing at one another hopelessly. The English went home convinced that the French were chimpanzees; the French said good-bye to them convinced that they were gorillas. The American conscripts came home disliking both, for the English of the English was almost as unintelligible to them as the French of the French.

What it costs the human race in hard cash to jabber in so many different tongues is hard to figure out: it must run to billions of dollars a year. At regular intervals an optimist arises with a new and easy artificial language and proposes that every one learn it at once, and so put an end to the loss. But these schemes never take hold. A few enthusiasts are converted, and presently it is announced that a bright girl in Palermo or Cape Town, having learned Volapük or Esperanto in four lessons, is corresponding actively with a young man in Buenos Aires or Seattle who learned it in two. But that is as far as the thing ever goes. In a few years the new universal language is forgotten and another has taken its place.

Other optimists from time to time announce that English (it used to be Russian) is making fast progress in all directions, and that in fifty or a hundred years everybody on earth will speak it, and the other languages will be abandoned. But that is immensely improbable. The fact is that English is nowhere displacing any other language. Here and there it is coming in as a second language, but nowhere is it going any further. Even the Dutch in South Africa cling to the Taal, despite the union, just as the Canucks in Canada cling to their bad French and the Filipinos remain faithful to Spanish. All these people learn English after a fashion, but they seldom if ever think in it. Thus a man who speaks it as his native tongue remains a foreigner to them, and they dislike him.

The progress of English is mainly along the world's trade routes. It becomes the universal language of commerce. But such languages of commerce have arisen in the past and then disappeared. They never displace the truly national language. Even Latin could not do it. It fastened itself upon the people of France and Spain only at the cost of becoming unintelligible to genuine Romans, and this corruption had such repercussions at home that it eventually ceased to exist as a living language. The Germanic dialects, farther north, beat it casily and completely.

The fact is that we are probably further from a universal language today than we have been since the dawn of the middle ages and that we are moving away from it instead of toward it. The revival of nationalism is everywhere working in that direction. Fifteen years ago every literate Czech transacted most of his business in German; now his children are studying Czech. The Walloons refuse to learn French and talk grandly of separating themselves from Belgium. The Norwegians revive an ancient peasant dialect and so strive to make themselves unintelligible to the Danes. The more visionary Irish plan to stamp out English in their country and return to Gaelic. And gabble of the same sort is heard from the Slovenes, the Finns, the Letts, the Basques, the Egyptians, and even the Corsicans.

Moreover, there is an obvious tendency for most of the more important languages of the world to split into dialects, especially English and Spanish. The Spanish spoken in Mexico, for example, now differs very considerably from the Spanish of Spain—to such an extent, indeed, that Spaniards find it very hard to understand. Its relation to correct Castilian is very much like the relation of the dialect spoken by the Appalachian mountaineers to the correct English of

London. On the one hand, it is full of archaisms, long abandoned in Spain, and on the other hand it bristles with neologisms, mainly borrowed from the Indian languages or from the English.

All the other countries of Latin-America have developed their own dialects, and the differences between them are in some cases very extensive. English has influenced all of them, especially in the matter of vocabulary, but most of their loan-words have come out of the Indian languages, which differ greatly from place to place. Most of these dialects show grammatical decay. In some of them the three conjugations of standard Castilian are reduced to two; in others some of the letters of the alphabet have changed their sounds. The educated people of Latin-America are all taught standard Castilian, but they speak it as seldom as educated Americans speak standard English.

English itself seems to be breaking into dialects, despite the heroic effort of purists to preserve its unity. This effort in the United States is largely inspired by a puerile Anglomania; it is very prevalent among university pedagogues with their eyes on Oxford degrees. On the lower levels it takes the form of an active propaganda for certain British affectations—for example, the pronunciation of *either* as *eye-ther*. This, in fact, is bad English as well as bad American. Historically the word is *ee-ther*, not *eye-ther*.

But in spite of all such bubblings and upwashings of the colonial spirit, American moves away from standard English very steadily, both in vocabulary and in pronunciation, and most English philologians make no effort to deny the plain fact. Some time ago one of the most intelligent of them, Mr. H. E. Palmer, linguistic adviser to the Japanese government, prepared a dictionary of English pronunciation for the use of Japanese students. In a vocabulary of 9,645 words he noted nearly 3,000 that were differently pronounced in England and American. And these were all ordinary words: he did not include any slang, or, indeed, any other neologisms.

This tendency to variation, as I say, is resisted stoutly by the birchmen told off to police the speech of sophomores, but it continues nevertheless, and at any moment some accident of international politics may change resistance to it into yielding and even support. A war with England, which is certainly not impossible, would work a miracle upon these pedagogues. Overnight, with the espionage act hanging over them, they would discover elements of a deleterious and even revolting nature in standard English, and a few weeks would see them alert for every *eye-ther* and rushing to the Polizei with news of it. During the revolution there were American patriots who proposed seriously that English be abandoned altogether in America, and either Hebrew or Greek, both sacred languages, substituted. There will be no need to go that far next time, for American will be ready to hand.

(May 29, 1927)

THE EMPEROR OF DICTIONARIES

Spies in my pay at Oxford university send me news that preparations are under way there to celebrate the completion of that behemoth of all books, the Oxford English Dictionary. There will be military exercises, boxing matches between the dons, orations in Latin, Greek, English, and the Oxford dialect, yelling combats between the different colleges, and a series of medieval drinking bouts. The ceremonies will begin with discharges of artillery and end with displays of fireworks. In St. Stephen's house an embryo missionary will be butchered and boiled. The master of Magdalen will fiddle jigs. There will be barbecues in the yards of Brasenose and Corpus Christi.

In all this rejoicing there will be relief as well as exultation, for the Oxford dictionary has been hanging over Oxford for nearly fifty years. It has taken longer to write, in fact, than any other book ever heard of, at least in English, and has enlisted the time and labor of more men. Its beginning actually goes back to 1857, when the Philological society appointed a committee to collect words; since 1870 it has been actively in progress, first under the late Sir James Murray, then under Dr. Henry Bradly, then under Dr. William A. Craigie, and now under Mr. C. T. Onions. Just how many scholars have had a hand in it I don't know—probably thousands. A general appeal for help was made at the start, and contributions and suggestions have been pouring in ever since.

Now the end approaches. The great work is finished from A down to Unforeseeable, and parts of W and all of V, X, Y, and Z are almost complete. In a year, or two years, or maybe three—for things are not rushed at Oxford—the whole will be assembled in eleven immense volumes. And what volumes they will be! Each of the ten already issued weighs ten pounds and is as large as an old fashioned family Bible. There will be 15,000 pages in all, each of three columns—more than seven miles of text, 5,000,000 lines of type, 200,000,000 letters and figures, not counting punctuation marks!

The title page of the Oxford says that it is a "New English Dictionary on Historical Principles." This means that its chief function is to trace the history of English words. To this end all the written records of the language were ransacked and laid under tribute, from the earliest times—not only printed books, but also public records, manuscripts, and even private papers. Obviously, no single scholar, nor any workable combination of scholars, could do all the necessary reading. It was for that reason that an appeal was made for volunteer helpers. They responded by the thousand, and for years their contributions poured into Oxford from all parts of the world.

There these contributions were carefully arranged in alphabetical order, and each letter in succession was handed over to a competent scholar, with a large staff of etymologists, lexicographers, proofreaders, and other experts to aid him. Thus the collection was gradually organized. Under every word everything that could be found out about it was arranged—its first occurrence, its changes in form and meaning, its origin, its relations to similar words in other languages, its mutations in various dialects, the varying fashions in its spelling and pronunciation, its employment in compounds and derivatives. And every change, however slight, was illustrated by an example.

The result is somewhat forbiddingly visible in the treatment of very common words, for example—*so. So* has no less than fifteen columns in the dictionary—enough matter, almost, for a small book. It is traced back into the very abyss of time, and there are examples of its use in writing

that go back to the year 700 A.D. At least fifty different uses
of it are distinguished, and every one is supported by clear
examples. One feels that *so*, at the end, has been squeezed
completely dry—that absolutely nothing more remains to
be said about it, or thought about it.

Obviously, such a dictionary is not for ready reference.
The reader who consults it finds himself swamped in detail;
worse, he finds himself seduced into sitting down with it for
an hour's curious reading. He cannot consult it casually to
find out how this or that difficult word is spelt. If he looks
to it for guidance in pronunciation he is confused by its scientific impartiality—its failure to choose between authorities. And its etymologies, he will quickly discover, are full
of doubts and unresolved alternatives. In brief, it is a work
for scholars, not for general readers.

Nevertheless, it is a work of immense and inescapable
value, even to the general reader, and once it is finished no
library of any pretensions will be able to do without it. For
it fills all the gaps that are in every other dictionary, great or
small; it covers the whole range of the English language almost completely. The ordinary dictionary, confronted by alternatives, has to make some choice, and whenever it
chooses it opens the way for error. The Oxford simply presents the whole evidence and lets the reader choose for
himself. It is a colossal mine of information about words. It
gives everything that is worth knowing about them. And it
adds a great deal that is simply strange and curious.

The amount of labor that went into it is appalling to
contemplate. The material came in in a huge flood, inchoate
and often contradictory. It had to be sorted out, its contra-
dictions had to be compared and weighed, and the innumerable gaps in it had to be filled. Sometimes the editors

spent months searching out the meaning of some obscure and half forgotten word. Not infrequently all this diligence went for naught in the end: the problem had to be put down as insoluble. The business involved consultations with experts in a thousand far flung fields and a gigantic correspondence. And when, at last, the text of a volume was complete and it was put into type, there remained the staggering drudgery of the proofreading.

The work, as it stands, is almost miraculously accurate. I have plowed through it for hours without finding the ghost of an error. Nor have I encountered many omissions, save of purely American words. Here the fault lies, not with the editors, but with their American collaborators. Until a few years ago there was an idiotic notion among American philologians that the study of Americanisms was somehow low. No professor of any pretensions engaged in it; it was left to laymen, and they all lacked the equipment that it demanded.

When Thornton's dictionary of Americanisms came out, the editor of the Oxford laid it under tribute at once. But that was not until 1912, and the Oxford was already three-fourths done. In consequence, it remains lamentably weak in the American department. I search in vain, for example, for the word *bootlegger*. It has been in common use in the United States for at least fifty years, and of late it has got into the standard English of England. The London *Times* uses it regularly, and it will probably get into the next revision of the Book of Common Prayer. But it is not in the Oxford dictionary. It is not there because the American philologists who sent in contributions back in 1887, when the A–B volumes were under way, were too stupid to recognize a good word when they saw it.

Now the deficiency of the Oxford is to be remedied by the preparation of a dictionary of Americanisms, with Dr. William A. Craigie, editor of the N, Q, R, Si–Sq, U, and V sections of the Oxford, in charge of it. Dr. Craigie faces a formidable task. He himself, naturally enough, has no first hand knowledge of the American language; it will take him two or three years to make himself understood in it. And he will quickly find that most of the corn-fed philologians of the country know even less about it than they know about standard English.

(March 7, 1926)

VII. MISCELLANY

※

Here is the widely ranging critic casting a caustic eye on architecture, motion pictures, cooking, marriage, and the telephone habits of his associates.

Read now, the essay entitled "On Connubial Bliss" strikes a poignant note that the author never intended.

In 1930, subsequent to writing these pieces, Mencken married Sarah Powell Haardt, an accomplished and attractive young writer from Montgomery, Alabama.

It was the tragedy of his life when she died five years later.

THE AMERICAN SCENE

SOME TIME AGO, in the pursuit of my gloomy duties as an itinerant theologian, I made a journey covering ten states. Most of my traveling was done by day, and so I had a good chance to observe the landscape. Save for a few spots, none of them of any extent, it was unbrokenly lovely. In more than one place, indeed, it was genuinely entrancing. I saw beautiful mountains, I saw beautiful river valleys, and I saw even more beautiful plains. But nowhere in those ten states did I see a beautiful town. One and all, they were hideous.

Why should this be so? I'm sure I don't know. In all the countries of Europe, even Spain, the villages along the way are charming, but in the United States they are almost uniformly appalling. The only exceptions that I know of are in the older sections of the Atlantic seaboard, and especially in New England, Pennsylvania, and Maryland. Here, along the limestone belt, one occasionally encounters a village that is clean, substantial, dignified, and soothing. But not often. Pennsylvania, which has some of the most sightly small towns in the United States, also has some of the worst. Maryland, of late, has succumbed to improvement and becomes indistinguishable from Ohio or New Jersey. The whole of New England is in decay. There is nothing anywhere else.

Certainly poverty is not the cause of this depressing ugliness, for prosperity is widespread in America, and even the farming sections share it, despite the yowling of yokels yearning for *panem et circenses*. There are gaudy filling stations in every village in the country, and plenty of pretentious and expensive buildings. But the more pretentious they are, the uglier they are. They sit upon their lots absurdly. They are painted in the wrong colors. They show no feeling whatever for architectural form. And they commonly swear at their neighbors.

The cities of the United States, in recent years, show a vast improvement in this department. Most of them have still to discover the full virtues of architectural unity and coherence. Their tall buildings downtown grow more graceful year by year, and they show a new feeling for beauty in their residence sections. But the villages seem to grow worse and worse. When they attempt anything ambitious it is usually a warehouse made of concrete blocks—certainly the most horrible building material ever invented—or a bank building with a false Romanesque front. Their new dwelling houses are mainly bungalows—with pillars in front almost fit for the Parthenon. Everywhere is barbaric painting, and everywhere is cheapness and imitation.

In Europe, from Scandinavia to Sicily, the village churches are always graceful, and often they are very beautiful. I can recall no exception. But in America they are usually even worse than the dwelling houses and stores. On my brief journey I saw village churches in North Carolina, and again in Ohio and Indiana, that were downright staggering. They seemed to have been designed by the devil himself, and as a practical joke upon the Christians frequenting them. Half of them were raised idiotically on stilts, and practically all of them had grotesque and preposterous steeples, mainly of scantlings and clapboards. Not one in fifty showed decent surroundings suitable to a house of worship. The churchyards, indeed, were even worse than the churches.

Of late there has been some attempt to improve the country churches, especially in the south and middle west. The southern Baptists have a committee at work upon the problem, and it has had competent architects prepare some very charming designs, well within the means of a small town congregation. The Lutherans of the Missouri synod have undertaken the same reform in their territory, and no doubt other denominations have done likewise. But so far, I can only report sadly, there is little evidence of practical results. Traveling more than 2,000 miles through the heart of a rich and smiling country, I saw only half a dozen churches that did not suggest dog houses.

One reason why they are so bad, of course, is that there are too many of them. Very few European villages, even in the Catholic south, have more than one church. It represents the joint wealth and piety of the whole population, extending over generations, and so it is substantially built, and gets a certain grace and beauty out of its very solidity. But in the average American village there are three, four, and sometimes even six or eight churches put up by the warring sects, and all of them cheap and bad. These sects, trying vainly to outshine and exterminate one another, all remain poor. They rush into church building before they can afford it, and the usual result is simply one more libel upon God, with a debt hanging over it and no money to keep it decently painted.

The Catholics, to be sure, are free from that criticism. They never build a church until they are sure of the money to pay for it, and once it is consecrated it is commonly kept in good order. But in the main they seem to patronize very bad architects, for their churches are usually harsh in design and very ungraceful. Even in the big cities, in truth, the Catholic churches are seldom as beautiful as they ought to be, considering how much money is spent upon them. Large numbers of them are of gray granite—a stone which needs expert handling to avoid making it look like cast iron. That expert handling, I fear, is not often given to it.

But the Protestant churches are the worst, for they are the cheapest and look it. If they are made of stone, then it is the dullest, least vibrant stone that the vicinity affords; if they are of brick, then it is laid like the brick in a sewer manhole; if they are of wood it is badly sawn and worse painted. And always, or nearly always, there is a complete absence of taste in design. The European peasant seems unable to put up even a hog house without making it somehow graceful; his American descendant is apparently quite unable to build even a church without giving it something of the abominable clumsiness and sickliness of a tar paper house along the railroad track.

I offer no remedy for this unpleasant state of affairs, for I know of none. It might be improved, at least theoretically, by setting up authorities to control architecture, whether public or private, but I am cynical of all such authorities— and they do not seem to be needed in Europe. Will time educate and civilize the yokel and make an aesthete of him? I doubt it. Judging from present evidence, its influence actually runs in the other direction, for the oldest villages in America are the most beautiful—not only because age gives even a bad building a certain dignity, but also and more importantly because the early buildings were better than the modern ones. The whalers of New England coast towns and the Pennsylvania Dutch farmers of Pennsylvania seem to have been alike gifted with a faculty for design; their surviving churches and homes are all lovely. But their progeny build bungalows.

It is a pity, for the American landscape is almost uniformly beautiful. In very few parts of this immense country is there any natural ugliness. Even the pine woods along the south Atlantic seaboard and the monotonous reaches of the western prairie have their high qualities, and it is not surprising to hear that there are men and women who love them. The more broken country is everywhere of great beauty, from the hills and lakes of Maine to the last flutters of the Georgia highlands, and from the gorgeous Piedmont of Virginia to the cliffs that frown down upon the Pacific. Some time ago I spent a summer morning riding through the blue grass country of Kentucky. Where is there anything in Europe more lovely? In color as in contour it is almost perfect.

But its villages, like those of all other parts of the republic, are mainly hideous. They sprawl absurdly; their trees are badly planted; their houses leap out of the ground like flying fish; they show colors that nature would be ashamed of; they fade into outskirts that are not only frowzy but also filthy. A few seemly and winning towns are there, but not many—not a tenth as many as there ought to be. Such a landscape deserves the reverence of man as a beautiful woman deserves it. He ought to be ashamed of doing anything to mar it. But in the blue grass, as in the green grass, the American peasant flings himself barbarously upon it and tries his level damndest to make it revolting.
(August 28, 1927)

ON CONNUBIAL BLISS

THAT SOMETHING is wrong with the ancient estate of holy matrimony, so long in high esteem in the world, seems to be the unanimous view of all the self-constituted experts upon the subject, male and female, who now rage through the republic. My mail is filled with the fulminations of these professors, many of whom appear to believe that, because I happen to be a bachelor by the grace of God, I am also a contemner of connubial bliss, and even an advocate of free love, that dreadful wickedness. The females among them, I observe without surprise, mainly argue that the American wife and mother of today is a slave, and ought to be set free. The males, going counter to this revelation, argue that the husband and father is a slave, and ought to be set free.

Most of these evangelists, naturally enough, back up their projects with concrete legislation, and not a little of it is already before the great and good men who make our so-called laws. The bills thus proposed by the more savage sort of suffragettes, if they are ever enacted, will reduce the ancient lord and master of the family to a role both onerous and ignominious. Whenever his lady, after consultation with her familiars (chiefly, I take it, spinsters), decides to favor posterity, he will be summoned. His duty done, he will be dismissed. Meanwhile, his whole earnings will be hers, to dispose of as she pleases, and the child or children issuing from her condescension will be completely under her control.

The partisans of the male are no less revolutionary. As things stand, they argue, an American husband is already so far gone in slavery that he has scarcely any rights at all. While his marriage endures, his property, like his life, is at the mercy of his wife, and when she throws him out she is able, under our laws, to make off with nine-tenths of it in the form of alimony. They propose to get rid of this curse by abolishing alimony—or, at all events, by restricting its payment to ex-wives who are actually helpless and in need. The rest, they argue, can work, as their husbands must work. If there are children, they can help to support them. No other scheme, it appears, is equitable.

Unluckily, I find myself out of sympathy with most of these reformers, and especially with those of the suffragette wing. Where they run aground is in mistaking the nature of marriage. They seem to believe that it is a purely contractual relation, and that its terms, in consequence, may be changed like those of any other contractual relations—either by free bargaining, or by duress of law. It is, in fact, nothing of the sort. Marriage is not a contract; it is a way of life. Its essence, when it is sound, is a complete surrender of many of the natural rights of the individual. It is not comparable to buying an automobile or joining the Elks; it is comparable to entering a monastery or enlisting for war.

Most of the malaises that now afflict it among us are palpably due, it seems to me, to imprudment efforts to change its unescapable terms. Of such sort are all the dodges that sentimentality has put upon the law books of late years, each and every one of them designed to lighten the alleged burdens of the wife. Have they actually benefited wives? I doubt it. They have simply increased the number of rebellious and fugitive husbands. For they are all based upon the assumption that the husband dislikes his wife, and is trying to escape from her clutches. So long as that assumption is false they are supererogatory and insulting. And the moment it becomes true they are useless.

Here, as in other fields, legislation is mainly nonsense. Its basic theory seems to be that when a man is uncomfortable and trying to rid himself of the things that make him so, the way to cure him is to make him more uncomfortable. Human nature, I fear, does not really work in that manner. So long as a man loves his wife and children, there is no need of laws to make him support and cherish them: he will do it at any cost to himself. Contrariwise, when he hates the one and is indifferent to the other, no conceivable law can wring out of him the full measure, nor even a tenth measure, of the devotion that he owes to them.

The trouble with the divorce laws in most American states, it seems to me, is not that they facilitate the breakup of marriages, but that they make it difficult, and often almost impossible, to break up marriages completely. The average decree, far from resolving the matter, is simply the beginning of even worse raids and forays than those that have gone before. The wife has a claim on her husband's property—not infrequently a very vexatious and burdensome claim—and the husband continues to have a vested interest in his wife's conduct. Each can annoy the other, and three times out of four they do so. The worst hatreds that I have ever encountered in this world issued out of just such post-connubial combats.

Are they unavoidable? I don't think so. They could be avoided by abandoning half measures for whole ones—that is, by making every divorce complete and absolute, as an annulment is complete and absolute, with each party restored to the *status quo ante*, and neither, in consequence, with any claim on the other. But suppose the wife has no means of support? Then let her find one: women without husbands have to do it. If marriage has been simply her device for making a living, and nothing more, then let her marry again, just as a lady of joy, losing one client, seeks another. Certainly it is unfair to ask her husband to go on paying for services that he is no longer getting.

But the children? My belief is that their sufferings are far more poignant in moral statistics than they are in real life. In nine divorce cases out of ten, no children are heard of. When they exist, they have been grossly damaged already, and perhaps incurably. Their dispositions should not be beyond the talents of a judge of reasonable sense. In cases wherein neither of their parents volunteers to care for them, prudence will suggest sending them to some comfortable orphan asylum or reformatory, where they will at least encounter decenter adults than they have been living with.

My point is that the law, like the social reformer, is quite unable to introduce conditions and precautions into so ancient and instinctive an institution as marriage. It is, perhaps, essentially a banality, but it is a banality of the most powerful authority. If it is not swallowed whole, it had better not be swallowed at all. Every effort to attach reservations to its complete submergence of interests and personalities is bound to lead to disaster. If it is a true marriage, those reservations are irrelevant and impertinent. And if it is not, they can do nothing to preserve it against the natural forces that seek its destruction.

In this department the reformers are even more unwise than the lawmakers. They are forever suggesting modifications of what they call the marriage contract, to the end that neither party may be put under any duress by the desires of the other. But that is simply trying to convert marriage into something that it is not. In anything rationally describable as a true marriage, it must be obvious that each party is not only willing, but eager to yield to the desires of the other. That, indeed, is the essential basis of the relationship. It is not a mere exchange of bribes and concessions. It is a mutual renunciation, with mutual happiness as its end.

I am romantic enough to believe that this happiness is very often attained, though it is, at least in part, of such a character that it does not appeal very forcibly to my private tastes. But the happy wife is not that one who has driven a hard bargain with her husband, supported by laws that put him at her mercy; she is that one whose main desire is to be amiable and charming to him, and whose technique is sufficient to accomplish it. And the happy husband is not that one who has wrung from his wife a franchise to disport himself without regard to her peace and dignity, but that one whose devotion to her makes it impossible for him to imagine himself willingly wounding her. Such couples, perhaps, are not as numerous as they ought to be. It is hard for even a happy marriage to survive the insane laws and idiotic propaganda that now flourish.

(March 20, 1927)

DREAMS OF PEACE

MY MAIL is filled of late with the literature of the various societies devoted to the great cause of international peace. I read it attentively, but for some reason or other the impression it makes upon me is precisely like that made by the literature of the New Thought. No doubt that is because both sets of propagandists are obviously convinced that words are more powerful than facts. Facing the incurable, they seek to cure with the rhetorical. The peace fanatics, if anything, are more naïve and preposterous than the New Thoughters. The latter at least refrain from proposing that all doctors be hanged. The former advocate abolishing the army and navy, and trusting wholly to eloquence.

In detail, as in gross, their schemes are full of transparent and tedious puerility. For example, a large part of their persuasiveness is aimed at the clergy, and especially at the evangelical wing thereof. But it must be plain to every one that the clergy no longer make public opinion in America, save in a few backward areas of the south and middle west. Elsewhere they are tolerated, but certainly not heeded. It would be far more intelligent to try to fetch the vaudeville actors of the republic, or the radio announcers, or the writers of movie titles. Even the newspaper editors, despite their excessive dubiousness, are probably more influential, at least upon the generality of morons. But the peace advocates concentrate upon the clergy, and evidently hope to dispatch Mars in the Sunday schools.

That hope, as I hint, is vain. For it not only relies upon the help of partisans who are impotent; it also relies mainly upon the force of arguments that are feeble and without appositeness. The whole peace propaganda, in fact, is full of mush. It is based upon sentimentalities that are effective only against half-wits. It dodges what is palpably true, and embraces absurdly only what is sweet and lovely. I don't believe it is making any progress.

The best of all schemes for making war unpopular that I have yet heard of was set forth by Dr. George W. Crile, the Cleveland surgeon, in 1919, in a little book called *A Mechanistic View of War and Peace*. Dr. Crile is the complete antithesis of a New Thoughter. He believes that the human body is almost as much a machine as an automobile engine, and that thought itself is mainly a physical function. Nevertheless, he also believes that an idea from without, coming into the brain, can condition the ideas that it secretes itself, and upon this notion his plan for getting rid of war is based.

In brief, he proposes that the land be flooded with literature showing war precisely as it is—with literature and pictures, and especially with pictures. What the young hear of the thing now, he says, is chiefly romantic and inaccurate. They see heroes marching off with their shoes shined and the flag waving; they see them coming back neatly bandaged, with medals covering their façades. But they see nothing of war itself. The movies never show a portrait of a soldier with his face shot off. There is no attempt to convey the smell of the trenches. The radio does not bring in the remarks of men at the moment that bayonets are thrust through their gizzards.

Dr. Crile, as a surgeon engaged in the late war, accumulated a large collection of actual war pictures, and he gives some of them in his little book. One is a portrait of a French soldier struck in the face by a German one pounder shell. Another is a view of forty or fifty soldiers who gave their lives for democracy, and were subsequently permitted to lie out in the rain and mud for a couple of weeks. Yet another (perhaps eloquent only to youngsters privy to the elements of histology) shows a cross section of the brain of a hero who retreated before the Germans for six days and six nights, and then died horribly of hunger, thirst, fatigue, and fright.

Obviously, a portfolio of such views, printed in huge editions and distributed in the public schools, would do more to make war loathsome than all the pious argument ever heard of. Exhibited to a youth just entering his teens, it would scare him half to death, and the shock would abide with him all the rest of his life. Put into the form of stere-opticon slides, the pictures would paralyze any Sunday school in the land. No conceivable harangue by the pastor could ever be so eloquent, or leave so powerful an impression behind it. Not a few of the attending scholars, perhaps, would drop dead or go crazy, but the rest would be immensely safer against Creel Press Bureaux and artillery fire than they were before.

More, the scheme would be perfectly legal, and the warlocks would have a dreadful time putting it down. Dr. Crile's own book went through the mails unmolested, and is to be purchased in any book store today. A more popular volume, widely distributed and with more (and perhaps worse) pictures, would arouse, of course, a great deal of indignation among professional patriots, and no doubt the Dogberrys of the postoffice would try to suppress it, but the chances are very good that they would be beaten. The resultant uproar would give the book an immense circulation, and bring it to hundreds of thousands who might otherwise not hear of it.

The movies offer another sweet and facile means of propaganda. There are plenty of films in storage showing the revolting realities of war, and if it turns out to be impossible to get at them, then others may be obtained abroad. Would the various state censors intervene? I don't think they could do it if no charge were made for admission. But even if they could there would remain the grand old American device of bootlegging. Films showing prize fights are now forbidden in at least three-fourths of the states, and yet, as every one knows, they are shown everywhere. So are films showing even more sinful transactions.

I offer these suggestions to the friends of international

peace in a purely disinterested spirit, for I am personally no opponent of war, but an advocate of it. All the peace propagandists that I have ever read or listened to seem to me to be dotty. Their case is not only maintained in a stupid and ineffective manner; it is intrinsically weak, and even ridiculous. The objections to war that they offer, even the objection that it is cruel, seem to me to be feeble, and mainly irrelevant. The arguments in favor of it impress me as reasonable and sound. My one regret is that there is so much peace already.

But any cause, however bad, deserves to be carried on in an intelligent and persuasive manner, and here the peace advocates fall down badly. At the moment their chief argument seems to be that war is unprofitable, even to the victor, and in proof thereof they point to the situation of France. But all that is simply nonsense. France did not win the war; France lost the war. She was so badly beaten when the United States went to her rescue that another six months would have seen the Germans bathing at Biarritz and listening to the band at Nice. England was faring somewhat better. She might have gone on to a draw. But she could have no more won a clear victory, without American aid, than she could have beaten the United States itself.

Both of these great countries now suffer from their wounds. But what of our own great republic? It went in at the last minute and gained a cheap and easy victory. In every rational sense it won the war. Well, was the business profitable, or did it show a loss? I leave the answer to any Frenchman—or Englishman. The United States not only beat the Germans; it also beat the French and the English, not to mention the Italians and the Russians. Ever since it has been taking tribute from all of them, and it will keep on taking tribute from them for at least half a century to come. In the face of its colossal gains, it is a bald absurdity to argue that war is unprofitable. It is, under favorable conditions, the most lucrative enterprise that a nation can engage in. It made the British empire and it may make the American empire. The only grain of truth in the case of peace advocates lies in the fact that losing wars is expensive, and sometimes disastrous. But that was well known in the world long before Dr. Carnegie put up his peace palace. (*September 5, 1926*)

ON HUMAN PROGRESS

THOUGH WE LIVE in what is regarded as a go-getting and up-and-coming age, with novelties announced every day and a great deal of yelling and snorting always going on, it must be obvious that human progress, like every other sort of biological progress, continues to proceed at a very leisurely pace. Is the United States senate appreciably superior to the Roman senate, either in learning or in integrity? Is Dr. Frank Crane actually a profounder philosopher than Socrates? Is the religion on tap in the anti-evolution belt any better than the religion practiced and believed in the Teutoburger Wald? Can a modern Kansan leap higher, or run faster, or drink harder, or spell better, or die with greater style and finish than an ancient Assyrian?

It is highly improbable. In fact, it is plainly not so. Nevertheless, it would be idle to deny that progress has been made, and doubly idle to deny that it has been sound and abiding. The governments in vogue in the world today, though they are certainly still far from perfect, are a great deal better than anything ever heard of in the world of the Ptolemies, or even in the world of Elizabeth. They are still inordinately extravagant, incompetent, and corrupt, and they are still run mainly by inferior men. But it is at least less difficult than it used to be to keep those inferior men within bounds. A certain fear of consequences has got into them; they step a bit more softly than their predecessors. Do they yet plunge the human race, at intervals, into insane and disastrous wars? Then it is not as often as aforetime.

It is, indeed, the average man, the plain citizen, who has got the most out of human progress. He is safer than he used to be, and by the same token he is cleaner and fatter. In the genuinely civilized countries famine no longer menaces him, save in time of war. His meals are secure, even when his immortal soul is in danger. Wild beasts no longer devour him; he cannot be butchered save by a long process and with the consent of his fellows; he is no longer haunted by ghosts and demons; plagues seldom alarm him.

I say that he is no longer haunted by ghosts and demons. This is not saying, of course, that he has ceased to believe in them. I think it would be quite safe to guess, indeed, that at least 90 per cent of the people of the United States still have some sort of belief in supernatural powers, especially those of an inimical character. Not many Americans encountering an angel or an archangel up a dark alley would fail to emit low whistles of astonishment and incredulity; but nine-tenths of them, seeing a ghost, would grant its bona fides instanter. It is the theory of every religious sect in good repute among us that a man, on dying, continues to exist, and it is the theory of all save the Unitarians and Universalists that there are such things as demons, and that, under easily imaginable conditions, they may work evil.

This belief in supernatural agencies, I am convinced, will survive in the world for long ages—so long, indeed, as the destiny and agonies of man remain unintelligible, which will probably be forever. It is simply impossible for the human mind to imagine an effect without a cause, and to all save an inconsiderable minority of men a cause is indistinguishable from an intent. Thus the major mysteries will continue to be ascribed to the will of God, and the minor mysteries, many of them of such a character that it would be hard to think of a dignified God having any hand in them, will be blamed upon demons of various tribes.

The notion that the belief in witches has died out on earth is a great mistake. The number of Americans who actually disbelieve in them is probably as small as the number who actually disbelieve in democracy, and no doubt it is made up of much the same individuals. They are the natural skeptics of the race, and, taken as a whole, they are a somewhat unpleasant party. The rest of humanity, as the phrase goes, is more open minded. Its belief in evil spirits and their human allies is not, to be sure, an ever present ingredient of its thought, like its belief in its current Coolidges, Lenins, and Mussolinis; but it is always ready to grant their existence on proof—and that proof need not be very massive.

But even in this department there has been some progress since the days of the Babylonian empire, though we must resort to subtleties to describe it. Let me put it in these terms: that the ancient human belief in spooks and demons, though it has not been obliterated, has at least been made unfashionable. In other words, it has been converted from a public vice into a secret vice, and thus, by the moral theory prevailing in the world, has been rendered less discreditable than it used to be. There was a time when any man who believed in witches or ghosts said so openly, and was respected accordingly. But now he keeps it quiet, as he keeps quiet, say, the fact that he sleeps in his underwear, reads the serials in the tabloid papers, is afraid to walk under a ladder, or loves his wife.

This has been the main effect of skepticism in the world, working over long ages: that it has become *gauche* and embarrassing to admit certain indubitable facts. Their unpopularity is due not to their destruction or abandonment but simply to the forensic talent of the skeptics, a bombastic and tyrannical sect of men, with a great deal of cruelty concealed in their so-called love of truth. It is not altruism that moves them to their assaults upon what other men hold to be precious; it is something no more than a yearning to make those other men leap. The fundamentalists of Tennessee are thus right in denouncing Clarence Darrow. Mr. Darrow, I have no doubt, loves the truth—but it is with a passion comparable to that a man has for an amiable maiden aunt. When he went to Tennessee he went on safari, which is a Hindu word signifying the chase.

The skeptics, pursuing this immemorial sport, have driven certain congenital beliefs of the human race under cover, and made them furtive and apologetic. When they tackled the belief in witches, two or three hundred years ago, it was as respectable as going to church; now it is so dubious that those who continue to cherish it keep the fact to themselves. In the course of time, perhaps, they will reduce the belief in democracy to the same disrepute, but I don't think they will ever obliterate it.

However, there is no call to deplore this essential failure of skepticism, for so long as it succeeds on the surface it succeeds for all practical intents and purposes. Human progress is never complete, but only partial: the upper level moves much faster than any below it. We see before us, even in this year of the enlightenment, how vigorously the larger masses of mankind resist accepting the veriest commonplace of scientific knowledge. What every schoolboy is supposed to know, as he knows that the world is round and that the sun rises in the east, is actually forbidden by law in two American states.

What is too often overlooked is that even Christianity, after two millenniums of ostensible acceptance by all the more civilized nations of the west, is still but imperfectly assimilated by nine Christians out of ten. Certainly no one would argue seriously that its ethical principles are anywhere put into practice in the world today; even its chief spokesmen abandon them at the first temptation, as in time of public war or when they are themselves engaged in controversy with other spokesmen. The old pagan ethics have been driven under cover by an assault comparable to that made by skeptics, but they are still there, and they crop up whenever the band begins to play, or there is a dollar to be made. So on the theological side. The lofty and somewhat tenuous mysticism of Christianity is nowhere converted into an actual way of life, save by small groups of odd persons; on the lower levels, though it is official, it has little reality. When the test comes it always turns out that the majority of men actually believe in something far more elemental. The hell they fear goes back to Pleistocene times, and so do the demons. And the God they profess to venerate is hard to distinguish from the Grand Juju worshipped in the swamps of the Congo.

(*April 17, 1927*)

THE SOUTH REBELS AGAIN

FUNDAMENTALISM, Ku Kluxry, revivals, lynchings, hog wallow politics—these are the things that always occur to a northerner when he thinks of the south. They are all he sees when his eyes are cast across the Potomac. It seems to him that civilization is completely dead down there—that an empire almost as large as western Europe, and as rich as the Byzantium of the Isaurians, is snoring through the cultural night of Albania or Guatemala. He reads about the grotesque doings of Coca Cola bishops, or hordes of imitation Billy Sundays, of whole hierarchies of imperial wizards and illustrious goblins. He observes that Cole Blease has been elected to the United States senate, that Ma Ferguson is governor elect of Texas, that William Jennings Bryan has willed his bones to Florida. And he shrugs his shoulders.

In all this disdain there is some justice. The south, at bottom, deserves it. All over this great and puissant nation, of course, frauds and fanatics flourish, but nowhere else are they taken so seriously as in the late Confederacy. I try to think of a governor of Massachusetts or New York inviting a tin pot evangelist to the executive mansion and holding public orgies in the state reception room. It is impossible to imagine it—yet it happened in North Carolina. I try to think, again, of the president of a state university—say, in Michigan or Pennsylvania, or even in Nebraska—serving on a committee to welcome Billy Sunday. Again I buck—but it happened in South Carolina.

The south, indeed, still suffers from the goose-stepping that went with slavery. It still puts too much trust in prestige, position, authority. A plowhand admitted to holy orders instantly becomes an expert upon all ethical and sociological questions, however abstruse. A pedagogue is full of learning *ipso facto*; a bishop, is divinely inspired. In most parts of the north a United States senator enjoys a rank somewhat like that of a banker or a bootlegger: he is under suspicion, but has the benefit of the doubt. In the south, despite the examples of a dozen Vardamans and Bleases, he yet carries around a certain ante-bellum dignity, and his views upon foreign exchange, the diversification of crops, and the destiny of the human soul are accepted with gravity.

Such is the south as the north sees it. The picture in its main outlines is probably correct enough. But important details are overlooked. What the north misses, in brief, are the scattered rebellions that now arise all over the land of cotton—the gallant efforts that small but pertinacious minorities make to break through the cultural fog, and let in some sanitary sunlight. Such minorities exist in every southern state, even the most backward. In some they still struggle desperately for a mere foothold, but in others they are out in the open, battling gallantly and effectively, and in a few they have already done excellent execution.

The excesses of the nether mob, in fact, forced them into action, and they are resolute in proportion to the density of the imbecility to be combatted. The south produced the Klan, but the south was also the first to fall upon the

Klan. Is it so soon forgotten that the wizards and dragons swept Maine at the last election, and lost Texas? Or that the fight against the Invisible Empire in the Democratic national convention was forced and led not by the delegates from New York but by those from Alabama—that the most devastating of all the attacks made upon it from the floor came from a man from South Carolina? Or that its wave of malignant balderdash, striking two southern states, Virginia and Maryland, instantly broke and washed back?

In this department, of course, the battle has been mainly political—that is, it has been between rival job seekers—and sometimes the foes of the Klan have been almost as bad as its own kleagles, kligrapps, furies, terrors, and genii. But in other directions the division between the Davisbund and the Philistines has been more clearly marked—so clearly, indeed, that the Philistines of all wings have massed for the common defense. Nowhere is that defense effective today. All over the south the minority is emancipating itself and having its say, and in more than one state it is making cruel practice upon the poor whites and their pastors. What one observes is the rise of a new aristocracy, and it is sounder than the old one because it is based upon better brains.

It would be possible to call an impressive roll of enterprises and personalities, taking in almost every state south of the Potomac—the appearance of the *Reviewer* at Richmond, of the *Double Dealer* at New Orleans; the revival of the *Texas Review* as the *Southwest Review* at Dallas (its first number contained a truly astonishing treatise on Texas politics by a Methodist preacher!); the multiplication of poetry magazines and other small *Tendenz* journals; the massive phenomenon of Cabell; the rapid recovery of the more intelligent southern newspapers from the Ku Klux, fundamentalist, and prohibition terrors; Mrs. Peterkin's re-discovery of the Negro in fiction; the new school of realistic history set up by Professor John D. Wade at the University of Georgia; the sudden appearance of Negro writers of gen-uine dignity, notably Walter F. White.

But the whole movement may be best observed, per-haps, in one salient example—the launching of the *Journal of Social Forces* at the University of North Carolina, with a Georgian, Dr. Howard W. Odum, at the helm. This Odum was slow in coming to maturity and rebellion. He took his degree at Columbia fifteen years ago, and for a long while he was known only as the author of a single remark-able dissertation, *The Social and Mental Traits of the Ne-gro*. It was a book of real distinction, but it had no immedi-ate successors. The author had disappeared into his native fastnesses, and was apparently lost with all hands. Nothing whatever came from him; nothing was heard of him. But finally, four years ago, he was called to the University of North Carolina, and there, in a short while, he began to make a stir. First he set up a school of public welfare, and began to make a realistic study of the state of Christian cul-ture among the Tar Heels. Then he began to gather stu-dents about him, and to put them to the same work. Then he got help from outside the state. And then he established the *Journal of Social Forces*.

This *Journal* comes out four times a year, and is bound in a drab paper that makes it look like a government report. But inside it is full of dynamite, for what it presumes to do is to upset all assumptions upon which the thinking of North Carolina, and indeed of the whole south, has been grounded since the civil war, and to set up a new theory of the true, the good, and the beautiful upon a foundation of known and provable facts. For the first time there is a complete end to cant and sentimentality. For the first time the south is getting a whiff of the true scientific spirit.

I daresay Dr. Odum had some uneasy moments during the first days of his venture, but it was not long before he began to attract recruits, and now he has a band of earnest and competent workers about him, and his *Journal* is the most comprehensive and interesting publication of its kind, and by long odds, in the whole United States. One of the first collaborators he found was Gerald W. Johnson of Greensboro, one of the best journalists the south has produced in years. The result is that the *Journal* is not only soundly scientific but also well written. More, it is widely read, and the University of North Carolina is officially behind it, and so it seems likely to survive.

Its appearance is a phenomenon of the first importance, for what it reveals is the collapse of the old morbid sensitiveness of the south and the rise of a disposition to examine its problems anew and in a realistic manner. Dr. Odum is by no means a mere muckraker. He remains a thorough southerner, wholly devoted to the south. What he has introduced down there is simply the doctrine that the ancient evasions, the timeworn platitudes, the hoary sentimentalities have outlived their protective usefulness—that the south can now afford to look the facts in the face, and go about seeking remedies for its troubles without pretending idiotically that the patient is in the pink of health. It is a significant sign of the times that a southerner should have thrown himself into the propagation of that idea. It is a sign of far more significance that it should have been received not with yells for the police but with applause.

Other Odums hatch out day by day all over the late
Confederacy. The very heat of the fundamentalist and Ku
Klux fury is hurrying them out of the egg. I advise the no-
bility and gentry of the north to keep an eye on those regions, so black and desolate only yesterday. There are watch
fires burning, and brave spirits ready for the barricades.
(*December 7, 1924*)

THE SAD CASE OF TENNESSEE

SOME TIME AGO, writing in this place, I lamented the intellectual darkness that prevails in the great state of Tennessee, and proposed that measures be taken to dispel it. The
reply of the state press was a deluge of abuse. I was denounced as a bolshevik, an atheist, and a scoundrel. One
editor hinted I was a Russian by birth and one of the diabolical elders of Zion. Another dared me to come down to
Nashville (or was it Knoxville?) and meet twenty or thirty
brave Tennesseeans in fair combat. A third demanded to
know how many Liberty bonds I had bought during the war
and where I got the money. The rest simply roared.

Such arguments, perhaps, are powerful in Tennessee,
but as for me, I can only say that they leave me undissuaded.
I still believe that my chance and casual remarks were apposite and sound. More, I am confirmed in that belief by
the yells and tall talk that greeted them. For one of the best
ways to test the enlightenment of a state, I believe, is to
look at its newspapers. If they are well informed and sensi-

ble, if they see what is in front of them clearly and discuss it honestly and courageously, then you will find a general interest in ideas and a disposition to hear new ones, as well as old ones. But if they are ignorant and bellicose, if they seek to put down discontent and heresy with the weapons of the professional patriot and hedge evangelist, then you will find only idiocy.

There was a time when most of the southern states were cursed by newspapers of the latter type. It was a time of intellectual stagnation, of depressing dullness, and sloth. There arose eventually, usually against great opposition, papers of a different and better sort—and wherever, they arose, that part of the south was roused from its long sleep. It is the misfortune of Tennessee that other southern states have gone ahead of it in this matter. It has one or two excellent papers, but the level of its state press is very low. Thus the anti-evolution law crept upon it, and the Scopes trial. And thus its very name is a hissing and a mocking today from pole to pole.

There is a moral in all this for other states, and I believe that not a few are well aware of it. That moral is to the general effect that it is extremely dangerous to seek to dispose of evils by denying that they exist and by denouncing those who call attention to them. The barbarous ignorance that came to its final flower in the anti-evolution law had been visible in Tennessee for a long while—in fact, since before the civil war. The educational machinery of the state was defective. Its chief political offices were held by ignoramuses, chiefly out of the poor white trash. The people of its uplands, in so far as they came into contact with ideas at all, had to take them from the rustic pastors, themselves on all fours intellectually with city street car conductors. The gods worshipped were such grotesque mountebanks as the late William Jennings Bryan.

Those Tennesseeans who were educated and in contact with the rest of the world were not unaware of these things. They deplored the backwardness of the state and suggested remedies. They proposed that the ruling political charlatans be turned out and decent and competent men put in. They opposed the imbecile voodooism of the bucolic theologians. But to what effect? To the sole effect that they were themselves denounced raucously by the state press. This discontent with the swinishness about them, it appeared, was unpatriotic and hence abominable. It was their duty, as good Tennesseeans, to declare that all was well and give three cheers. Anything short of that was treason.

The consequences of this nonsense are now known to every one. Abused beyond endurance, the civilized Tennesseeans took refuge in silence, and so the hill billies and their pastors had their way. There ensued the ludicrous attempt to put down learning by law. There ensued the Scopes obscenity, with Tennessee all over the first pages of the world. And there ensued, finally, the emergence of Tennessee as a joke state, laughed at even by Haitians and Dominicans.

When I argue that all this might have been prevented by an intelligent and courageous press I do not indulge in mere speculation, for it has been prevented by an intelligent and courageous press elsewhere. But wherever the press is inferior—as in Mississippi, for example—the same thing is being repeated. Worse, it seems likely to be repeated in Tennessee itself. For the hill billies and their pastors, not content with the Scopes trial, now propose to set up a Bryan

Fundamentalist university at Dayton—i.e., an immense engine for putting down intelligence, deliberately and relentlessly—and the state newspapers, far from opposing the scheme as an insult, appear to welcome it.

What will be the net effect upon the state, imagining this bizarre institution actually set up and in full function? Obviously, that effect will be disastrous. All sorts of fanatics and half-wits will swarm in, and all the surviving members of the enlightened minority will get out. The state will become a sort of Holy Land for imbeciles, and their imbecility will color all its laws and the whole fabric of its government. Its governor, Peay, seems an absurd fellow today, with his toadying to the ignorant and his shameless defense of the anti-evolution law. But if the Bryanites pour in they will be giving all the state offices presently to jackasses ten times worse than Peay.

The end is easy to discern. The very name of Tennessee will become a jest. Its more intelligent sons—and it still has plenty of good blood—will move out, and having moved out, they will be anything but eager to let it be known where they came from. At home there will be no opposition to the fundamentalists and their moron followers. Journalism in the state, flattering the mob as it does now, will become a mere conspiracy against sense—puerile, without dignity, and preposterous.

The point is that nothing is more imprudent than trying to put down facts by denying them. They have a habit of breaking through even the most violent denial and of taking on force in the process. The more they are opposed the more dangerous they become. The way to deal with them is to meet them frankly and squarely. Once they are clearly understood, it is possible to deal with them effectively. But so long as they are concealed and obscured there is no dealing with them at all.

Herein lies the prime value of free speech. It makes concealment difficult and, in the long run, impossible. One heretic, if he is right, is as good as a host. He is bound to win in the long run. It is thus no wonder that foes of the enlightenment always begin their proceedings by trying to deny free speech to their opponents. It is dangerous to them, and they know it. So they have at it by accusing those opponents of all sorts of grave crimes and misdemeanors, most of them clearly absurd—in other words, by calling them names and trying to scare them off.

Only too often, alas, they succeed. They have succeeded apparently in Tennessee. But their success is never very secure. It is always possible, given pugnacity enough in the heretics, to reopen the question, and once it is fairly reopened the obscurantists are easy game. Their fury is their undoing. It leads them into extravagant excesses. They argue nonsensically. They became absurd. Thus all that is needed to unhorse them is pertinacity. They must win by assault or they can never win at all.

In Tennessee they seem to be trying assault. Their apparent aim is to so overwhelm the state with bilge that all civilized Tennesseeans will give up in despair and clear out. It will be interesting to see what happens. My guess is that blackguard journalism, supported by the mob, will achieve what appears at first glance to be an overwhelming victory, but that suddenly it will come a cropper and go down to wreck.

(*March 14, 1926*)

THE MOVIES

AT SHORT INTERVALS one hears news that the movies are about to be uplifted. Does it ever actually happen? It does not. The movies today, if the accounts of those who frequent them are to be believed, are as bad as they have ever been, and in more than one way they grow worse. Has the threat of censorship purged them of their old frank carnality? Perhaps. But in place of it there is only imbecility. Of late, unable to endure the actual films, I have been reading some movie scenarios—that is, the scenarios of movies currently on view, and most of them successes. What I found in those scenarios, at the best, was precisely what the servant girls of my youth used to find in the *Fireside Companion*. In other words, what I found there was simply mawkish and maudlin bilge.

There are, to be sure, films of a better sort, but how many? Certainly not enough to give any color to the general run. In that general run one finds only fodder for half-wits. The transactions depicted all lie upon the level of kitchen wench romance. That play of rational and amusing ideas which one encounters occasionally in the drama, and very frequently in the novel, is simply not there. The best movie ever heard of, put beside the worst play by a Bernard Shaw or the worst novel by a Cabell, become sheer idiocy. The worst sinks so low that no other art, not even that of the architect of suburban filling stations, can show a parallel to it.

Where do the authors come from who concoct such depressing drivel? Some of them seem to be recruited from the ranks of the dramatists, and others are novelists of more or less dignity in their own craft. But when they write for the movies something seems to happen to them—or, at all events, something happens to what they write. It may start out, for all I know, as plausible stuff, even as charming stuff. But by the time it gets to the movie parlor it is only garbage. No author of any decent position has ever written a movie that added an inch to his stature as an artist. But many an author, going into the movies, has been ruined.

Why should this be so? I can discern no sound reason in the nature of things. It is perfectly easy to imagine an intelligent and amusing movie, with an idea in it at least as sound as that in the average stage play, and enough ingenuity in its details to hold the attention of a civilized spectator. The technic of the movie, true enough, is still a bit stiff and unnatural, but so is the technic of the opera. Yet there are plenty of operas that do not insult the intelligence. They have true beauty in them; they conceal the clumsiness of their own form; they have intellectual dignity. One may endure them without throwing one's self into the mood of a hotel chambermaid on a holiday. Slightly intoxicated, one may even enjoy them.

But the movies never rise to that level. In order to enjoy them without treason to the higher cerebral centers one must take on so vast a dose of stimulants that one cannot see them at all. Why? If the experts who profess the subject are to be credited, it is because every movie, before it gets to the screen, must be filtered through a dozen intelligences—and many of them are not intelligences at all, but simply vacuums. It is because the confection of movies is not entrusted to artists, nor even to competent artisans, but to gangs of blacksmiths and pants pressers. These blacksmiths and pants pressers decide what is to be played, and then they decide, in detail, precisely how it is to be played. The result is the aforesaid garbage.

No art, however sturdy, could conceivably survive such murderous sabotage. If an opera librettist had to submit his work to a committee of trolley conductors, and the composer had to write every note under the eye of a church choir tenor and an auctioneer, and if the resultant composition had to be produced by a designer of hot dog stands, and the singers rehearsed by an oyster shucker, then opera would be what the movies are today. In brief, they are idiotic because their production is mainly in the hands of idiots—with a few cynics interspersed to watch for the times when even idiots show some sense.

The bondage of the movies to men wholly incapable of grasping the nature of a fine art, and of no more native taste or intellectual dignity than so many curve greasers or Anti-Saloon league congressmen—this bondage is not due to the movies themselves, but simply to a chain of perfectly obvious natural causes.

The movie business, starting out a generation ago on a shoestring, quickly plunged, like most new enterprises, into an era of wildcatting. Any man with money enough to hire a loft above a livery stable could set up a movie parlor, and any man who could borrow a second hand camera and induce a few jobless actors to trust him was ready to make films. The result was a saturnalia of speculation and roguery. Patents were worth nothing to the wildcatters; copyrights were worth nothing; contracts were worth nothing. To take the word of a movie man, in those gay days, was like believing the oath of a prohibition agent.

But among them were some men of greater rectitude,

and, what is more, of greater talent for business—mainly men who had been petty tradesmen, but still fellows with some grasp of business principles. They tried to reorganize and stabilize the movie industry, and after long and desperate struggles they succeeded. It was no mean task, and they well deserved the profits that flowed in upon them. The trade today, so its leaders boast, is as sound as the steel business, and even has its code of honor. There are movie men in Rotary; there will be a movie window in the Cathedral of St. John the Divine.

But the bookkeeper of an opera house, alas, is seldom competent to select its repertory or to rehearse its caterwaulers. The movies, today, suffer from that profound and inconvenient fact. The men who organized them as an industry now attempt to operate them as an art—and the result is exactly the same as that which follows when a rich hog fattener, having decided to retire to the county seat, designs his own house, including the wall paper and the steeple, and loads a fowling piece to make sure that the workmen carry out his plans.

In other words, the movies languish as a fine art because the men who determine what is to get into them haven't the slightest visible notion that such a thing as a fine art exists. Having learned by experience that certain classes of imbecilities fetch the mob and make a great deal of money, they conclude that such imbecilities are somehow worthy and laudable and so admire them themselves. Hence their honest wonder when the movies are denounced: they can no more imagine than you could that what pleases them should be disgusting to other persons. And hence their vigorous, paralyzing policing of the authors, scenario writers, directors, and actors who are their slaves. The ideas of these gentry alarm them, as they would alarm a Baptist evangelist or a policeman. They prefer their own.

But soon or late the authors, scenario writers, directors, and actors—that is, those among them who have any intelligence, which is not many—will have to revolt against this bondage. Soon or late the movie as an art will have to emancipate itself from the movie as a vast, machinelike, unimaginative, imbecile industry. Soon or late the artist must get his chance. He is halted today by a delusion borrowed from his enemy—that movies are possible only on a great scale, that they must inflame the morons or have no being at all. This is nonsense. The theater, once beset by the same folly, has been liberated by the so-called Little Theater—that is, by the amateur. The movie, I suspect, will be liberated in much the same way. Some day some one with an authentic movie mind will make a cheap and simple picture that will arrest the notice of the civilized minority as it was arrested by the early plays of Eugene O'Neill. When that day comes the movies will split into two halves, just as the theater has split. There will be huge, banal, maudlin, idiotic movies for the mob, and no doubt the present movie magnates will continue to produce them. And there will be movies made by artists, and for people who can read and write.

(July 3, 1927)

THE TELEPHONE NUISANCE

THE OTHER DAY I was summoned to the telephone to answer a long distance call from Cleveland. I could recall no business with any one in that great city, but the local operator (rather unusually) spelled and pronounced my name correctly, and so I put the receiver to my ear and waited. Four or five minutes passed. There was, it appeared, some sort of trouble on the line. I could hear the local long distance operator howling at the Cleveland operator, and the Cleveland operator whispering back. At the end of nine minutes the Cleveland operator addressed me directly. She was sorry, she said, but the call could not be completed. The unknown in Cleveland, growing tired of waiting on his end, had gone out to lunch.

What is to be made of such manners? Here was a man who summoned me uninvited from my work, let me wait with a telephone to my ear for ten minutes, and then calmly walked off. Who he was I don't know, and shall probably never know, for I served notice on the telephone company on the spot that no long distance call from Cleveland would be answered at my house for six months. But, though one town is thus shut off, all the rest remain open, and at regular intervals I'll hear from them. On days when I am hard at work against time, and making heavy weather of it, I'll be hauled to the telephone to wait upon the peppery dialogues of long distance operators, and the pleasure of bounders I don't know and don't want to know. Idiots who, if they wrote me letters, would get no answers, and who, if they came to my house, would be kicked out by my chaplain, will be free to call me up day or night, and if the ex-

perience of the past counts for anything scores of them will
do it.

The thing, indeed, becomes an unmitigated curse. The
telephone has become as great a boon to bores as the movies
are to morons. It enables them to practice their depressing
art and mystery upon any one who has a telephone in his
house, whether they know him or not, and they take advantage of the privilege up to the extreme limit of human
endurance. It has been rarely, during the last few years,
that I have sat down to a meal at home without suffering
their intrusion; it has literally never happened that I have
escaped them during two consecutive hours of work.

My home is in Baltimore and my office is in New York.
In the latter city the excessive number of calls, especially
during the morning hours, makes the service very bad, but
that fact doesn't seem to discourage the town nuisances in
the slightest. The moment I get to my office in the morning
the shrilling of the bell begins, and it keeps up without
pause until late in the afternoon. Often it is so bad that I
find it almost impossible to get through my mail. As for
any work requiring a greater alertness and concentration, it
is wholly out of the question. Day after day I am forced to
flee to my hotel for enough quiet to get through the banal
operations whereby I make a living.

There are, of course, devices for escaping this barrage.
Many men have secretaries to take their telephone calls.
When a call comes in the secretary finds out who is calling
and then asks for instructions; it is not until after that that
the boss himself is reached. I practice the scheme myself,
but it has many disadvantages. For one thing, the secretary's
report on a call is almost as distracting an interruption as

the call would have been itself. For another thing, the secretary of a man who does any actual work in his office is very busy herself, and the calls greatly interrupt and impede her work. And for a third thing, it seems to me to be grossly impolite to force a man making a legitimate call to wait while its legitimacy is being discussed.

But in New York, I fear, politeness is a lost art. It is the almost universal custom in the town to relay calls through secretaries. One hears that one is wanted by Mr. Blank, and then one discovers that one is talking to his secretary. While she goes to fetch him, one waits. At least two times out of seven, in my experience, the connection is broken while he is being sought, and so the whole business is in vain. Five minutes later the secretary calls again, and it is repeated. I have had as many as four such calls in a row. Time consumed: twelve minutes. Penalty for the attendant swearing: 10,000 years in hell.

Of late a new complication is invented. The bore instructs his secretary to call up his chosen victim, and the secretary asks the switchboard operator to get his number. When the victim gets to the telephone he finds that he is talking to the operator, and so he has a double wait: while the operator gets the secretary, and while the secretary gets the bore. It frequently happens that the bore forgets the call in the meanwhile, and cannot be found. Or he has gone into conference. Or he is operating upon some other victim, and his line is thus busy.

Naturally enough, such elaborate hocus-pocus is mainly practiced by third rate men—that is, by the sort whose calls are seldom of any importance. The secretary fever now rages in the United States, and every white collar slave has one. They transact, indeed, nine-tenths of the business of the country. One of the chief occupations of these secretaries is calling up people who don't want to be called. Their idiot employers obviously get a magnificent satisfaction out of this privilege. It makes them seem busy and important. It puts them on a footing of equality with their betters. So the bells jangle all day long, and men with actual work to do are driven half frantic.

The schemes that have been proposed for getting rid of the nuisance are all full of defects. There is, for example, the plan of putting in a so-called silent telephone—that is, one whose number is not listed in the book. But it has the disadvantage of cutting off many calls that are really necessary and would be welcome; moreover, it does not impede the bores, for all the true professionals know every silent number for miles around. There is, again, the plan of having no telephone at all. But that is cutting off one's nose to spite one's face. The telephone, in the modern world, is far more than a mere convenience; it is an absolute necessity. Without it one wastes more time than it ever wastes itself, even when it rings all day. And one misses many charming contacts, and many sweet titbits of gossip.

The true remedy, I think, lies in other directions. What is needed is a national secret organization, with members bound by a bloody oath to avoid telephone calls whenever possible and to boycott all persons who make them unnecessarily. Even without this secret organization much could be accomplished. On July 1 next, at noon precisely, I shall put into effect a little plan of my own. From that instant I shall answer no calls made by switchboard operators or secretaries. The instant I hear the dulcet feminine inquiry, "Who is this?" I shall hang up, and for ten minutes thereafter I shall answer no calls at all.

This scheme, to be sure, will annoy many of my friends, but I am sure that they will bear with me: they must suffer that I may survive at all. I am as busy as they are, and yet I never make telephone calls by way of a secretary. Whenever I wish to call any one I make the call myself, and am at the telephone, ready for discourse, the instant the party called responds. This seems to me to be only common politeness. Nevertheless, it appears to be somewhat rare in the world, and especially in New York. Very often, so calling a man, I find him surprised into temporary speechlessness by the fact that I am talking to him myself. He expects a preliminary parley with a secretary. He is prepared to give his full name and address, and to answer various other questions. When I bust in upon him at once he is somehow shocked.

But life in this grand and incomparable republic would be far more comfortable if such shocks were so common that they ceased to shock at all. The telephone is undoubtedly the most valuable of American inventions. It is worth a dozen airplanes, radios, and talking machines; it ranks perhaps with synthetic gin, the movie, and the bichloride tablet. But here again, once more and doubly damned, we becomes slaves to a machine. What I propose is simply a way of liberation.

(April 10, 1927)

VICTUALRY AS A FINE ART

SOME TIME AGO, functioning as a magazine editor, I essayed to get hold of some articles on the American cuisine. At once I discovered that the number of American authors capable of writing upon the subject, charmingly and at first hand, was so small as to be substantially equal to the number of honest prohibition agents. After six months' search, in fact, I found but three, and one of them had been living abroad for years and another had lived there since childhood. Even the first was scarcely a 100 per cent American, for he had traveled extensively, and though he was holding a public office in Washington when I found him he confessed in the first sentence of his article that he wished the Volstead act were repealed and the Hon. Mr. Volstead himself in hell.

I speak here, of course, of authors competent to write of victualing as a fine art. Of cooking-school marms, of course, we have a-plenty, and we also have a vast and cocksure rabble of dietitians, some of them more or less scientific. But it must be obvious that the cooking-school marm knows very little about voluptuous eating, and that the dietitian is its enemy. The marm, indeed, seldom shows any sign that the flavor of victuals interests her. The thing she is primarily interested in, to borrow a term from surgery, is the cosmetic effect. In the women's magazines she prints pretty pictures of her masterpieces, often in full color. They look precisely like the dreadful titbits one encounters in the more high-toned sort of tearooms, and at wedding breakfasts. One admires them as spectacles, but eating them is something else again.

Moreover, the marm is primarily a cook, not an epicure. She is interested in materials and processes, not in gustatory effects. When she invents a new way to utilize the hard heel of a ham, she believes that she has achieved something, though even the house-cat may gag at it. Her efforts are to the art of the cordon bleu what those of a house painter are to those of a Cézanne. She is a pedagogue, not an artist. The fact that she is heeded in the land, and her depressing concoctions solemnly devoured, is sufficient proof that Americans do not respect their palates.

Why this should be so I don't know, for here in this great republic we have the materials for the most superb victualry the world has even seen, and our people have the money to pay for it. Even the poorest Americano, indeed, eats relatively expensive food. His wife knows nothing of the hard pinching that entertains her French sister. He has meat in abundance and in considerable variety, and a great wealth of fruits and vegetables. Yet he eats badly, gets very little enjoyment out of his meals, and is constantly taking pills. The hot dog is the *reductio ad absurdum* of American eating. The Sicilian in the ditch, though he can never be President, knows better: he puts a slice of onion between his slabs of bread, not a cartridge filled with the sweepings of the abattoirs.

The national taste for bad food seems all the more remarkable when one recalls that the United States, more than any other country of the modern world, has been enriched by immigrant cuisines. Every fresh wave of newcomers has brought in new dishes, and many of them have been of the highest merit. But very few of them have been adopted by the natives, and the few have been mainly inferior. From the Italians, for example, we have got only spaghetti; it is now so American that it is to be had in cans.

But spaghetti is to the Italian cuisine simply what eggs are to the Spanish: a raw material. We eat it as only those Italians eat it who are on the verge of ceasing to eat at all. Of the multitudinous ways in which it can be cooked and garnished we have learned but one, and that one is undoubtedly the worst.

So with the German sauerkraut—a superb victual when properly prepared for the table. But how often, in America, is it properly prepared? Perhaps once in 100,000 times. Even the Germans, coming here, lose the art of handling it as it deserves. It becomes in their hands, as in the hands of American cooks, simply a sort of stewed hay, with overtones of the dishpan. To encounter a decent dish of it in an American eating house would be as startling as to encounter a decent soup.

What ails our victualry, principally, is the depressing standardization that ails everything else American. There was a time when every American eating house had its specialties, and many of them were excellent. One did not expect to find the same things everywhere. One went to one place for roast goose, and to another for broiled soft crabs, and to another for oysters, and to yet another for mutton chops. Rolls made the old Parker House in Boston famous, and terrapin à la Maryland did the same for Barnum's and Guy's hotels in Baltimore.

This specialization still prevails in Europe. The best restaurants in Paris—that is, the best in the epicurean, not in the fashionable sense—do not profess to offer the whole range of the French cuisine. Each has its specialty, and upon that specialty the art of the chef is lavished, aided by prayer and fasting. His rivals in other places do not try to meet and beat him on his own ground. They let him have his masterpiece and devote themselves to perfecting master-pieces of their own. Thus victualing in France continues to show a great variety and a never failing charm. One may eat superbly every day and never encounter a dish that is merely eatable. The Parisians look forward to dinner as a Tennes-seean looks forward to his evening bout with the Scriptures.

But in America the public cooks have all abandoned specialization, and every one of them seems bent upon cooking as nearly as possible like all the rest. The American hotel meal is as rigidly standardized as the parts of a flivver, and so is the American restaurant meal. The local dishes, in all eating houses pretending to any tone, are banned as low. So one hunts in vain in Boston for a decent plate of beans, and in Baltimore for a decent mess of steamed hard crabs, and in St. Louis for a decent rasher of catfish. They are ob-tainable, perhaps, but only along the wharves. One must take a squad of police along to enjoy them in safety.

What remains? A series of dishes fit only for diners who are hurrying to catch trains—tasteless roasts, banal beefsteaks, cremated chops, fish drenched in unintelligible sauces, greasy potatoes, and a long repertoire of vegetables with no more taste than baled shavings. The bill of fare is the same everywhere, and nowhere is it interesting. Within the last year I have been in the heart of New England and in the heart of the south. In both places the hotels offered the same standardized cuisine. In neither was there any culinary sign that I was not in Chicago or New York. In New England the brown bread was indistinguishable from the stuff served on Pullman dining cars, and in the south there was no corn bread at all.

I dare say that the Pullman diner has done much to bring in this standardization. Distances are so great in the federal union that the man who does much traveling eats most of his meals on trains. So he gets used to dishes that all taste alike, whatever their ostensible contents, and ends by being unable to distinguish one from another. Thus he is indifferent to novelty, and perhaps hostile to it. The hotels give him what he wants. If he protested often enough and loudly enough they would turn out their present crews of street railway curve greasers and locomotive firemen and put in cooks.

I leave the meals served on Pullman diners for a separate treatise. They are botched by the effort to give them the delusive variety of the appalling meals served in American hotels. In a kitchen two feet wide and eleven feet long four or five honest but uninspired Aframericans try to concoct fifteen or twenty different dishes. They naturally spoil all of them. On the continent of Europe all meals served on trains are table d'hôte. Their principal dishes are cooked, not on the train, but at the terminals. They are always appetizing and often excellent. Light wines or beers wash them down. The dining cars are hideous with gaudy advertisements—one sees inside what one sees outside in America—but the chow does not insult the palate. At home I have to eat many meals in Pullman diners. I always order the same thing. It is impossible for even a Pullman cook to spoil ham and eggs.

(June 13, 1926)

ON CONTROVERSY

ANY MAN engaged habitually in controversy, as I have been for twenty years past, must enter upon his declining days with a melancholy sense of its hollowness and futility. Especially in this great republic, where all ideas are suspect, it tends almost inevitably to degenerate into a mere exchange of nonsense. Have you ever examined carefully the speeches made by the candidates in a presidential campaign? If so, you know that they are of bilge and blather all compact. Now and then, true enough, one of the august aspirants to the Washingtonian breeches is goaded or misled into saying something pungent and apposite, but not often. His daily stint is simply balderdash.

It is rare, indeed, to encounter a controversialist who states his own case clearly, or who shows any sign of understanding his opponent's. Turn, for example, to the current combat between the fundamentalists and the modernists—an academic and puerile duel in our great Sodoms and Ninevehs, but raging like an oil fire in the Bible and hookworm belt, where men are he and hell yawns. Both sides wallow in pishposh. The fundamentalists, claiming a monopoly of faith, allege that they believe the whole Bible verbatim et literatim, which is not true, for at least 99 per cent of them reject Exodus xxii, 18,* to say nothing of I Timothy v, 23.† And the modernists argue that there is no conflict between science and Holy Writ, which is even less true.

This controversy, in fact, is almost classical in character. Neither side is able to stick to the question at issue.

---

* Thou shalt not suffer a witch to live.

† Drink no longer water, but use a little wine for thy stomach's sake and thine often infirmities.

Each tries to dispose of the other by delivering mighty wallops below the belt—the fundamentalists by passing laws converting the modernists into criminals (that is, as criminality is now defined by American jurisprudence), and the modernists by depicting the fundamentalists as a horde of gibbering baboons, sworn to uproot civilization and not above suspicion of cannibalism.

I have had a hand in this great battle of scattered wits myself, striving in an austere and lofty manner to introduce the sublime principles of Aristotle's "Organon" into it. I have got the traditional reward of one stopping to preach in front of a house afire. The more extreme modernists—which is to say, the professional atheists—discontented because I haven't advocated hanging the fundamentalists, denounce me as a Crypto-Calvinist, and hold me up to obloquy in their papers. The fundamentalists, suspecting me of a secret partiality for Darwin, accuse me of trying to upset the ten commandments, and one of the most eminent of them was lately hinting that I have personally had a bout with No. 7, and come to grief in the manner described by the late Dr. Sylvanus Stall in his well known work on pathology, *What Every Boy of Fourteen Should Know.*

This last accusation was novel, but, as they run in such affairs, very mild. The usual charge against an opponent, in the America of today, is that he is a bolshevist, and in receipt of Russian gold. It has been leveled at me so often that probably a majority of the persons who have heard of me at all believe it, and there are even dismal days when I half believe it myself, though I have been denouncing socialism publicly for twenty years, and am, in fact, an incurable Tory in politics. A short while ago a Boston critic, becoming aware of the latter fact by some miracle, at once proceeded to denounce me because my radicalism, as he thought he had discovered, was bogus.

During the period 1908–1920 I was chiefly engaged in literary controversies, and so my politics were aside from the issue. But when the great wave of idealism engulfed the United States in 1917 I was at once bawled out as a German spy, and open demands were made that my purely esthetic heresies be put down by the Polizei. My principal opponent, in those days, was an eminent college professor, now unhappily dead. He not only attempted to dispose of my literary judgments by hinting that they were inspired by the Kaiser; he even made the same charge against the works of the writers I was currently whooping up. And so did many of his learned colleagues. I met the attack with an elaborate effort to prove that all college professors were asses.

The issue of this forgotten combat was characteristic: thus all controversies in the realm of ideas end. The moment the great war was over there came a revulsion against its idealism, and so it was no longer damaging to accuse me of taking the money of the Hohenzollerns. Thus the professor that I have mentioned found his principal ammunition gone, and in an effort to unearth more he began reading the books I had been advocating. To his surprise he found that many of them were works of high merit, whereupon he began whooping for them himself, and even going beyond my loudest rah-rahs. In the end he was actually searching them for evidences of Teutonic influence, and hailing it with enthusiasm when found.

His poor fellow professors, meanwhile, were the goats. I ceased to revile them, once the war was over, and devoted myself mainly to political and moral concerns, but various other controversialists took up the jehad, and in a short time it was raging from coast to coast. It got far beyond anything I had myself dreamed of. Indignant publicists, quite unknown to me, began grouping all professors with chiropractors, congressmen, and spiritualists as quacks. In dozens of colleges large and small, north, east, south, and west, the students began holding meetings and flinging insults at their tutors. Scores of college papers, for flouting them in contumacious terms, had to be suppressed. In several great institutions of learning the thing actually reached the form of physical assault.

When the smoke cleared away, the college professor, once so highly respected by every one, found himself a sort of questionable character, and he remains so today. In many cases, I believe, he actually is, but surely not in all. The point is that the virtuous have suffered with the guilty. Many an honest and God fearing professor, laboriously striving to ram his dismal nonsense into the progeny of Babbitts, is bombarded with ribald spitballs as a result of a controversy which began outside his ken and speedily got far beyond the issue between the original combatants.

Such are the ways of war in the psychic field. Why they should be so I don't know, but so they are. No controversy, to my knowledge, has ever ended on the ground where it began. Even the historic one between Huxley and Wilberforce, two of the most eminent men of their time in England, ranged all over the landscape before the contestants had enough. It began with Huxley trying to prove that Darwin's *Origin of Species* was a sound book; it ended with Bishop Wilberforce trying to prove that Huxley's grandfather was a gorilla. All its steps are paralleled in the current combat between the fundamentalists and modernists.

Some time ago, contemplating a trip to the west, I wrote to a friend in a California town, telling him that I would visit him. He mentioned the fact casually to a newspaper acquaintance, and the latter suggested to one of the town Babbitts that I be invited to address the local Rotarians. The Babbitt, thinking to have some harmless fun with me, agreed that it was a good idea, and the next day the local morning paper announced my invitation as a fact. That afternoon the evening paper was full of indignant protests. My friend in the town is a Socialist. I am certainly not, but because he is my friend I was denounced as a dangerous radical, and plans were instantly made to prevent me speaking. The row is still raging as I write, with brother against brother. Meanwhile, no one has actually invited me to harangue the Rotarians, and I'd certainly decline if I were asked.

Once, in an effort to keep controversy on a lofty plane, another Socialist and I wrote a book jointly. He advanced the Marxian arguments, and I tried to meet them. We were excessively polite, and kept strictly to the matter in hand. We both spent hard labor upon the writing, and went to great trouble to verify every fact adduced. The book was praised by the reviewers as full of information and extremely high toned. It sold less than 200 copies in eight years. Then the publisher unloaded his stock upon a cut rate bookseller, and copies went for ten cents.

(*October 24, 1926*)

GLOSSARY

Abelard: Peter Abelard (1079–1142), French philosopher and theologian emasculated by the canon of Notre Dame whose niece, Héloïse, was involved with Abelard in a celebrated love affair.

Abrams, Dr. Albert: San Francisco physician (1863–1924) and discoverer of what he called Abrams's reflexes and electronic reactions.

Aldrich: Thomas Bailey Aldrich (1836–1907), American poet and editor of the *Atlantic Monthly* (1881–90) who also wrote novels and short stories.

Ashford, Daisy: Margaret Mary Ashford, English author who wrote a book (published 1919) at the age of nine; it was called *The Young Visiters; or Mr. Salteena's Plan.*

Bennett, the elder: James Gordon Bennett (1795–1872), founder of the New York *Herald* (1835) and pioneer in journalistic techniques.

Blease, Cole: Coleman L. Blease, United States Senator (1925–31) from South Carolina; James F. Byrnes unseated him in the state's 1930 Democratic primary election.

Borah, Senator: William E. Borah, Republican United States Senator (1907–40) from Idaho; pacifist and leading opponent of United States participation in the League of Nations.

Brack, Judge: character in Henrik Ibsen's play *Hedda Gabler.*

Brandes(es): Georg Morris Brandes (1842–1927), Danish lit-

279

erary critic and historian; champion of materialism and disciple of Taine.

Brennan: George M. Brennan, banker who campaigned vigorously for the nomination of Alfred E. Smith by the Democrats (1928) and served with the War Finance Corporation (1923–8).

Brooks, Van Wyck: American writer, critic, and Pulitzer Prize winner (1936).

Cabell: James Branch Cabell, American novelist who derided conventional history and invented a country of medieval fantasy called Poictesme, used as a setting for some of his works.

Cagliostro: Count Alessandro Cagliostro (1743–1795), Italian impostor and alchemist whose real name was Giuseppe Balsamo.

Capper: Arthur Capper, journalist and publisher who was Governor of Kansas (1915–19) and United States Senator (1919–49).

Carnegie, Dr.: Andrew Carnegie (1835–1919), Scottish-born American industrialist and philanthropist who built and equipped many public libraries.

Carroll, Earl: American theatrical producer (1893–1948) and song-writer known for his productions titled *Earl Carroll's Vanities.*

Chambers, Robert W.: American author (1865–1933) who produced forty-five novels in his first twenty years as a writer.

Chautauqua: an adult-education movement that originated at a Methodist meeting in Chautauqua, New York.

Cobb, Irvin: American humorist (1876–1944) whose best-known works, such as *Old Judge Priest,* were set against a rural Kentucky background.

Crane, Dr. Frank: American minister who wrote a syndicated daily inspirational column for newspapers from 1909 to 1928.

Creel Press Bureau: United States government propaganda bureau under President Wilson known officially as The Committee on Public Information and headed by George Creel.

Curtis(es): Charles Curtis (1860–1936), American politician from Kansas who became Vice-President (1929) under Herbert Hoover.

Daugherty, Harry M.: Harding backer and United States Attorney General (1921–4), tried and acquitted on charges of conspiracy to defraud the United States government (1927).

Davis: John William Davis, American lawyer and public official who was nominated for President at the Democratic convention of 1924.

Debs: Eugene V. Debs (1855–1926), Socialist labor leader nominated as a presidential candidate five times; he spent three years in prison (1918–21) under an espionage-act conviction.

Drew, Daniel: American capitalist (1797–1879) who suffered financial ruin in the 1873 panic.

Fox sisters: Leah, Catharine, and Margaret Fox, who toured Europe and the United States claiming contact with the supernatural world. Margaret confessed that their act was a hoax, then retracted the confession.

Gary, Judge Elbert H.: chief organizer and chairman of the United States Steel Corporation (1903–27).

Godey: Louis Antoine Godey (1804–1878), American publisher who helped found what later became *Godey's Lady's Book*, the first famous and successful women's magazine.

Gracchi: Roman statesmen and social reformers of the second century B.C. Cornelia, wife of Tiberius Sempronius Gracchus the Elder, is still remembered for her maternal pride in their two sons—"These are my jewels."

Harvey, Col. George: Wealthy magazine editor and publisher who founded *Harvey's Weekly* in 1918 to launch attacks on Woodrow Wilson.

Heliogabalus: Roman emperor (218–222) who imported the cult of the sun god, shocking and disgusting Romans by the indecency of the rites and his own private life.

Herrick, Myron T.: politician active in nominating both Mc-Kinley and Harding for President. Herrick was United States Ambassador to France (1912–14, 1921–9); was also Republican Governor of Ohio (1903–5).

Howells: William Dean Howells (1837–1920), American novelist, editor, critic, and leading literary figure of his time.

Jenkins: Charles Johns Jenkins (1805–1883), Georgia Governor removed by General George G. Meade for refusal to implement a Reconstruction convention in his state.

Johnson: United States Senator Hiram Johnson, California Republican who sought the presidential nomination (1920); was Governor of California (1910–17) and one of the founders of the Progressive Party of the United States.

Johnson, Magnus: Swedish-born American politician who was United States Senator from Minnesota (1923–5) and United States Representative (1933–5).

Koch, Robert: German bacteriologist (1843–1910) who devised a method of staining specimens with aniline dyes and established the bacterial cause of many infectious diseases.

La Follette, Dr.: United States Senator (1906–25) Robert M. La Follette of Wisconsin, who ran for President on the Progressive Party ticket (1924), drawing five million votes in losing.

Lamont(s), Tom: Thomas William Lamont (1870–1948), American banker who helped transact loans from the United States for foreign countries.

Lodge, Henry Cabot: (1850–1924) United States Senator from Massachusetts and close friend of Theodore Roosevelt.

Lowden: Frank O. Lowden, Republican Governor of Illinois (1917–21) whose deadlock with General Leonard Wood helped make possible Harding's successful candidacy for the (1920) Republican presidential nomination.

Marbury vs Madison: United States Supreme Court case (1803) which placed a limitation on the power of the Supreme Court.

Meredith, George: English novelist and poet (1828–1909) who first came to wide public recognition with the publication (1885) of his *Diana of the Crossways*.

Milligan case: A case decided by the United States Supreme Court (1866) in which the federal courts of Indiana were given jurisdiction in a matter that the military had attempted to pre-empt.

Nasby, Petroleum V.: pseudonym for David Ross Locke (1833–1888), American satirist and journalist.

Nye, Bill: Edgar Wilson Nye (1850–1896), American humorist who wrote and lectured, founding and editing the *Laramie Boomerang* (1881–4) in Wyoming.

Palmer, A. Mitchell: Attorney General of the United States (1919–21) and candidate for nomination (1920) by the Democratic Party for President.

Pater: Walter Horatio Pater (1839–1894), English essayist and critic whose brilliant style was widely admired.

Patti, Adelina: coloratura soprano (1843–1919) who was the most popular and highly paid singer of her day.

Peay, Gov.: Austin Peay, Governor of Tennessee (1923–7) who, during a campaign for re-election, bought full-page newspaper ads to quote Mencken's attacks on him.

Peffer, Whiskers: William A. Peffer (1831–1912), editor of the *Kansas Farmer*; he had a luxuriant beard; was elected United States Senator from Kansas (1890) on the People's Party ticket.

Penrose: Boies Penrose (1860–1921), United States Senator from Pennsylvania who played a leading role in Republican national politics.

Pepper: George Wharton Pepper, United States Senator from Pennsylvania (1922–7).

Pestalozzi: Johann Heinrich Pestalozzi (1746–1827), Swiss educational reformer whose theories laid the foundation of modern elementary education.

Peterkin, Mrs.: Julia Mood Peterkin, American novelist whose sympathetic novel about Gullah Negroes, *Scarlet Sister Mary,* earned her a Pulitzer Prize (1929).

Reed: David Aiken Reed, Pittsburgh lawyer appointed as Republican member of the United States Senate (1922) and elected to two more terms (1923–9, 1929–35).

Reed: James A. Reed of Missouri (1861–1944), Democratic Senator who opposed United States participation in the League of Nations and lost the presidential nomination (1928) to Alfred E. Smith.

Sacco: Nicola Sacco, Italian immigrant, executed (1927) with Bartolomeo Vanzetti for murder after a celebrated trial in which the leftist leanings and foreign origins of the defendants figured prominently.

Satie, Eric: Erik Alfred Leslie Satie (1866–1925), French musician who employed unusual progressions and curious titles in his compositions.

Scopes, Infidel: John T. Scopes, a Tennessee biology teacher who was tried (1925) for teaching the Darwinian theory of evolution.

Simpson, Sockless Jerry: Kansas farm politician (1842–1905), elected to Congress three times (1890, 1892, 1896); references to the silk socks of a banker opponent earned him his nickname.

Smoot: Reed Smoot (1862–1941), first Mormon elected United States Senator; co-author of the Hawley-Smoot tariff act (1930); he was from Utah.

Spencer, Anna Garlin: American educator, feminist, and Unitarian minister (1851–1931) who was a leader in woman-suffrage and peace movements.

Stall, Sylvanus: Lutheran minister (1847–1915) who was the author of books with such titles as *What a Young Boy*

Ought to Know (1897), *What a Young Husband Ought to Know* (1899), and *How to Pay Church Debts* (1880).

Sterne, Laurence: British author (1713–1768) of *The Life and Opinions of Tristram Shandy.*

Stone, Lucy: American reformer and abolitionist (1818–1893) who fought for women's rights; she retained her maiden name after her marriage, and her followers were called "Lucy Stoners."

Taine(s): Hippolyte-Adolphe Taine (1828–1893), French philosopher and critic whose passion for scientific truth had a marked influence on French thought.

Thaw, Harry: Pittsburgh playboy convicted in the triangle slaying of architect Stanford White (1906) on the roof of Madison Square Garden, New York.

Timrod(s): Henry Timrod (1828–1867), one of the chief Southern poets of the Civil War and editor of the Columbia *South Carolinian.*

Torquemada: Tomás de Torquemada (1388–1468), theologian who defended supreme papal authority and directed the Inquisition in his native Spain.

Vanzetti: see *Sacco.*

Vardaman(s): James Kimble Vardaman, Governor of Mississippi (1904–8) and United States Senator (1913–18) who opposed President Wilson and his World War I policies.

Vare, Senator-elect: William Scott Vare, Pennsylvania Republican, elected to the United States Senate (1926) but denied the seat after an investigation of campaign expenditures in the primary.

Vesalius: Andreas Vesalius (1514–1564), Flemish anatomist whose many discoveries in human anatomy were based on studies made by dissection.

Virchow: Rudolf Virchow (1821–1902), German politician and scientist; founder of cellular pathology.

Volstead Act: The legislation that enforced the prohibition of the sale, manufacture, and transportation of liquor under the Eighteenth Amendment to the Constitution.

Walsh: Thomas James Walsh (1859–1933), American statesman who began service in the United States Senate in 1913 and is best known for his work in the Senate Investigating Committee in exposing the Teapot Dome scandal.

Ward, Artemus: pseudonym of Charles Farrar Browne (1834–1867), American humorist who used misspelled words and quaint turns of speech in his essays.

Warren, Charles Beecher: American jurist who served as assistant United States attorney general (1914–18) and as a special master in important cases decided by the Supreme Court.

Watson, Jim: James E. Watson, United States Senator from Indiana (1916–33) who was majority leader (1929–33) for the Republican administration.

Weller: Republican United States Senator (1921–7) Ovington Eugene Weller of Maryland.

Wheeler, Wayne B.: general counsel of the Anti-Saloon League of America (1915–27) and adviser to President Harding on Prohibition enforcement.

Wilberforce, Bishop: Samuel Wilberforce (1805–1873), English Bishop of Oxford; a talented orator whose persuasiveness earned him the popular sobriquet "Soapy Sam."

Wister, Owen: American author (1860–1938) of the bestseller *The Virginian*.

Wood: General Leonard Wood, chief of staff of the United States Army (1910–14), prominently mentioned (1920) as Republican presidential candidate (see *Lowden, Frank*).

Young, Brigham: Mormon leader (1801–1877) who guided the migration of the church faithful west (1846–7) and became director of the Mormon settlement at Salt Lake City, Utah.

H. L. MENCKEN

was born in Baltimore in 1880 and died there in 1956. Edu-cated privately and at Baltimore Polytechnic, he began his long career as journalist, critic, and philologist on the Balti-more MORNING HERALD *in 1899. In 1906 he joined the staff of the Baltimore* SUN, *thus initiating an association with the* SUN *papers which lasted until a few years before his death. He was co-editor of* THE SMART SET *with George Jean Na-than from 1908 to 1923, and with Nathan he founded in 1924* THE AMERICAN MERCURY, *of which he was editor until 1933. His numerous books include* A BOOK OF BURLESQUES *(1916);* A BOOK OF PREFACES *(1917);* IN DEFENSE OF WOMEN *(1917);* THE AMERICAN LANGUAGE *(1918—4th revision, 1936);* SUPPLEMENT I *(1945);* SUPPLEMENT II *(1948); six volumes of* PREJUDICES *(1919, 1920, 1922, 1924, 1926, 1927);* NOTES ON DEMOCRACY *(1926);* TREATISE ON THE GODS *(1930);* TREATISE ON RIGHT AND WRONG *(1934);* HAPPY DAYS *(1940);* NEWSPAPER DAYS *(1941);* HEATHEN DAYS *(1943); A* MENCKEN CHRESTOMATHY *(1949); and* MINORITY REPORT *(1956). Mencken also edited several books; he selected and edited* A NEW DICTIONARY OF QUOTATIONS *(1942). He was co-author of a number of books, including* EUROPE AFTER 8:15 *(1914);* THE AMERICAN CREDO *(1920);* HELIOGABALUS *(a play, 1920); and* THE SUNPAPERS OF BALTIMORE *(1937).*

PRINTER'S NOTE

This book is set in ELECTRA, *a Linotype face designed by* W. A. DWIGGINS. *This face cannot be classified as either "modern" or "old-style." It is not based on any historical model, nor does it echo any particular period or style. It avoids the extreme contrast between "thick" and "thin" elements that marks most "modern" faces, and attempts to give a feeling of fluidity, power, and speed.*

The book was composed, printed, and bound by THE PLIMPTON PRESS, *Norwood, Massachusetts. The paper was made by* S. D. WARREN COMPANY, *Boston. The typography and binding are based on original designs by* W. A. DWIGGINS.